# Twitter® Marketing

## FOR

# DUMMIES®

## by Kyle Lacy
with contributions from
Manny Hernandez

**WILEY**

Wiley Publishing, Inc.

**Twitter® Marketing For Dummies®**

Published by
**Wiley Publishing, Inc.**
111 River Street
Hoboken, NJ 07030-5774

www.wiley.com

Copyright © 2010 by Wiley Publishing, Inc., Indianapolis, Indiana

Published by Wiley Publishing, Inc., Indianapolis, Indiana

Published simultaneously in Canada

For general information on our other products and services, please contact our Customer Care Department within the U.S. at 877-762-2974, outside the U.S. at 317-572-3993, or fax 317-572-4002.

For technical support, please visit www.wiley.com/techsupport.

Wiley also publishes its books in a variety of electronic formats. Some content that appears in print may not be available in electronic books.

Library of Congress Control Number: 2009938251

ISBN: 978-0-470-56172-0

Manufactured in the United States of America

10  9  8  7  6  5  4  3  2

WILEY

# About the Author

**Kyle Lacy** loves everything about social media and the Internet. He believes in the massive potential to communicate and change the world in which we live by using online tools. Kyle started his obsession with social media and marketing at Anderson University, where he helped run a start-up record label called Orangehaus Records. With Kyle's leadership, the marketing team dove into the world of MySpace and Facebook in order to gain recognition for their artist, Jon McLaughlin, who was eventually signed to Island Records in New York City.

After graduating college in December 2006, Kyle and his good friend, Brandon Coon, decided to start a graphic design and marketing company called Brandswag in July 2007. Brandswag started out designing identities for small businesses and collateral. In August 2008, the social media wave busted through the doors of Brandswag, and the company took off. Six people currently work at Brandswag, and the company is mainly working on Web development and social media strategy and consulting.

Kyle loves the idea of educating business owners and C-level employees on the power of social media (mainly Twitter). He writes a regular blog at www.kylelacy.com and www.getbrandswag.com/blog, and is a regular contributor to Smaller Indiana (www.smallerindiana.com). His blog has been featured on the *Wall Street Journal*'s Web site and Read Write Web's daily blog journal. He was also recently voted the top Generation Y marketing blog on the Internet by Viralogy.com, as well as ranked in the top 150 social media blogs in the world.

# Dedication

To my parents and my family (middle-America and the northwest). I would not be where I am today without your continuing support and encouragement.

# Author's Acknowledgments

First off, I would like to thank the awesome team at Wiley — Amy Fandrei, Jean Nelson, and Kim Darosett — for putting up with my hectic schedule and my early, early, early morning writing habits. Also, thanks to Manny Hernandez (@askmanny) for helping with the content of the book from a technical side. Manny is the man!

Secondly, a huge thanks to Sarah Buckner! Without her referral, this book would have never happened. I owe you big, Sarah!

A huge thanks to Erik Deckers, who helped me with the content for this book. He is an excellent writer and helped reign in my crazy mind. I could not have done this without him.

To my business partner, Brandon Coon, who put up with my lack of attention (for a brief moment) on our business. Also, thanks to our wonderful team at Brandswag — Amy Rowe, Stephen Coley, Jon Mobley, and Austin Wechter. We could not ask for better employees!

To all my Anderson Friends (3FDW) for listening to me on a Friday night rant about Twitter and marketing.

To all my Indianapolis friends and mentors: Without your support through the past two years, I would not be where I am today. I am blessed to have wonderful friends from college and beyond.

Last, but not least, to all the social media nerds and fanatics out there. Your content has opened up doors that could never have been imagined! Keep up the good fight and remember communication is key!

## Publisher's Acknowledgments

We're proud of this book; please send us your comments at http://dummies.custhelp.com. For other comments, please contact our Customer Care Department within the U.S. at 877-762-2974, outside the U.S. at 317-572-3993, or fax 317-572-4002.

Some of the people who helped bring this book to market include the following:

### Acquisitions and Editorial

**Project Editors:** Kim Darosett and Jean Nelson

**Acquisitions Editor:** Amy Fandrei

**Copy Editor:** Laura K. Miller

**Technical Editor:** Michelle Oxman

**Editorial Manager:** Leah Cameron

**Editorial Assistant:** Amanda Graham

**Sr. Editorial Assistant:** Cherie Case

**Cartoons:** Rich Tennant
(www.the5thwave.com)

### Composition Services

**Project Coordinator:** Sheree Montgomery

**Layout and Graphics:** Joyce Haughey, Melissa K. Jester, Ronald Terry, Christine Williams

**Proofreaders:** Debbie Butler, Melissa Cossell, Evelyn W. Gibson

**Indexer:** Steve Rath

---

### Publishing and Editorial for Technology Dummies

**Richard Swadley,** Vice President and Executive Group Publisher

**Andy Cummings,** Vice President and Publisher

**Mary Bednarek,** Executive Acquisitions Director

**Mary C. Corder,** Editorial Director

### Publishing for Consumer Dummies

**Diane Graves Steele,** Vice President and Publisher

### Composition Services

**Debbie Stailey,** Director of Composition Services

# Contents at a Glance

# Table of Contents

# Introduction

· · · · · · · · · · · · · · · · · · · · · · · · · · · · · · · · · · · · · · · · · · · · · · ·

**G**reetings, and welcome to *Twitter Marketing For Dummies*. You have officially entered into the joyous world of marketing on Twitter. If you want to think about the tool in terms of celebrity, Twitter is the Oprah of social-networking sites. Twitter is huge in both the number of users and excitement.

This idea of communicating on the Internet is continually evolving, and with Twitter, you have the opportunity to reach millions of people in a matter of seconds. The future of online communication is rendering business owners lifeless because of how slow they are to adopt new technology for communication. What if your customers stopped using the phone and moved somewhere else? Would you be ready? Would you read about Twitter if your competitors bought this book? Guess what — they already did.

This book is full of ideas created by the masses about how to communicate through Twitter. Success is the only option, and Twitter can help you with your business goals and aspirations.

So, is Twitter life, and the rest just details? Not exactly, but Twitter can help you create a sustainable communication model to drive more leads, revenue, and customer evangelists to your product. And the best part is, you don't have to spend countless hours researching how to use Twitter to market your products. I did it for you!

## About This Book

If you've received your citizenship papers from Twitter and are just starting to dip into the world of 140-character communication, this book is for you. It gives an in-depth look into the world of marketing on Twitter. The majority of the concepts discussed deal with combining Twitter with your traditional marketing plan, creating your following of brand evangelists, and finding the best tools for productivity on Twitter. Most of all, you discover how Twitter can transform the way your business communicates with clients (both current and potential) and increase your sales.

Twitter offers a fun way to communicate with your followers, but it also has huge business potential. This book deals with Twitter as a business tool. As a famous rapper once said, "We are makin' it rain benjamins." To the layman, this expression means one-hundred-dollar bills are falling from the ceiling (which probably makes the cash a little awkward to gather).

I wrote this book to help you gain traction on Twitter and to drive revenue to your business. If you can successfully market through Twitter, you can drive more leads and potentially more business to your door! Do you have a specific topic that you want to find out about, such as building your followers? Jump to the chapter that discusses assembling your Twitter posse (Chapter 7, if you want to go there now).

Avoid blinding yourself with the light bulb that bursts above your head when you read this book. If you tear a page out to post on your wall, or put sticky notes and highlights all over the pages of this book, I've done my job. In fact, flag and highlight as many pages as you want. Consider this book a reference guide to help you define and improve your marketing concepts, goals, and communication strategies on Twitter.

Also, this book doesn't look good gathering dust on a bookshelf. Use it! (Everyone knows the color yellow doesn't blend well with anything.)

# Foolish Assumptions

Every author has to assume a few things about his or her audience when writing a book. I made the following assumptions about you:

- You're an awesome individual because you picked up this book. Either way, you're way ahead of the game!

- You either already have a Twitter account or are planning to create one soon.

- You own a small business, or you work in marketing or sales for a large business.

- You want to combine the two preceding bullets and use Twitter to market your business and/or products.

- You are sending out tweets but have no idea what type of return you are getting on your time investment. Further, you have no idea whether your boss is going to fire you the next time she finds out you're using Twitter.

I also assume you have some basic Web-fu skills, such as knowing how to surf the Web. I assume that you may have your own Web site and/or blog, and that you may even have a few social media sites that you visit and update frequently (such as Facebook, MySpace, LinkedIn, and so on).

# Conventions Used in This Book

I know that doing something the same way over and over again can get boring, but sometimes consistency is a good thing. For one thing, consistency makes stuff easier to understand. In this book, those consistent elements are *conventions:*

  ✔ I use *italics* to identify and define new terms. (I even used this convention to explain the word "conventions" in the preceding paragraph!)

  ✔ Whenever you have to type something, I put the stuff you need to type in **bold** so that you can easily tell what you need to enter.

  ✔ When I type URLs (Web addresses), code, or e-mail addresses within a paragraph, they look like this: www.wiley.com.

# How This Book Is Organized

The idea of marketing on Twitter has a wide variety of subject matters and ideas, which is part of the reason why this book is broken down into parts, chapters, and sections. The whole point of organizing the book in the *For Dummies* way is for quick reviewing and reading. If you want to know about creating one or two accounts, you can go directly to the section that discusses that topic in Chapter 2. If you want to know about creating a Twitter marketing plan, head to Chapter 4.

The following sections describe how the book is organized.

## Part 1: The Future of Twitter in Business

If you need to understand the concepts and future trends of Twitter as a business tool, this part is for you. I discuss the ideas of business development, the growing number of Twitter users, and what Twitter means to your business. This part also describes ideas about how to use Twitter effectively for *noobs* (people who are new to a given situation or technology). If you're not new to Twitter, you can skip Chapter 2, which discusses how to get signed up for an account and create a profile.

## Part II: Building and Implementing Your Twitter Marketing Roadmap

Part II is the most important part of the book. You absolutely must plan your Twitter marketing strategy before you dive directly into the churning waters of Twitter marketing. Twitter can be a powerful marketing tool if you plan your roadmap to success. Read and reread Part II in order to gain the knowledge that you need to successfully implement the rest of the ideas in this book.

## Part III: Devising Online Strategies for Twitter Marketing Domination

From building your following to implementing communication strategies, Part III takes a look at how you can use Twitter to grow your business. Does it matter whether you have quantity over quality in your followers? Should you use the auto-direct-messaging feature? (Please don't.) This part provides many answers for you. You need to successfully implement an online strategy before you try to implement that strategy (which Part IV covers). Mastering the online use of Twitter is your key to success.

## Part IV: Implementing Twitter Strategies for Offline Marketing Domination

Integration, integration, integration. Nothing can help you market your business more than the combination of an offline and online strategy. Twitter can become much more powerful when you use it to push offline marketing strategies, as well as online strategies. If you want to use Twitter to execute a live event, add spice to your brochure, or strengthen your offline network, you can. This part shows you how to integrate and strengthen all your marketing endeavors by using Twitter, online and off.

## Part V: The Part of Tens

Tradition. Plain and simple. The Part of Tens caters to a couple of traditions. First, the *For Dummies* books all have a Part of Tens, which sums up the more important information to help you on your Twitter journey. I guide you through the top ten don'ts of Twitter, such as annoying people with a hard sell. (Don't do it!) Second, Internet communication lends itself to placing things in numbered lists, so the chapters in the Part of Tens are concise and to the point.

## Appendix

Hundreds of people contributed to the appendix. Twitter users from around the world gave their opinion on how to use Twitter for marketing. You can find more than 100 of their ideas near the back of this book for your perusing enjoyment. You can really make the most of driving business and ideas through Twitter by implementing some of these ideas.

# Icons Used in This Book

I use the following icons throughout the book to highlight paragraphs that you should pay particular attention to.

A Tip is kind of self-explanatory, right? The Tip icon points out information that can help you use or implement your ideas differently. You may find these simple suggestions very useful.

I look at Remember icons as massive tips to remember. These icons mark information that you really should commit to memory when you use Twitter for marketing purposes.

The Technical Stuff icon marks information of a highly technical nature that you can normally skip over. I don't read the technical stuff for anything! So why should you? Honestly, who reads the directions?

The Warning icon is the equivalent to the warning label on a lawnmower that tells you not to stick your foot underneath the blades. Warnings help you along your way so that you don't cut off your little Twitter legs.

The Case Study icon points out real-life examples of how companies have used the Twitter marketing concepts and techniques discussed in this book.

# *Where to Go from Here*

You're ready, my young Jedi. Go forth into the world of Twitter and dominate your efforts in marketing and driving business through the Internet. But where should you start?

If you already know the basic Twitter ropes, you can skip Part I. But I strongly suggest that you read Part II before you start trying to use Twitter as a marketing tool. You must have a plan in place that measures your Twitter marketing success rate and how you use the tool. Part II describes how to plan and develop a strategy.

If you have a specific topic in mind that you want to know more about, check the Index or the Table of Contents, and then flip to that chapter, section, or page and start reading. And, of course, you can always just start your Twitter marketing adventure at Chapter 1.

If you have any questions regarding marketing on Twitter, feel free to check out my blog at www.kylelacy.com or e-mail me at kyle@getbrandswag.com.

# Part I

# The Future of Twitter in Business

## The 5th Wave     By Rich Tennant

"This is getting downright annoying. He tweets me every time he's about to go down a chimney."

# In this part . . .

You're stepping into the world of Twitter marketing. You know that Twitter is one of the most popular social-media sites on the Internet, but how can you use it to drive business? What's the difference between micro-blogging and blogging? Who's on Twitter, and why are they using it? I answer these questions in this part.

In Chapter 1, you get a glimpse into the world of using Twitter for business. If you haven't already signed up for Twitter, Chapter 2 helps you sign up and get going. So, grab a cup of coffee or tea (or a 12-hour energy drink), and jump into Twitter marketing.

# Chapter 1

# I Tweet, You Tweet, We All Tweet: Twitter and Your Business

*In This Chapter*

▶ Discovering Twitter

▶ Marketing your business on Twitter

▶ Throwing out traditional marketing methods

*I*magine a world in which millions upon millions of potential customers are talking, sharing ideas, and shaping new realms of communication. This new online platform has blasted through traditional marketing and communication concepts and created a world in which collaboration and customers are king. This world exists as Twitter (www.twitter.com).

Twitter has exploded, with growth rates of 1,382% year-over-year and over 6 million members as of this writing. All those Twitter users are potentially waiting for you to communicate with them. When you start using Twitter for your business, you're entering a new phase of Internet marketing in which you discuss your brand on a daily basis and send out your thoughts in bursts of 140 characters or less. You're on the leading edge of a communication and cultural transformation in the business landscape of the world. Isn't this exciting?

Twitter has disrupted the traditional marketing process and placed the customer in control of the marketing message. But don't fret! The future of marketing is bright — never before have you had such possibilities for growing your business. Twitter enables you to find potential customers quickly and easily and communicate with them with only a few keystrokes.

This chapter introduces you to the key concepts of marketing your business and products by using Twitter. (For help signing up with Twitter, see Chapter 2.)

# Understanding How Twitter Works

*Twitter* is a social network that gives you the ability to post messages of 140 characters or less. Because Twitter is a network with members throughout the world, when you send out a message, Charles in London and Mary in California can read it at the same time. Imagine the possibilities for your business!

If you understand the concept of sending a text message from phone to phone, you can pick up Twitter easily. The same rules that apply to texting also apply to the world of Twitter, with one exception: On Twitter, you're limited to 140 characters to communicate a concrete thought.

## Micro-blogging (tweeting)

Twitter is built on the concept of *micro-blogging,* in which people write short, frequent posts (often by using a cell phone) that don't exceed 140 characters. Those 140-character posts are known as *tweets;* Figure 1-1 shows a few tweets from several Twitter users.

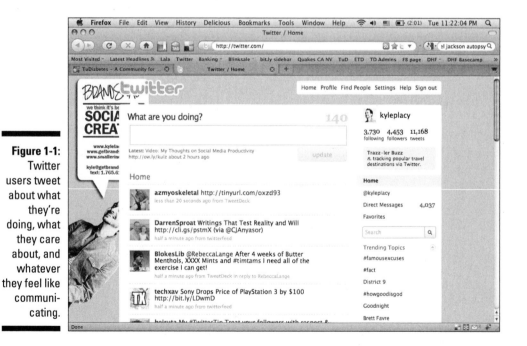

**Figure 1-1:** Twitter users tweet about what they're doing, what they care about, and whatever they feel like communicating.

Tweets are a form of micro-blogging that have enabled users to share massive amounts of content in the form of short text messages that they send to unique sets of people or entire groups. Twitter is one of the original platforms for micro-blogging, and it has ruled this space since its creation in 2006. Micro-blogging has increased the speed of information ten-fold, in contrast to writing a blog post or writing an in-depth consumer report.

Blogging is a more elaborate approach to information sharing and marketing on the Web. Micro-blogging is a short-term approach that's ideal for quick and thoughtful communication. Blogging and micro-blogging should work hand-in-hand to create a platform that you can use to spread your business ideas to your customers and potential market.

## Following others and being followed

When you *follow* somebody on Twitter, his or her tweets appear on your Twitter timeline (much like you can see your friends' status updates on your Facebook feed), as shown in Figure 1-2. The big difference between Twitter and Facebook is that you don't need other people's approval before you can follow them on Twitter, as long as they've set their Twitter accounts to public status.

**Figure 1-2:**
You want to follow many people, but you also need to be sure that you follow the right kind of people.

Being followed on Twitter has very little to do with being followed in real life, when you feel like someone is shadowing your every move. Every time you post a tweet, it appears on the Twitter timeline of all the people who are following you. If you're posting on Twitter as a business, you need followers on Twitter so that you can get your message out about your company, products, and services. Twitter also gives you the ability to have conversations with current and potential clients.

So, you just need to follow as many people as possible and start tweeting about your products like there's no tomorrow, right? Not so fast. You need to have a plan, a strategy to make the most of Twitter, before you start following a bunch of people (or *tweeple,* as they're sometimes called in the Twitterverse).

## *Sharing with your followers and retweeting*

When you start following others on Twitter, you need to share useful information with them so that they want to follow you, too. The information that your followers are interested in may vary, depending on their focus and interests. But they're probably not dying to read a ton of tweets in a row in which you praise your products and services: If you take that approach, prepare to be *unfollowed* massively on Twitter.

You need to strike a balance between your marketing message (naturally, you want to promote your company, products, and services — otherwise, you wouldn't be reading this book), useful information about your industry, and some personal elements to give people a feel for the human side of your company. Along with all these elements, you also need to share useful tweets that

## Twitter community demographics

People who use Twitter for marketing purposes include marketing experts, celebrities, public-relations professionals, writers and authors, business owners, and employees. More importantly, the majority of Twitter users are your customers and peers. A popular myth is that Twitter is made up of Generation Y Internet users (ages 18 to 27). However, the Pew Internet & American Life Project has placed the median age of Twitter users at 31: Generation X (ages 28 to 45) has taken hold of Twitter.

What does this statistic mean for your business? It gives you insight into the kind of people who are using Twitter.

others post on Twitter. Sending your followers a tweet that you've received is called *retweeting,* and it's considered part of the social currency on Twitter. You can see an example of a retweet in Figure 1-3.

Retweeting goes well beyond giving credit to whoever shared something: It indicates that you respect or like this person's opinion, thoughts, or whatever he or she tweets about. Also, when others retweet something you've posted, you can start to get your message out in the Twitter world — but you have to start by retweeting messages posted by other people before you can ask them to retweet your messages. For a more in-depth look at using retweeting in your marketing plan, check out Chapter 8.

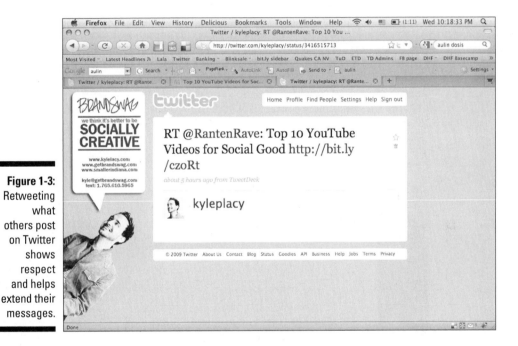

**Figure 1-3:** Retweeting what others post on Twitter shows respect and helps extend their messages.

# Using Twitter in Your Business

You can use Twitter as a valuable marketing tool for your business, whether you have a small, medium-sized, or large business. Also, Twitter can help complement your company's current PR and customer service efforts. The following sections describe several ways that you can use Twitter for your business.

## Sharing news and stories

Because Twitter gives you the ability to share 140-character thoughts in a split second, you can easily share links to PR releases and stories about your business, service, or product. But in order to make your tweets interesting and diverse so that you can hold on to and increase your followers, consider sharing news and stories about the industry that you serve. You can become a reference for people who are looking for information about the topic, and that status can ultimately gain you more followers who may become your customers.

You can also branch out into general news stories, keeping an eye on trending topics on Twitter, as described in Chapter 10. Tweeting about more than just your business and industry can help show the human side of your company; however, depending on what your Twitter marketing strategy is, keep your brand in mind when you use Twitter and consider what your tweets say about your brand as a whole. Make sure that you enhance and complement your brand's story through your tweets. The tweets by @brandswag in Figure 1-4 help tell the story of its brand, as summarized in the Twitter user's bio:

```
Ideas Infecting Business through Social Media, Marketing,
and Design
```

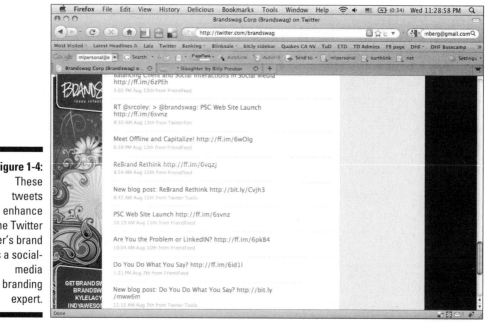

**Figure 1-4:** These tweets enhance the Twitter user's brand as a social-media branding expert.

## Empowering your fans

Twitter gives you the ability to take a single thought and share it with millions of people. And your customer *evangelists* can spread your message, as well as their opinions about your company's greatness, to as many people as possible.

Your evangelists can help you get your message out, but you must first find out who they are and remember to give to them (by retweeting their interesting messages) before you ask for their support.

You can spot your fans and evangelists by keeping an eye on who retweets your posts most often. (Chapter 8 introduces some tools that can help you track that information.) Also, monitor Twitter trends in your industry so that you can spot the people you need to be listening to; see Chapter 10 for details.

Through a disciplined balance between listening to others and retweeting their useful contributions, eventually you earn the right to ask for their support in return. The reward may be as big as having your brand story go viral and getting picked up by thousands or millions of potential customers, as described in Chapter 9.

## Customer service

Twitter can help you turn your company's customer service into a competitive advantage, as Comcast and Zappos have done through their highly personal and accessible customer service reps on Twitter. You can see an example of how Comcast offers customer service through Twitter in Figure 1-5.

If you involve the right people in your company on Twitter — and train them in time management and empower them to talk openly to customers — you can save both your customers and yourself time, money, and frustration: a true win-win situation.

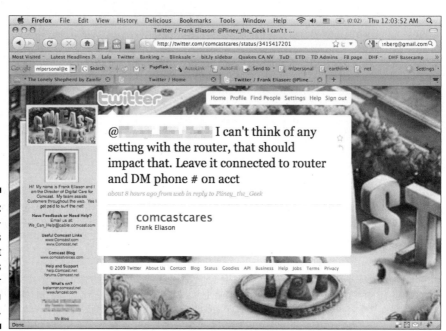

**Figure 1-5:**
@Comcast-
Cares offers
Comcast
users
customer
service via
Twitter.

## Finding a fit for your business

Examples of businesses that use Twitter can help you see how Twitter might fit with your business model. The following list describes just a few of the companies that have revolutionized the way businesses use Twitter customer service, business-to-consumer marketing, business-to-business marketing, and public relations:

- ✔ **Customer service:** Zappos (www.zappos.com), an online shoe retailer, is almost obsessed with customer satisfaction. Unsurprisingly, it adopted Twitter as a channel to communicate with its customers and offer customer service.

- ✔ **Business-to-consumer marketing:** Ford Motor Company is getting the word out about its new Fiesta model through the Fiesta Movement. If you visit www.fiestamovement.com, you can see how Twitter is a critical component of this promotional campaign.

- ✔ **Business-to-business marketing:** Duct Tape Marketing (www.ducttape marketing.com) started several years ago as a book and blog aimed at small businesses. Today, it uses Twitter as part of its toolkit to deliver valuable information to its audience.

✔ **Public relations:** Louis Vuitton (@LouisVuitton_US) embraced Twitter as part of its social-media–centric PR strategy that was born by forging relationships with popular and content-heavy fashion bloggers in Paris.

# Marketing on Twitter

In old-school marketing, the idea was that the more you broadcasted a marketing message, the more your sales grew. Because of this idea, marketing departments of many companies ran much like machines. Yes, some creative thought was involved, but the communication model was more machine-like than most marketing professionals would care to admit.

They (the marketing machines) churned out hundreds of thousands of ideas in order to plaster on the public's minds the benefits of their products and services. More often than not, this approach worked because there was a more limited number of products and a more limited number of channels through which companies could market those products. So, you could more easily reach your audience. It was the age of broadcast, in which you sent the message in only one direction, and everyone on the receiving end consumed it.

In this age of social media (which Twitter is a part of), the machine is slowly morphing and giving way to a more sophisticated school of thought. The customer is now crafting brand messages. People are talking to other people. They share good and bad experiences, tips and tricks, and do's and don'ts — and you can only do so much in terms of pushing messages because everyone's attention has become incredibly fragmented. Millions of products compete for a slice of attention on a gazillion channels and Web sites, making it nearly impossible (and unreasonable) for a company to broadcast effectively anymore.

Instead of selling a message to a group of consumers, on Twitter you rely on your customers to talk about your product and help you reach others through word of mouth. Twitter is now at the forefront of the customer experience, where customers sell to customers. Companies no longer craft the thoughts and ideas of brands in the board room. Consumers create personal representations of brands in their living rooms, restaurants, and gathering places, and on their keyboards.

Marketing on Twitter works in a very different way than traditional marketing. Of course, you can help shape the dialogue: You certainly can (and should) participate in the conversations about your company, products, and services. But you no longer have absolute control over what gets said about them.

In this social-media world of marketing, you have to take responsibility for your mistakes, correct them, and try to make sure they don't happen again. If you try to hide your mistakes, social media can come back to bite you. For example, if a customer shares a negative thought about your company and you don't respond, the backlash could be significant. The crowd mentality can take a negative idea, whether true or not, and ruin your brand reputation. If you're transparent about your errors, customers see it and may respect you more for it.

# Chapter 2

# Getting Started with Twitter

## In This Chapter

▶ Signing up for Twitter and creating your profile

▶ Understanding the basics of using Twitter

▶ Looking into Twitter software

*T*witter is starting a revolution in terms of how and why your company communicates with customers and potential clients. Where do you start? Where do you jump into the massive world of the direct message and the tweet?

It all starts with your profile.

Creating a Twitter profile is a little bit different than signing up for MySpace or Facebook, where you list your favorite bands, books, movies, and funny photos of you and your family. Just as you have less room (140 characters) to share your message on Twitter, you also are constrained by how much information you can enter in a Twitter profile; however, that doesn't mean your Twitter profile is not important.

The information you include in your Twitter profile introduces you to others on Twitter and may be the reason why others choose to follow you (or not). Therefore, you need to give it careful thought.

The whole idea behind Twitter involves packing big ideas into small spaces, so you need to fit the most important information about your business in a small space — a photo, a 160-character bio, and a URL.

In this chapter, I walk you through the process of signing up for Twitter and creating a profile. I also break down the most important parts of the profile and where you should focus your time. And I give you some tips to help you choose the best Twitter pictures.

# Signing Up with Twitter

To start your Twitter journey, you need only a computer, an e-mail address, and an Internet connection. If you don't have any of the three, you're pretty much out of luck when it comes to starting a Twitter profile. (Yes, you can use a mobile phone with Twitter, but it is far more convenient to get your Twitter account started on a computer.)

## Creating a Twitter account

You can use this quick, easy, slick, and state-of-the-art process to create your very own Twitter account! Just follow these steps:

1. **Go to www.twitter.com.**

2. **Click the green Sign Up Now button.**

   When you click this button, a page opens that launches you on a brand new adventure of communicating with and meeting new people, forming new relationships, and creating opportunities for yourself and others.

3. **Enter the information Twitter is asking, nay, begging you for, as shown in Figure 2-1.**

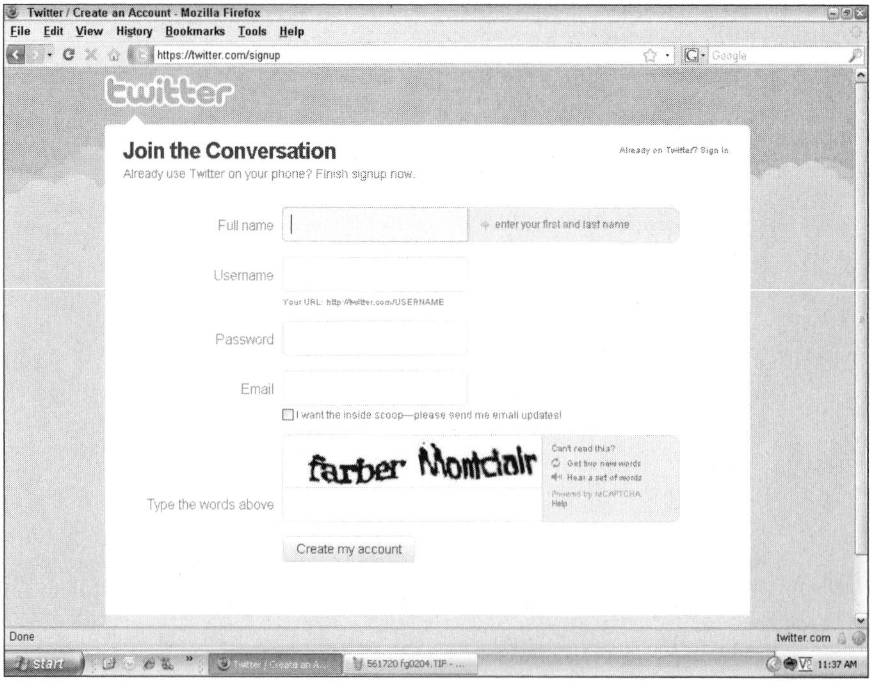

**Figure 2-1:** Sign up for your Twitter account.

To create your account, you have to enter the following pieces of information:

- *Full Name:* Type your first and last name. Alternatively, you can use your company's name here, but I recommend using a business name only if you're creating a corporate-only account. (If you're interested in having both a personal account and a business account on Twitter, you can use software that allows you to run both accounts simultaneously. I discuss that software in Chapter 5). See the "What's in a name?" sidebar, later in this chapter, for more about how to choose a name for your Twitter account.

- *Username:* Type a username for your Twitter account. Your username becomes part of your personal URL, for example, `www.twitter.com/kyleplacy`.

The majority of Twitter users include their own names or company names as part of their usernames. When you're debating what to use for your Twitter name, remember that people need to remember the name in order to find you. But you may find that someone already uses your actual name as their Twitter username. If this is the case, a red sign that reads "Username Has Already Been Taken" appears next to the username you entered, as shown in Figure 2-2.

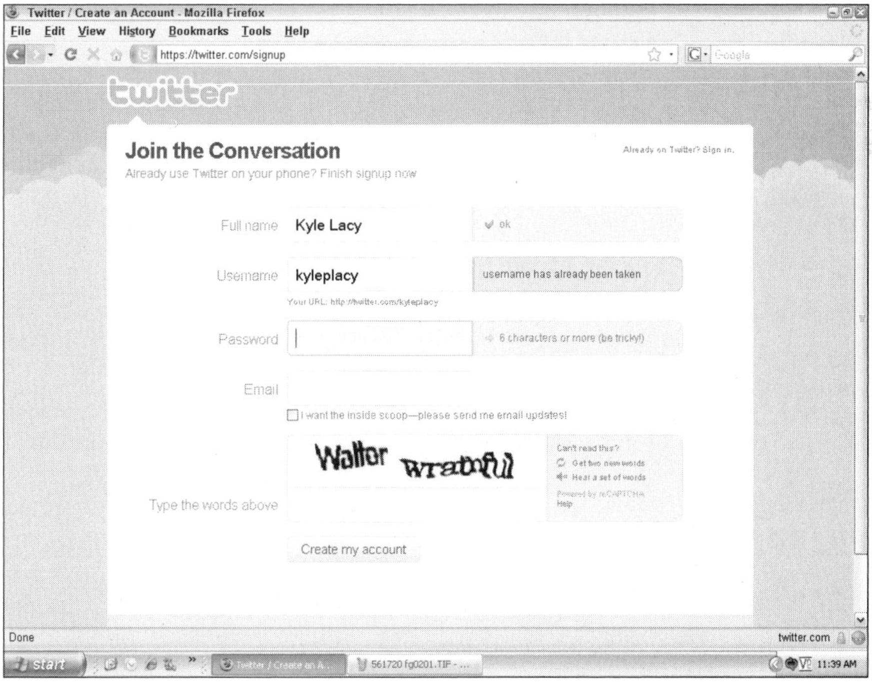

**Figure 2-2:**
With so many Twitter users, it is possible that your preferred username is taken.

If this happens to you, you've either found a name stealer or happen to have the same preference for a username as someone else on Twitter (John Smith, you have my sympathy). To get yourself out of this situation, try a new username including your middle initial or a number after your name, such as @kylePlacy or @kylelacy1984, in place of the first username you entered.

Although it can be as long as 15 characters, try to pick the shortest name possible. Remember, people have only 140 characters in a tweet, including your name if they're replying or retweeting one of your messages. And if you have @JohnJacobJingle for a username, that leaves only 124 characters for somebody to respond.

- *Password:* Type a password. Your password is your key to your Twitter Empire (Twempire?). Use strong password guidelines: Make it over six characters in length and add a capital letter, numbers, and/or punctuation marks. (An example of a strong password is Fr@nk5inatr@.)

- *Email:* Type your e-mail address. In order to receive alerts and information regarding your Twitter account, you have to enter a valid e-mail address you have access to. Below the Email text box, you can check the I Want the Inside Scoop – Please Send Me Email Updates check box to receive notifications from Twitter.

- *CAPTCHA:* Type the weird swirly smoke letters that you see underneath the Email text box. These letters are the Twitter security system called a CAPTCHA — Completely Automated Public Turing Test to Tell Computers and Humans Apart — which allows Twitter to protect against computers from automatically signing up massive numbers of accounts. It's basically there to confirm that you're a human.

 **4. Click the Create My Account button.**

 After you create your account, Twitter opens a new page that allows you to upload contacts from different e-mail platforms. (See the following section for the steps you can use to search your contacts.)

 You also get a welcome e-mail message at the e-mail address you entered, confirming your username and Twitter profile page, along with links to let you activate your phone to use Twitter and invite your friends.

## Using the Find People Email search

When you start finding and following people, the fun really begins! Twitterati unite! If you're in a hurry, you can skip the Find People – Follow Them section by clicking the Skip This Step link at the bottom of the page. However, I recommend that you let Twitter build your list with your current e-mail contacts. If you need to build a list quickly, this is a great way to do it, especially if you already have an e-mail list of customers and potential customers.

Twitter gives you the ability to use your Gmail, Yahoo!, or AOL e-mail account to search your database of e-mail contacts for people who already use Twitter. You have the ability to find your friends! And Twitter doesn't share your username and password with anyone other than you. It's extremely secure.

After you click the green Create My Account button on the Twitter signup page, follow these steps:

1. **On the Find People – Follow Them page that appears, enter your e-mail account's password in the Email Password text box.**

   Select an e-mail platform you have an account with (Twitter supports Gmail, Yahoo!, and AOL) and enter your e-mail address and password, as shown in Figure 2-3.

---

## What's in a name?

You can make your full name an important part of marketing on Twitter. Your name may not break a campaign or a sales lead, but you always have that possibility. Remember that in order to create a real and lasting relationship with your customers on Twitter, you need to be open and honest about your identity.

I discuss the importance of a good Twitter username in more depth in Chapter 4, but plain and simple: people buy from people. Would you rather have someone know you as Hickory Bob Huskie or Joe Smith? People connect with people, and social media (including Twitter) provide you a great place to make a connection that can help you sell. People buy from people they know, like, and trust. And it's hard to know, like, and trust people with names such as HansumDude1978. Stick with your real name.

However, if you're starting a business account, use your business name as your username. If people are searching for your business on Twitter, you want them to find you easily. Just don't use Hickory Bob Huskie. If your company name is Hickory Bob Huskie, please go to your local bookstore and pick up *Branding For Dummies,* by Bill Chiaravalle and Barbara Findley Schenck (Wiley).

---

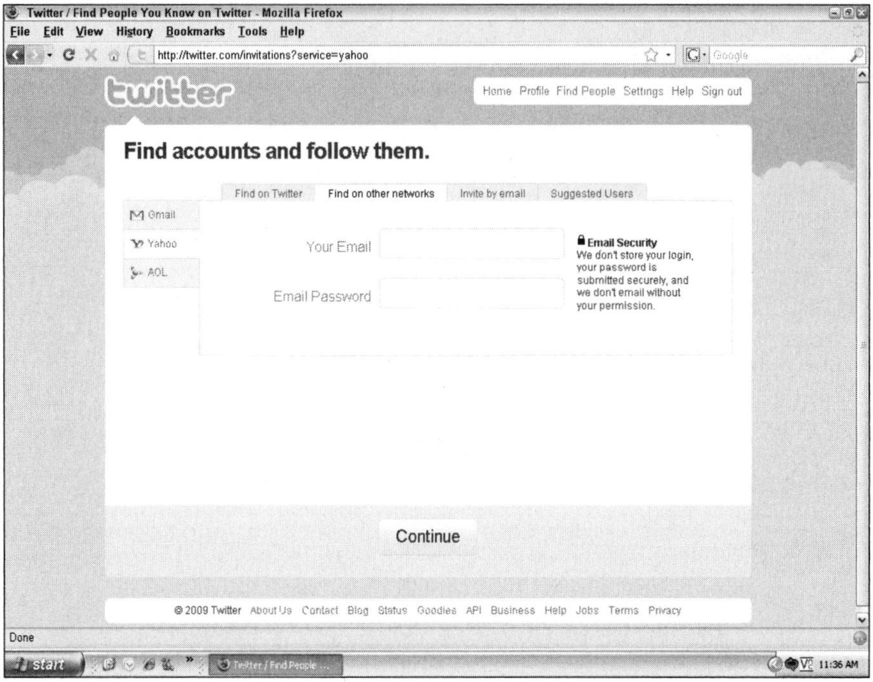

Figure 2-3:
Enter your
e-mail and
e-mail
password
to search
for people
you know on
Twitter.

2. **Click the Continue button.**

   Twitter searches your e-mail address book and shows you which contacts have Twitter accounts (if any of them do) so you can conveniently
   follow them. You can see what the results page looks like after Twitter is
   done searching your e-mail address book.

3. **To follow a contact returned by the search, make sure the check box
   to the left of his or her avatar is checked and, when you are done
   selecting all the people you want to follow, click the green Follow
   button, as shown in Figure 2-4.**

If you get a direct message or a tweet from someone who says he or she is from
Twitter and asks for your password, report that user because Twitter never
asks for that information. (They already have it, so they don't need to ask.)

**Figure 2-4:**
Twitter
makes it
easy for
you to fol-
low people
you already
know.

You may be concerned that someone can steal your e-mail address or personal identity from Twitter. If so, create a new e-mail address just for Twitter.
Use Gmail, Yahoo!, or AOL to create a new address. Just remember to monitor
it regularly because all the notifications about account activity — including
people who start following you — are sent to that e-mail address.

## Finding people to follow

After you have followed those people that you already know who have
Twitter presence, on the Find People – Follow Them page, there are additional ways to find people that match what you are looking for.

As shown in Figure 2-5, by clicking the Find on Twitter tab, you enter a username, first or last name (this can also be a business name), to be able to find
an existing Twitter user.

Clicking the Invite by Email tab allows you to invite people whose e-mail
addresses were not included as part of your e-mail address book. You can
enter multiple e-mail addresses in the Enter Some Email Addresses text box;
be sure to separate the addresses with commas.

**Figure 2-5:**
The Find
on Twitter
page lets
you search
for people
who already
have a
Twitter
account.

Lastly, clicking the Suggested users tab presents you with a list of users recommended by Twitter. This list is quite varied — it can include celebrities,
news outlets, political figures, and more. As shown in Figure 2-4, to follow any
of the suggested users, check the check box next to the avatars of the users
you want to follow and then click the green Follow button.

## Writing your 160-character bio and more

You use the bio to let the world know who you are. If you're using Twitter for
personal communication, talk about who you are, what you like, and what
you do. What are your hobbies, your interests, and your passions? If you're
using Twitter for business, what does your business do? Use plain language
and keywords that people would normally search for. Do you sell real estate
in Michigan's Upper Peninsula? Put that in. Are you a corporate travel plan-
ner for veterinarians? Put that in.

Don't use jargon that normal people don't use, and don't make commercial
statements such as *We Help You Make Money Overnight*. It puts people off, and
they're less likely to follow you.

To enter a bio, click the Settings link at the top of the page. This takes you to
your Account page, as shown in Figure 2-6.

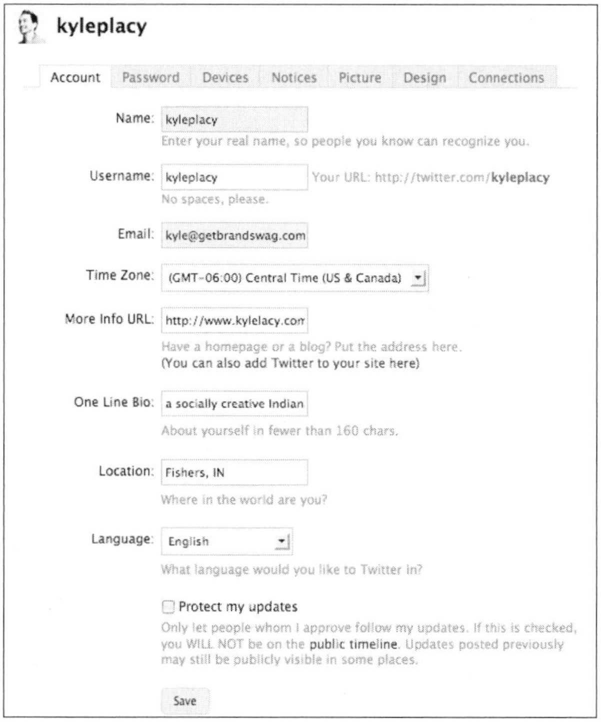

**Figure 2-6:**
The
Account
page lets
you add a
URL, a One
Line Bio,
and more.

In the One Line Bio text box, you have up to 160 characters to talk about yourself. If you have a Web site you can link to, it is a good idea to do so in the One Line Bio text box. Be sure to enter the URL in the More Info URL text box, too.

Also on this page, you get the opportunity to change the time zone you are tweeting from, add a location to your profile page, and designate what language you plan on writing your tweets in. (As of this writing, English and Japanese are the only available language options.)

Lastly, you can choose to protect your updates by checking the Protect My Tweets check box. This makes your Twitter updates visible only to those people that you approve — not the wisest idea for a business, if you ask me, but it's there in case you wanted to know.

## Adding a picture

You know how they say "a picture speaks a thousand words?" That holds very true in Twitter, and as a result, few things are a bigger turnoff on Twitter than profile pages that haven't picked an original avatar to substitute Twitter's default avatar, shown on Figure 2-7.

**Figure 2-7:**
The Twitter default avatar apparently is based on the o_O emoticon, which means "Left Raised Eyebrow."

To change your Twitter picture, follow these steps:

1. **Click the Settings link at the top of the page.**

   This takes you to your Twitter Account page.

2. **Click the Picture tab, shown in Figure 2-8.**

3. **Click the Browse button.**

   A dialog box appears that lets you browse for an image on your computer. You're limited to JPG, GIF, and PNG image files that do not exceed 700k in size. It's a good idea to select a square image, but you don't have to upload a small thumbnail: Twitter takes care of sizing the image for you.

**Figure 2-8:**
The Picture
page lets
you upload
your own
Twitter pro-
file picture.

4. **Select the image you want and then click the Open (or OK) button.**

5. **Click the Save button.**

   After a few moments, Twitter displays your new avatar on your profile page. It may take a few seconds to display your Twitter profile picture. Be patient and your beautiful face (or logo) will be displayed in due time.

Your profile picture is meant to help others identify you easily and tell a bit more about you to those who may not know you. A logo for your business or product may be a good choice for your picture, but if your company has a spokesperson or image of an individual that people can relate to, use a photo of this person. Think how you can make the photo as interesting as possible. For example, crop a portion of the photo or show an unusual angle to get people's attention.

If you want to get catchy and flashy, you could try to add your logo to your picture. Use a picture of yourself and add your logo to the left or right side of your profile picture.

Whatever image you choose, make sure you have permission to use it to avoid getting in trouble. Copyright issues and pretending you're someone you're not are two bad mistakes for a business using Twitter. By breaking the Twitter law, your account could be deleted or suspended. Remember your followers! You don't want to be deleted or suspended.

# Understanding Twitter Basics

I don't go into a lot of detail about how to use Twitter in this book because it's very easy to use, and *Twitter For Dummies,* by Laura Fitton, Michael Gruen, and Leslie Poston (Wiley), covers it in depth. But here are the Twitter basics:

- ✔ **Tweets:** A *tweet* is a message. You have 140 characters, including spaces, to put down your thoughts. Type your message in the What Are You Doing text box on your homepage and click the Update button to send a tweet, as shown in Figure 2-9.

Enter your tweet here.     Click this button to send your tweet.

**Figure 2-9:**
You can
type up to
140 charac-
ters in the
What Are
You Doing
text box.

Rules of grammar and punctuation fly out the window when you send a Tweet. Abbreviate *with* to *w/,* turn *people* into *ppl,* and even make *for* or *four* into *4.* You can make your messages deep and philosophical, clever, funny, informational, educational, a question, an answer, or what you had on your bagel for breakfast this morning.

✔ **@replies:** When you want to reply to a particular tweet, you can click the Reply button offered by all Twitter clients or the backward arrow next to the tweet you want to reply to on Twitter itself, as you can see in Figure 2-10.

Alternatively, you can type the @ ("at") symbol followed by the person's user ID, followed by your tweet, in the What Are You Doing text box, as shown in Figure 2-11. An @reply not only lets the rest of the world know who you're talking to, but it also lets the other person know that you're talking about him or her.

**Figure 2-10:** You can reply to a tweet, by clicking on the backward arrow next to it.

Reply button

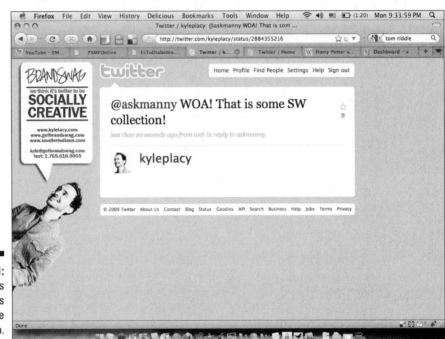

**Figure 2-11:**
@replies
show others
who you are
talking to.

If you're using a Twitter client such as TweetDeck, you can see all your @replies in one column, instead of having to spot them in the general timeline.

✔ **Hashtags (#):** You can use hashtags to create groupings and help generate popularity around a particular keyword or topic. You can create a hashtag about a city, local event, news event, brand, sports team, or anything you want by preceding it with the hash mark (#).

When you include a hashtag in a tweet, it becomes clickable. In Figure 2-12, you can see an example of a tweet with a hashtag.

✔ **Direct messages:** Also called DMs, *direct messages* let you communicate privately with other Twitter users. To send a direct message, type the letter **D** followed by the username of the twitterer you want to reach, and then enter your message in the What Are You Doing text box, as shown in Figure 2-13.

Don't make the mistake of typing **DM** and then the message. Beginning a message with DM still sends it out to the general timeline. A Web site called dm fail (http://dmfail.com) searches for all messages that started with DM and displayed them for all to see — angry messages, breakups, and Twitter sex.

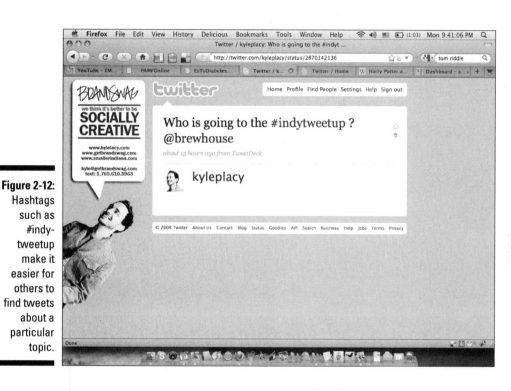

**Figure 2-12:** Hashtags such as #indytweetup make it easier for others to find tweets about a particular topic.

**Figure 2-13:** Direct messages give you a private means to communicate with others on Twitter.

✔ **Link shorteners:** If you have 140 characters, you don't want to use 50 of them by including a long URL. You need to shorten the URL so that you can save yourself some characters. Most URL shorteners shrink the links to anywhere from 16 to 20 characters.

Programs such as TweetDeck (`http://tweetdeck.com`) and Web sites such as `http://bit.ly` can shorten a URL for you. I talk about Twitter clients in the following section, but if you're looking for a desktop client, pick one with a built-in URL shortener.

Get a URL shortener that offers tracking so that you can see how many people have clicked on your shortened links. One of my favorites is `www.twitalyzer.com`, which uses the `http://bit.ly` URL shortener.

# Twitter Software You Can Use

Twitter's homepage has a Web-based interface that lets you send tweets and DMs directly from its window. However, you can only see a few tweets at a time, and Twitter's interface lets you create groups or see @replies, which means if you're following a lot of people, you're going to miss a lot of messages. The solution? Use software that makes reading, replying, and (of course) tweeting easier. All these products are free, unless otherwise noted:

✔ **TweetDeck (`http://tweetdeck.com`):** TweetDeck is a popular client that lets you create groups of people you want to follow, save a search for a particular keyword by creating a column for that search word or twitterer, and even shorten URLs by using one of six different URL shorteners. It also organizes everything into columns so that you can see everything on one screen. TweetDeck allows you to manage multiple accounts and update your Facebook status. TweetDeck uses Adobe AIR as its engine, which means it can run on Windows, Macintosh, and Linux.

✔ **twhirl (`www.twhirl.org`):** A desktop client that lets you manage multiple accounts by keeping multiple windows open at the same time. twhirl also lets you update different social media notifiers such as Ping.fm (which in turn lets you update your status on several other social networking sites, such as Facebook, MySpace, Identi.ca, and LinkedIn).

✔ **DestroyTwitter (`http://destroytwitter.com`):** Another Adobe AIR–based application. Destroy Twitter works just like TweetDeck, but it uses less memory. DestroyTwitter uses tabs — called canvasses — for different groups, and you are given the option to view your account in a column view, as you can in TweetDeck.

✔ **Spaz (http://getspaz.com):** This client works like other desktop apps, but it has different themes available. Spaz also has a mobile version available for the Palm Pre.

✔ **Twitterific (http://iconfactory.com/software/twitterrific):** A Twitter app for the iPhone or iPod touch. You can buy Twitterific for your Mac for $14.95 or download the iPhone version for free at the iTunes App Store.

You can find a lot of other desktop and mobile clients available, several of which use Adobe AIR. However, I just can't keep up with all of them and name them here. A quick Google search or even a tweet to your followers can help you find the client that's best for you.

# Part II

# Building and Implementing Your Twitter Marketing Roadmap

The 5th Wave          By Rich Tennant

"He saw your laptop and wants to know if he can check 'Twitter.'"

# In this part . . .

Perhaps you feel like you don't have enough time in the day to complete all the projects that you need to finish. You may feel like Twitter is just adding one more thing to your plate. Well, break the plate! In this part, you dive into the world of productivity, setting goals, and finding success in the world of Twitter marketing.

Millions of people use Twitter. How do you reach them in a strategic way? (If you don't want to use strategy, this part isn't for you.) You absolutely must have a strategy and set goals if you want to successfully market your business on Twitter. This part breaks down the topics of creating a Twitter marketing plan, building your followers, and taking best advantage of this wonderful communication tool.

# Chapter 3

# Combining New and Old Media Marketing

*In This Chapter*

▶ Using old-school marketing and principles on Twitter

▶ Working with new media tools and techniques

▶ Tweeting to find warm sales leads

▶ Deciding what to tweet about

**D**epending on whom you ask, Twitter and social media are changing the landscape of marketing. Old marketing is dead, new marketing is king. They're surprised people still advertise in the phone book, on TV and radio, and — gasp — on billboards.

"Everyone," they cry, "is online! Renounce your old ways and join us on the Interweb." (Because the really cool people call it the Interweb as a sort of irony.)

Meanwhile, the old-school marketers believe that the social-media craze is just a passing fancy and that serious business is still done with a handshake. They cite all sorts of numbers and reasons to continue to advertise in broadcast and print media. "Social media," grumble the curmudgeons, "is just a fad. People need to quit playing games and join the rest of us here on Earth."

But neither of these marketing views is entirely correct. Social media hasn't changed the marketing landscape, but at the same time, marketing can't completely go back to the way it was. The smart marketers — by which I mean you, the person who bought this book (see, that action right there already shows how brilliant you are) — understand that the tools may have changed, but the principles are still the same.

You still have the five P's of marketing — product, price, place (distribution), promotion, and people. The message is still more important than the medium. And you still have to provide a value to your customers; otherwise, they won't be willing to part with their money. Twitter is just one more tool in the marketing toolbox.

# Applying Old-School Marketing and Principles

Marketing has been around since Og and Zog were both competing in the blossoming wheel industry thousands of years ago. Og and Zog had to show customers how they'd benefit from a wheel (education) and how a wheel could provide value to them (sales), as well as offer customers excellent customer service (follow up).

The same techniques apply today. Marketers educate, sell, and service by using commercials, brochures, and Web sites. But now they have some new tools in the marketing toolbox.

So, what's the difference between old-school marketing and the new school? On the face, not much. The principles are still the same.

Say that you manufacture marbles and sell them to marble collectors. Thirty years ago, your marketing plan would have looked like this:

1. Find your ideal customer.

   Do focus groups, surveys, and data analysis. Find out who the typical marble collector is. Create a profile about what he or she likes to do, where he or she is likely to live, and whether he or she belongs to any marble clubs. Because collectors make up the majority of your customers, you need to focus most of your energy on them.

   You may have an ideal customer who is male, lives in a large city, is in his 30s or 40s, and likes sports.

2. Create a marketing campaign to reach those ideal customers.

   If it's in your budget, advertise during sporting events on TV, especially on ESPN. Put up billboards around the 15 biggest cities around the country. Buy a mailing list from the different marble clubs around the country and send them all a copy of your latest catalog. Put ads in print magazines that the ideal customer reads, including sports magazines such as *Sports Illustrated*.

3. Measure sales before and after the campaign.

   If sales went up, the campaign was a success. Also, if sales went down it is important to figure out what went wrong in the marketing process. Why did you lose money? Test. Retest. Try again.

4. Survey your customers.

   Find out where customers saw your ad. Continue to put money into the ads that worked. Don't pull the plug on the underperforming ads just yet, but make sure to keep a close eye on them for a bit longer, as they may turn out to be money sinkholes.

Marketers still follow the process in the preceding list to some degree. Even if companies have more advertising channels to choose from and they've gotten smarter about finding the ideal customer just by paying attention, every company still follows this basic plan.

But Twitter and the Internet have changed how you can target your customers. They've made marketing easier and cheaper. E-mail accounts and social networks such as Facebook are free to use. The cost of developing (and running) a Web site has dropped dramatically. And, thanks to the Internet, performing research, creating your message, and distributing it have become more affordable than ever before.

Here's what new-school marketing looks like:

1. Target your customers.

   Who cares what your ideal customer is like? You don't have to target people *like* them because you can target them directly. As you can see in Figure 3-1, you can do a search by using Twitterment (www.twitterment.com) and Nearby Tweets (http://nearbytweets.com). Follow people who are talking about marble collecting.

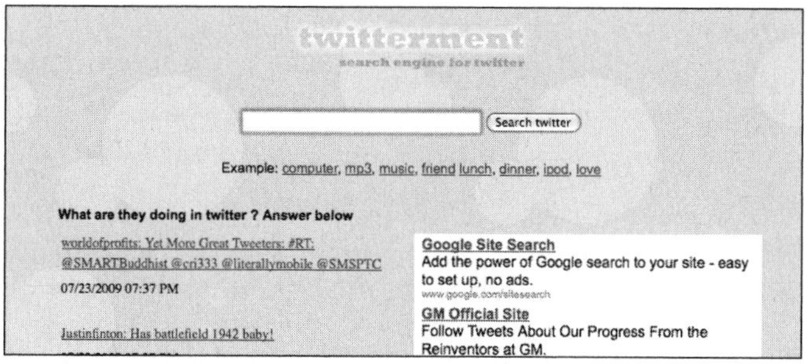

**Figure 3-1:** You can use Twitterment to find people that match your customer profile.

2. As long as you tweet about relevant content that these folks care about, there is a very good chance that they will follow you back.

3. Create a marketing campaign that involves a Web site and a blog, and create a Facebook and/or MySpace page. Invite people to join these groups.

    See *Web Design For Dummies,* 2nd Edition, by Lisa Lopuck; *Blogging For Dummies,* by Susannah Gardner and Shane Birley; *Facebook For Dummies,* 2nd Edition, by Leah Pearlman and Carolyn Abram; and *MySpace For Dummies,* 2nd Edition, by Ryan Hupfer, Mitch Maxson, and Ryan Williams, all published by Wiley Publishing, Inc.

4. Write regular blog content and use Twitter to post messages letting your followers know that you have a new post on your blog, as you can see in Figure 3-2.

**Figure 3-2:**
You can use Twitter to inform your followers about your recent blog posts.

You can shorten a really long Web address in a tweet. (I discuss URL shorteners in Chapter 6.) You can also track the shortened URLs, which means you can actually measure their effectiveness. By using a URL shortener such as http://bit.ly, the longer URL

```
http://www.marblemayhem.com/2009/06/marble-collecting-
          conference-boston
```

becomes

```
http://bit.ly/frpKw
```

Because you have targeted your customers, one of the many marble-collecting fans that follows you may retweet your message out to his 2,000 followers (many of whom also happen to be marble collectors). Some of them may retweet it to their followers and so on. If enough people are interested in what you have to say about marbles, with just a few mouse clicks, your post can potentially be read by 10,000 people.

In Figure 3-3, you can see what a retweet by one of your followers may look like. (The abbreviated form of retweet is RT, which appears at the beginning of a retweet post.)

**Figure 3-3:** On Twitter, others can help expand the reach of your message by re-tweeting it.

twitter  Home Profile Find People Settings Help Sign out

RT @Brandswag: New post: Marble collecting conference in Boston next month. http://bit.ly/frpKw

*less than 5 seconds ago from web*

kyleplacy

5. Measure your results.

   If you are not tracking and analyzing the traffic on your site, you should. You can do it using a platform such as Google Analytics (www.google.com/analytics), which lets you look at lots of information about your site's visitors. Using Google Analytics, find out which messages, which posts, which tweets, and even what time of day produced the best results, leading to the most sales. Armed with this information, you can put more energy and effort into the actions that generate more sales and drop the ones that don't produce such a good result. You can also try to figure out ways to improve nonperforming messages, posts, and tweets.

REMEMBER

Most of the ideas stay the same when you transition from old marketing techniques to tech-savvy ones: Find your customer, create a marketing campaign, create an effective message, and measure the results.

However, you can improve the return on your investment in some of these areas when you use social media as part of your marketing toolkit:

- ✔ Find your exact customer, not an approximation or ideal of one.

- ✔ Reach your customers right where they are, instead of advertising in places you hope they'll be.

- ✔ Send your message only to people who care about your product(s), instead of wasting ink and money on people who don't.

- ✔ Create frequent, even daily, content and get it to customers at all hours of the day, not once a month or only at game time.

- ✔ Don't spend thousands and thousands of dollars in print and broadcast advertising. Spend a small amount to no money on electronic marketing.

- ✔ Encourage retweets. This improvement is huge: Customers can easily share your message within their circles of influence.

Because of social media, you can share information with your friends much more easily than you could even five years ago. Back in the mid 2000s, if you wanted to share information with people, you had to e-mail links to Web sites or forward jokes countless times to each other. Now, you can share photos with friends and family. Upload a 5-minute movie of your 3-year-old explaining *Star Wars* and get a ton of hits. Write a blog post that 1,000 rabid marble collectors see or click a button that retweets a message to 10,000 people in just a few minutes.

Word of mouth was almost literally word of mouth 30 years ago. You called your friend about a great new restaurant. You asked a colleague whether she saw the billboard over on Massachusetts Avenue. You talked about the great new TV series. But you couldn't share articles or videos, unless you clipped an article out of a newspaper or magazine, or recorded a TV show on your VCR.

People didn't share 30 years ago like they do now. Thanks to social media's growth and tools such as Twitter, you can now easily share information with people who think like you and who like the same things you like. That's why some people are now calling "word of mouth" advertising "word of mouse." (Clever, huh?)

If anything is different about marketing today, it's not the tools, it's not the technology, and the medium isn't the message — the ability to share has given consumers a new voice. It has given consumers the power to talk about experiences and share them with thousands upon thousands of people. And you can make your business a success by sharing your stories, ideas, thoughts, and successes with the clients and consumers using Twitter for communication.

# Working with New Media Tools and Techniques

Thirty years ago, you could easily get your message to your potential customers. You advertised on the big three networks, on the radio, and in newspapers. People couldn't escape your message. They were in your world. You just had to repeat your message enough times for it to take effect.

Now, people have hundreds of channels on TV. They get their radio from the Internet, satellite, or one of a myriad of radio stations. Newspapers aren't faring very well: Both readership and advertising revenues have dropped, many newspapers have gone bankrupt, and people are questioning whether the newspapers will even be around in ten years.

But people are also online. In fact, if you need one place where you can find most people, it's online. More people are congregating on Facebook and MySpace every day. They're reading and writing blogs. And they're using Twitter.

If you want to reach your customers, you need to find out where they're located. Thanks to high-speed Internet and cheaper, faster computers, they're on social media, including Twitter.

## Understanding the potential of social media

Frankly, you can't escape social media. Not only are individuals getting involved, but small businesses and large corporations are jumping into the fray with both feet. Even the U.S. State Department has a Twitter account and a Facebook account, and it's even started a social networking site on its own server.

In the course of the past year, Twitter has been at the center of two major government protests, one in Moldova in April 2009 and one in Iran in June 2009. To show support for the Iran protests, many Twitter users made their avatar green, the same color used by the protestors, as you can see in Figure 3-4. (Okay, you'll have to trust me because this is a black-and-white book — the avatars really are green.)

AMSR12 HELP EACH OTHER! Stey by your people! Help the families who have their lovelies in prison or have lost their people!#iranelection
half a minute ago from web

maliheh__ @pattyblake Ahmadinejad may face confidence vote http://bit.ly/XasHn #iranelection #iran (via @cnn)
less than a minute ago from web

IranWitness Check out picture of Ahmadinijad poster with "HOPELESS" caption http://bit.ly/x3bxr #Iranelection, #Neda Times online
less than a minute ago from web

geologybabe RT @cnn Ahmadinejad may face confidence vote http://bit.ly/XasHn #iranelection
less than a minute ago from web

lovelranlove IMP. Ppl be aware.United4iran r this regime's rejects. Not our friends. Found out @the rally in NY. #iranelection #united4iran
less than a minute ago from web

**Figure 3-4:** As part of the Iran protest, thousands of Twitter users made their avatar green.

In both cases, the ruling governmental party was accused of election fraud, and the opposing party launched huge protests that caught the attention of the world. In both cases, people organized thanks to Twitter and Facebook. In fact, the Moldovan protest started with 6 people in a coffee shop in Chisinau (the capital city) and grew to 20,000 people just two days later.

Think about that: Six people turned into 20,000 people in 48 hours. Now, that's word-of-mouse advertising!

## Keeping your message real

You hear these words a lot these days: *authenticity* and *transparency*. People use them interchangeably, and they basically mean the same thing: Let people see what you're really doing and don't lie about it.

In the marble collecting example that I talk about in the section "Applying Old-School Marketing and Principles," earlier in this chapter, say that you buy your marbles from overseas. A dishonest or less-than-ethical company might lead people to believe that the company manufactures the marbles in the home office. But a transparent company tells people where the products come from.

Lying in the social media realm is the kiss of death because as quickly as you get your message to the public, word of your deception spreads twice as fast. Customers respect honesty. They might not like your product, but at least they won't accuse you of lying to them.

# Tweeting to Find Warm Sales Leads

Before social media, salespeople found prospects on mailing lists and phone lists, through their business networks and referrals, and by cold calling. They turned prospects into warm leads, and then into paying customers. Just like old-school marketing principles still apply today (as I discuss earlier in this chapter), old-school sales principles do, too.

## Searching for potential customers

Nowadays, you can find prospective customers by searching for them through Twitter's search feature (both, the one that you have access to within Twitter itself and the advanced search Twitter offers at http://search.twitter.com), Nearby Tweets (www.nearbytweets.com), and Twitterment (www.twitterment.com).

Though Twitter's search, Nearby Tweets, and Twitterment are excellent options to help you unearth prospects, new and improved Twitter search tools keep appearing all the time. Keep your eyes open for references to new resources you can use to expand your list of prospects.

To start your hunt for prospective customers, do a search to find people who are talking about your industry, field, or company. Going back to the marble collecting example, you can type in **marble collection** using the native search box on Twitter, as shown on Figure 3-5, or Twitterment's search box.

**Figure 3-5:** Twitter offers a convenient search box to help you find people to follow.

What are you doing?                                    140     kyleplacy
                                                                3,549   4,334   10,785
                                                                following followers updates

Latest: RT @casseracomm: RT @mashable HOW TO: Translate Your     update
Tweets http://bit.ly/10UYiF about 2 hours ago

Real-time results for **marble collection**    Save this search

kcorbammej Counting and sorting my **marble collection** for the first time in a long time.
about 19 hours ago from txt

susiesattic **marble collection** http://bit.ly/Zu3Q0
5 days ago from web

_Flik_ Just found my **marble collection** – I'm sad aren't I?!
5 days ago from dabr

Aleksandr_Orlov @Belleinthecity I see myself as businessKat. My desk is my wife, my **collection** of antique **marble** letter-openers, my mistress.
6 days ago from web

Tweets on tees
n. awesome crowdsourced shirts by Threadless.

Home
@kyleplacy
Direct Messages    3,769
Favorites
marble collection
Trending Topics
Harry Potter
Mexico
Comic-Con
G-Force
Gold Cup

— Search box

This search yields results that may be useful to a certain extent: After all, these are Twitter users who are talking about *marble collection.* But you may be interested in folks who are talking about this topic within your own geographical area. In this case, Nearby Tweets comes in handy, letting you enter a location, keyword, and search radius, as you can see in Figure 3-6.

**Figure 3-6:**
Nearby
Tweets
lets you
find nearby
Twitter
users.

If you need to get more specific with your search query, use the Twitter Advanced Search. To get to it, visit `http://search.twitter.com` and click the Advanced Search link beneath the search box. This takes you to a very detailed page (shown in Figure 3-7) that lets you find tweets based on the following parameters:

✔ **Words:** You can construct a query that contains all, any, or none of the words you enter. You can also find tweets that contain an exact phrase or a particular hashtag and tweets written in a specific language.

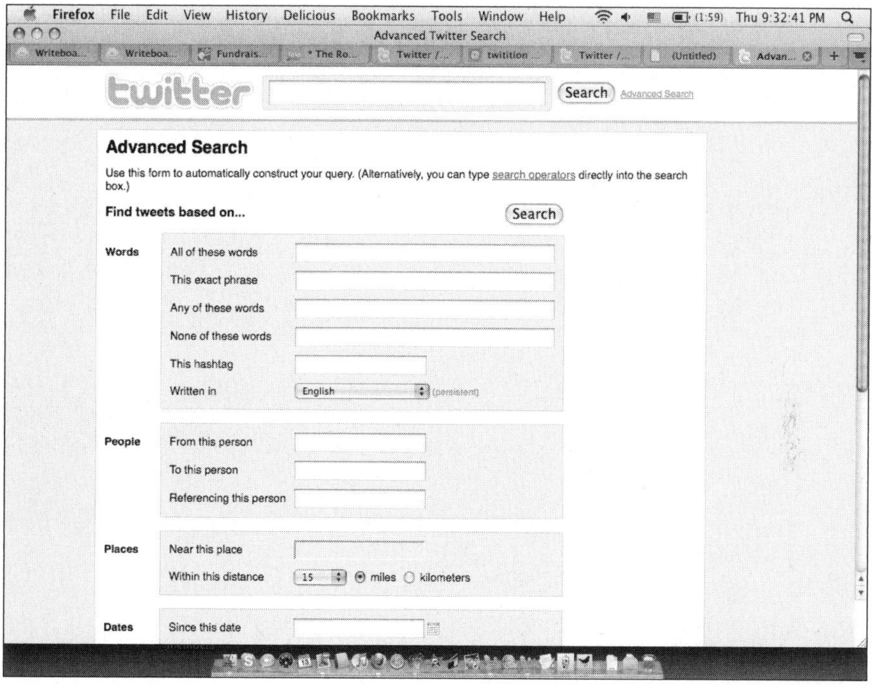

**Figure 3-7:**
Fine-tune
your search
on the
Advanced
Search
page.

✔ **People:** You can find tweets posted by someone, directed at someone, or referring to someone. Are there no secrets anymore?

✔ **Places:** In a similar way to Nearby Tweets, you can finds tweets posted a certain distance from a specific location.

✔ **Dates:** You can specify what dates you want to search for tweets. This search parameter can come in handy if you want to find out the response on Twitter to a campaign you are running.

✔ **Attitudes:** You can spot tweets with a positive or negative attitude as well as tweets asking a question. Can you imagine the power of learning how happy (or upset) your customers may be about your product?

✔ **Other:** You can filter your results to show only those that contain links or to limit the number of results per page.

## Turning prospects into warm leads

After you've identified potential customers, follow these people so that hopefully they'll follow you back. Engage them in conversation about anything and everything. Provide relevant content that they may be likely to find useful. As people get to know you, they'll become interested in what you do. And when that happens, they'll begin contacting you for information about what you do.

After you develop these relationships with people, they move from prospects — people you're following and who are following you — to *warm leads*. As leads, they've visited your Web site, signed up for your e-mail newsletter or blog, and even requested a catalog or downloaded your sales literature. What you do with them after that is up to you. (See *Selling For Dummies,* 2nd Edition, by Tom Hopkins [Wiley] for the scoop on making a sale.)

## Sending commercial messages on Twitter

As a general rule, don't bombard your customers and followers with commercial message after commercial message. That gets real old, real fast. If people think you're a spammer, they'll block and unfollow you. And if the folks at Twitter notice a pattern of a lot of people blocking or unfollowing you, they'll suspend your account and possibly even cancel it permanently.

However, this rule has a few exceptions. In some cases, your followers may actually expect you to send commercial messages. It can be okay to share a commercial message at random. Your followers will accept you pushing your wares or products across Twitter if you have not sandblasted them with content every hour of the day.

For example, @DellOutlet has been one of Twitter's marketing success stories, and the one that many people point to as the shining star among corporate Twitter users. @DellOutlet tweets nothing but major discounts for Dell computers and products (see Figure 3-8), and those discounts are available only on Twitter, not the Dell Web site or catalog. You can't even call in to ask for them.

In its first two years, @DellOutlet grew to nearly 1 million followers and sold $3 million worth of products, with $1 million of that being within a 6-month period. What's even more surprising about Dell's Twitter success is that they don't tweet every day, and they do actually communicate with their followers. They answer questions, recommend products and Web sites, and even send nice thank-you notes to people.

Some people scoff at the fact that @DellOutlet made "only" $2 million, compared to the $61 billion the entire company made in 2008. But think of it this way — when was the last time you made $2 million doing anything, let alone sending 140-character messages a few times a day?

**Figure 3-8:**
The tweets by @DellOutlet often contain exclusive offers.

# Deciding What to Tweet About

Figuring out what to tweet about can be tricky. Your first inclination may be to just start sending out message after message about your product or service. Come up with a clever statement, put a URL to your Web site, and repeat the process about three or four times an hour, right? *Wrong.*

This approach is actually the worst thing you can do. Oh sure, if you play the numbers game and trick thousands and thousands of people into following you, you might get a few sales this way. But if you try this technique, Twitter users will quickly label you a spammer, and Twitter will cancel your account and drop you completely.

The professional spammer is undeterred and just starts the whole mess over again, under a different name. But you don't want that to happen for your business. Your brand and reputation are important. You've worked hard to grow and maintain them, so you don't want to ruin them by blasting nothing but Twitter spam (which isn't called Twam, though I'm not sure why).

You can send out commercial messages, but you need to intersperse them with other types of messages. And you need to balance all the types of messages you send out. Share too much about yourself and you may come across as too self-centered. If you only tweet questions, you'll appear as someone who only takes and gives very little back. If you only retweet what others write, it may sound as if you don't have much to contribute on your own.

Keeping a balance between the different types of tweets will help you grow your follower base and fit in within the Twitter community.

## The five types of tweets

You can send out five basic types of tweets:

- ✓ **Personal messages:** Information about you, whether you tweet about work, home, or your personal life. You can share as much or as little as you want. Don't feel you have to share intimate details of your life — just share the parts that you don't mind other people knowing. This sharing lets people get to know the real you.

- ✓ **Retweets and replies:** Communicate with other people. Respond to their messages and carry on a conversation with them. Talk with these people the way you talk with your friends.

- ✓ **Questions:** Trying to decide which cell phone to buy? Need to know what the IRS mileage allowance is for your expense report? Want a recommendation on a restaurant to visit while you're in Boston? Tweet your question to your followers and see what comes back.

- ✓ **Commercial messages:** As I explain earlier, it's okay to send commercial messages on Twitter, just don't do it all the time. In fact, the recommended ratio is usually 1 commercial message out of 10 to 15 other types of messages. Any more commercial messages than that can make you come across as spammy.

- ✓ **Miscellaneous messages:** You can send out quotes that inspire you, links to articles you're reading, songs you're listening to, and anything that doesn't fit in the message types in the preceding bullets.

## Tweeting about what you know

When you're starting to tweet, you might feel like you have writer's block — especially if you take my advice to heart about not spewing your content all over the place. So, what do you talk about? Talk about what you know. Talk about hobbies or interests that involve your product(s); manufacturing of your product(s); shows, competitions, articles, and videos related to your product(s); and similar topics.

Using the marbles example that I introduce in the earlier section "Applying Old-School Marketing and Principles," if you sell marbles and you have marble collectors following you, talk about marble collecting, marble manufacturing, the results from the World Marble Shooting Tournament, and how Tim "Hammer Thumb" Murphy is considering coming out of retirement. Announce that you have a new post on your blog about how Italian glass marbles are more durable than Russian glass marbles, and ask for comments and a rigorous healthy debate. And once in a while, mention when your new line of shooters will be available on your Web site.

If you take the time to establish your reputation as a marble expert among other marble experts — speaking to marble collectors in the language of marble collectors about things that matter to the hearts of marble collectors — those marble experts will be more willing to listen when you talk about your business once in a while. But if you jump online and immediately begin blasting tweets about how your business offers 20 percent off the latest marble lines, users will ignore you more quickly than Hammer Thumb Murphy's patented Double Ambrose Spin can knock his opponent's marbles out of the ring.

# Chapter 4

# Planning Your Twitter Marketing Strategy

*T*he place to start when you need to develop a strategy for a business or a product is, of course, a business plan. Developing a Twitter marketing strategy helps you, your employees, and your business make marketing on Twitter successful.

The same concept applies to a traditional marketing plan. Every business in the world should write a business and marketing plan so that it can create a successful environment for the business. Think of your Twitter marketing strategy as a road map. You're developing a map, a sort of guide, that can lead you to the wonderful world of business success in the land of Twitter!

The first step to developing a successful journey is to decide where you want to go. Likewise, when you're developing a Twitter marketing plan, the first step is to determine your goal.

In this chapter, I tell you some of the tools and techniques that you can use to build and maintain a successful Twitter marketing strategy.

# Setting a Destination for Your Marketing Strategy

You can think about the concept of a destination for your Twitter marketing plan in a couple of ways. A good analogy is to think of your Twitter marketing strategy as a road trip. When you build a Twitter marketing strategy, the most important thing you do is set a destination — meaning the overall goal or specific goals that you can achieve by using Twitter.

## Choosing a target audience

If I were talking about the ABC's of business marketing, choosing a target audience would be A. This is also the first step in building a Twitter marketing plan. When you're trying to determine the target audience that your business reaches, answer a couple of questions:

- ✔ **Whom does your product or service appeal to?** For example, a travel company may be targeting retired individuals for vacationing. A video games company might target single men, ages 20 to 30.

- ✔ **Whom do you care about?** This may not be as relevant in the realm of traditional marketing, but it is in the Twitter environment because you're building relationships. So, in the case of the travel company, this may be the retiree who has been dreaming all his life of traveling to Hawaii. In the case of the video game company, this may be the guy who is willing to camp outside a store waiting for a new game to be released.

Review your current *demographic* (target audience) so that you can build an honest opinion of your client. Why reinvent the wheel? You either have a basic idea of your target audience or already have a specific group of people buying your product or service. For example, perhaps a typical client is Mary, a stay-at-home mom with three kids who buys your soccer balls. Or maybe it's Paul, the white-collar professional who works 90 hours a week, or Janice, the grandmother of your best friend. Or perhaps a segment of your clients are small-business owners.

Reviewing your current clients and placing them into the mix can also help you figure out whom you should target on Twitter. If you're starting a new business and you don't yet have a good idea of whom to target, review the questions included earlier in this section to help in your brainstorming process.

---

## Keep your content fresh

Offering your followers new content on a regular basis is a key component of a successful Twitter marketing strategy. You need to offer your Twitter followers fresh and relevant content that can help your Twitter domination quest. It will help you reach your marketing destination and set yourself up for success.

---

A concept many business owners or professionals fail to understand when it comes to brainstorming new strategies for business is to ask your clients' opinions. When you're figuring out who your target audience is on Twitter, look to your current clients. Are they on Twitter? Ask those clients who use Twitter for advice about whom you need to target on Twitter. Getting input from your current clients can go a long way to help you implement your strategy. You can send out e-mail surveys or just pick up the phone in order to get input from your existing customers. Whom do you communicate with currently? Now do it.

## Identifying your unique selling position

The next step in crafting a marketing plan is to think about what makes your business unique. Most businesses started on a concept of uniqueness. What sets you apart from the competition? What can you do while using Twitter that can set you apart from the other business owners or professionals who use the tool?

If you're in a unique niche, you can more easily build off your unique selling position on Twitter. Unlike traditional strategies, in which you'd make your unique selling position lowest price or club membership, a Twitter strategy involves combining what makes you unique as a business with unique content. How are you going to stand out from the millions of other people who use Twitter? (And no, frequent commercial tweets don't count as a good stand-out technique.)

You might offer a discount to Twitter users on your product or service. For example, offer a prize to the Twitter user who shares a certain blog post or comment the most with his or her followers. You could also offer a 10% discount to the first 20 people to click a link in one of your tweets.

If you want to decide what to offer your Twitter followers, you need to figure out why you're unique. What value does your product or service offer that your competition doesn't? (It's not your beaming personality, though customers do love that.) A couple of standard properties that can help you determine what makes you unique are:

✔ **Customer service:** This is still an important selling point in the business world. Even if you offer the same product as another company, if you have superior customer service, you can make it something that sets you apart on Twitter. To do this, monitor conversations about your company and your products on Twitter and use every opportunity to resolve the complaints of an unhappy customer and thank a happy one. You can see an example of an airline doing just this in Figure 4-1.

It's also important to train your customer service representatives to politely ask an irate customer to continue the conversation by e-mail or phone instead of on Twitter. You may even want to have your customer service reps give a standard answer to irate customers, such as "I'm sorry you're unhappy with your experience. Would you like to discuss the matter further via phone or e-mail?" The last thing that you want to happen is your representative getting into a public argument with a dissatisfied client on Twitter.

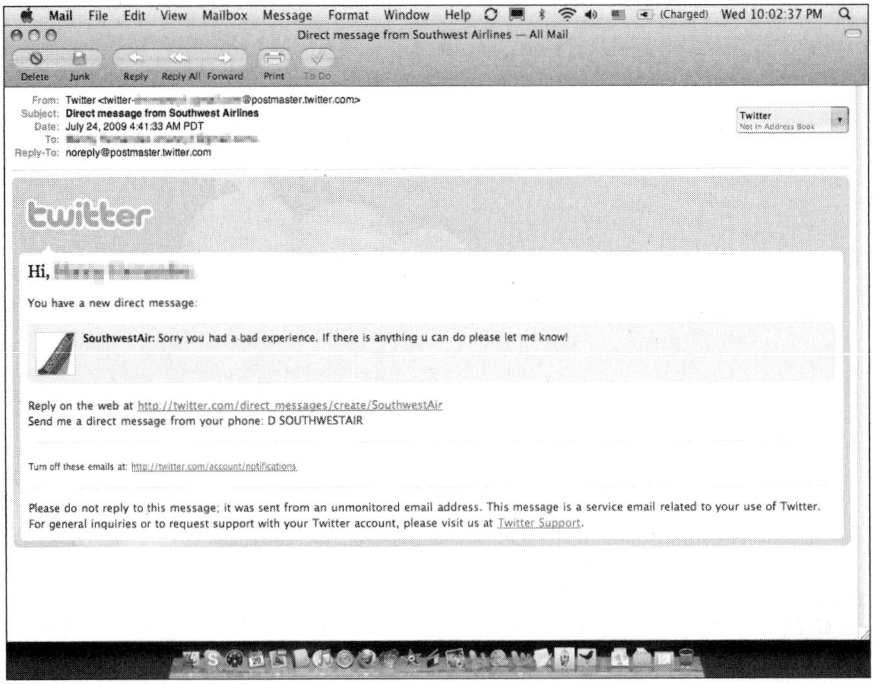

**Figure 4-1:** This Twitter user got a direct message from his airline after tweeting about a bad experience.

- **Upscale product offering:** You have a product or service that you sell to the upper echelons of society. This is what makes you unique, so you price your products or services *way* above the competition.

- **Downscaled product offering:** The Wal-Mart effect. If you have a downscaled product offering, you price your product below the average price offered by most of the industry. You can develop an extremely positive reputation when you use this approach to marketing on Twitter.

- **Longest track record:** You can use the age of your business as a unique selling position on Twitter. A long track record can be very valuable if you want to become a thought leader for your business niche.

- **Awards or prizes:** Have you or your company won any awards or prestigious plaques that tout your expertise in an industry? Those accolades make you unique.

- **Specialty:** If you offer a product or service that defines a niche market, you can turn this into a unique way to present yourself on Twitter. For example, Zappos.com (www.zappos.com) is almost a synonym for "online shoe store."

Write down the things that make you unique. You can refer to the list you create when you need help creating content for Twitter (described in the section "Crafting your message," later in this chapter) and building your following (covered in Chapter 7).

## Figuring out what your customers value

The age old question: What do your customers value? Don't worry; you can determine what your customers value pretty easily, but it's an important question to answer. In the world of business, you need to create a type of value that your customers can latch onto. By figuring out what your customers see as valuable in your company, you can create content on Twitter that can bring more customers and clients to your door.

What do your customers value when it comes to content? What do your customers value when it comes to products or services? You can easily determine the answers by asking your current customers. Have an open and honest conversation with your five best clients. They can tell you what they value in you or your company.

Figuring out what your customers value can also help you figure out your unique selling position — what would convince your customers to buy the product or service you offer as opposed to the one(s) offered by your competition.

The strategy to Twitter success involves producing content that takes into account the interests of your potential clients and customers. You want to share content that's directly related to your unique selling position.

# Implementing Your Plan

You can have all the ideas in the world, but without a good plan of implementation, you're going to fail miserably. But you won't fail when it comes to Twitter marketing if you adopt the principles in this book! Success is the only option. (Didn't George W. Bush say that one time? Too bad he didn't post it on Twitter.)

The first step in implementing your Twitter marketing strategy is to develop your content and the message that you want to share with the Twitter crowd. If you share the right content, the crow responds: They retweet it, click on your link, and buy your product, or they follow you.

## Crafting your message

When you implement your strategy, you need to plan your message. What are you trying to say to the Twitter groupies? You have endless possibilities for sharing your ideas, thoughts, and opinions through a communication technology such as Twitter.

Your voice drives your Twitter profile. You *are* the idea generator when it comes to sharing and producing content. Your business can benefit from establishing a connection with your followers that emphasizes the human side of your business: Putting a name and a face together, so to speak. They want to know that you're human and that you feel their pain. You feel their pain and can heal it — if they buy your product or service, of course.

To find your unique voice when it comes to communicating through Twitter, follow these steps:

1. **Take one of your unique selling positions and write it down.**

   A notecard or piece of scrap paper will do.

2. **Review your unique selling position.**

   What does it say? Are you the most personable realtor in the tri-state area? Are you the fastest plumber on planet Earth? Knowing your value position can help you find your voice.

3. **Write or type any stories you can remember in which you helped a client or customer by using your unique selling position.**

Think about your unique selling position like having a super power. Imagine being Superman or Wonder Woman, or better yet, the powerful Twitter Man or Twitter Woman. What super powers do you possess that help you in your quests to make clients happy?

Keep the stories, sentences, and ideas that you create in the preceding steps nearby. They can help remind you of how powerful your unique selling position is to your customers. The stories and ideas created by your business can help you create your unique voice for Twitter. JetBlue is a good example of this. Besides offering blue chips, their unique selling position involves caring for passengers, as shown in Figure 4-2, where they are answering a question that is not necessarily related to selling this customer a plane ticket.

**Figure 4-2:**
Your message on Twitter should be a reflection of your unique selling position.

Twitter is a place where you build relationships (unless you're a spammer). Relationship building is the key to your messaging on Twitter. So you should strive to cultivate relationships with your customers through your interactions with them on Twitter.

Content drives Twitter much like local, regional, national, and global stories drive newspapers. The content you create becomes the driving force of your Twitter marketing plan implementation. You have to directly relate that content to your unique selling position, your voice, and your industry. I discuss how to share, retweet, and create content in Chapters 6 and 10.

You have valuable content when it rings a bell with your followers (meaning your clients or potential clients) on Twitter. The content must have value that speaks to what customers are looking for on a daily basis. If you're a service provider, share content that has merit in your industry. For example, if you're a plumber, share a blog post with instructions on how to use duct tape to fix a leaky pipe.

 Valuable content surrounds the concept of talking about what you do — meaning what you (personally) do on a daily basis to help clients. Just remember: Don't try to push your product or service on Twitter. I deal some more with hard selling (another name for pushing your product or service) in Chapter 16.

## Defining the tactics

When you establish an overall idea about how to build the beginnings of a Twitter marketing plan, you need to define and refine the tactics associated with Twitter and your business.

In parallel with creating a presence on Twitter, you should also figure out what your competitors are doing in the world of micro-blogging. Also, you want to determine whether you should have separate accounts for your personal use and your business. Does it make sense to have both? The tactics define how you implement your strategy: This is the part where you roll up your sleeves.

### Performing a competitive analysis

You need to create a competitive analysis report for Twitter. What are your competitors doing that you can mimic (at the very least) or do better?

A *competitive analysis* involves finding out what steps your competition takes to use Twitter for lead generation. Determining the area of influence for your competitors can help in your quest for Twitter domination by letting you figure out where you stand in comparison to them.

The first step in building a Twitter competitive analysis involves finding out who among your competition is using Twitter. You can get this information in a couple of ways, but the best way is to use a tool called Twellow.

Also known as the Twitter Yellow Pages, Twellow (www.twellow.com) is a service that allows you to search for a specific name on Twitter. As shown in Figure 4-3, by using Twellow, you can find which companies are using Twitter in your business niche.

When you enter a personal or company name into Twellow, try your search with and without spaces. The two searches may return different results, all of which are typically useful.

**Figure 4-3:** Twellow can help you put together your Twitter competitive analysis.

After you find the Twitter name of all your competitors, you need to determine the amount of influence each competitor has. To find this information, you can use the tool called Twitter Grader (www.twittergrader.com) from the company Hub Spot, as shown in Figure 4-4.

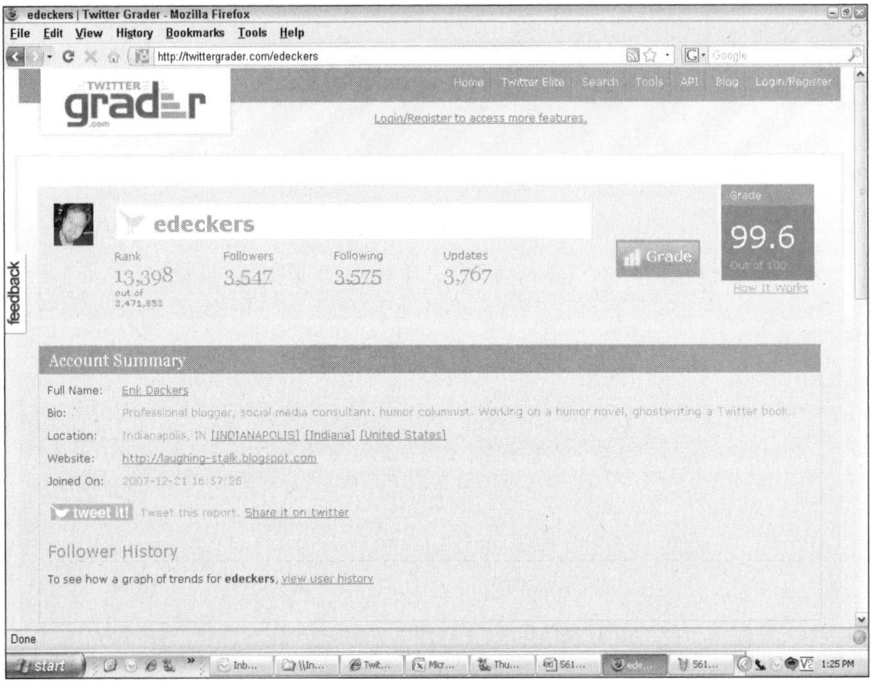

**Figure 4-4:**
Twitter
Grader
helps you
determine
your
competitors'
influence on
Twitter.

To use Twitter Grader to find your competition's area of influence, follow these steps:

1. **Open your browser and go to www.twittergrader.com.**

   The page that opens features a text box labeled Enter Your Twitter Username at the top of the page.

2. **Type a competitor's Twitter username in the Enter Your Twitter Username text box, and then click the Grade button.**

   A box pops up that says Off to the Races. Depending on the speed of your Internet connection, Twitter Grader may take a few minutes to finish the analysis.

   A new page appears, showing the rank of the Twitter user in comparison to all users that have been analyzed by Twitter Grader (nearly 3 million as I write these lines), as well as other useful information.

One of the most useful pieces of information returned by the Twitter Grader analysis is the user's grade (or score). This number is calculated by weighing elements such as the number of followers, the influence of the followers, the number of updates, the freshness of the updates, the ratio of followers versus users followed, and the number of times the user is being retweeted or cited. The rank information is based on the grade obtained by the user: A user with a higher grade will be higher in the ranking.

Another important piece of information you obtain from a Twitter Grader search is the Tweet Cloud. A *Tweet Cloud* is a list of generated words that a specific person uses the most, showing more frequently used words in larger font and less frequently used words in smaller font.

The Tweet Cloud gives you valuable hints as to what kind of content the user is writing about. For example, look at Figure 4-5. @edeckers's main tweets include the words *post, humor,* and *Indiana.*

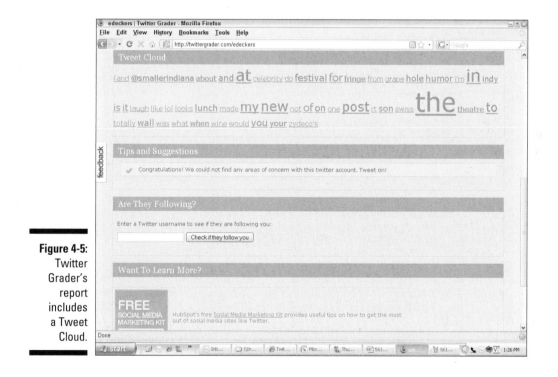

**Figure 4-5:**
Twitter
Grader's
report
includes
a Tweet
Cloud.

Because he has a pretty decent Twitter Grade (resulting in a good rank), if you were @edeckers's competition, you'd take into account the different words he's using on Twitter to help build your content strategy so that you can compete with him in the world of Twitter. For example, borrowing from @edeckers's Tweet Cloud, you may discover that his followers enjoy reading about local humor in Indiana. (Because you are his competitor, I am going to assume that learning about the comedy preferences of folks in Indiana is relevant to your business!)

Note what your competitors are writing about and be sure to follow them on Twitter: It's a great way to keep your pulse on the market and what types of messages are being presented to your potential or current customers.

### Creating a business profile, personal profile, or multiple profiles

How many accounts do you need when using Twitter? This topic is much debated in the Twitter world. If you're using Twitter for business, do you create a personal account and a business account, or do you use just one account? A lot depends on your specific case, and you should base your decision on your strategy and goals (which I discuss in the section "Setting Your Destination," earlier this chapter).

Here are some tips to remember when you try to decide on how many Twitter accounts you need:

- ✔ **Create a single account:** Stick with one account if you're a sole proprietor, artist, author, speaker, or any professional who *is* the business.

- ✔ **Create two accounts:** If you're a salesperson, an employee, or part of a company that has more than three employees, go with a personal account and a business account.

- ✔ **Create special accounts:** If your company is organizing a conference, you can make a Twitter account to drive traffic to that particular event or to highlight activities during the event.

  If you want to promote a book, whether you are the publisher or the author, it is also a good idea to have a dedicated account for it. For example, as you can see in Figure 4-6, @ningfordummies serves as the Twitter page for *Ning For Dummies* by Manny Hernandez (Wiley).

  You can also create accounts that pertain to a particular product. For example, Intuit (the maker of QuickBooks) has accounts for itself as a company, for its products, and for its customer service representatives.

**Figure 4-6:**
It is a good
idea to
create a
separate
account to
promote a
book or a
product.

You can explore the use of multiple accounts with an example company, XYZ Company. XYZ has six employees: an account representative, a graphic designer, a Web developer, a sales manager, a business development representative, and an operations manager. The account representative, sales manager, and business development representative are most likely to interact with clients on a daily basis. If your personal relationship with clients helps you develop business, create a specific account for your own personal use.

Given their more limited role facing the customers, the graphic designer, Web developer, and operations manager can either start a Twitter account or run the company account.

## Finalizing your marketing plan

Building your marketing plan takes time, but it's the most important thing you do when it comes to your Twitter domination! Now, for the important part: integrating your Twitter marketing plan with your offline strategy. You can make your Twitter marketing extremely successful if you combine it with your traditional marketing strategies.

Your offline strategy can include everything from direct mail to newspaper ads. You can combine some traditional strategies in order to promote your Twitter name offline:

- ✔ **Business cards:** Be very sure to put your Twitter username on your business cards. People use business cards as a marketing instrument constantly in the world of business.

- ✔ **Hire a sign holder:** You've probably seen guys and gals holding promotion signs for Domino's or Liberty Tax while dancing on the side of the road. You could hire one of these sign holders to promote your Twitter username. You also get an added benefit to hiring a roadside promotional person — they can be very entertaining when cars stop at a traffic light!

- ✔ **Buy a billboard:** Celebrity Ashton Kutcher bought multiple billboards to promote his Twitter username so that he could grow his list of followers. And it worked! Ashton has well beyond 3 million followers on Twitter at the time of this writing. If you can afford it, go for it.

- ✔ **Add to traditional marketing:** Add your Twitter username to every traditional marketing piece you send to potential and current customers — including direct mail, newsletters, and advertisements.

- ✔ **T-shirts:** Make a t-shirt to support your Twitter username. For example, you could have a t-shirt that features different tweets you've written about your niche topic. Create copies of the shirt and recruit ten people among your friends, employees (and perhaps even customers) to wear those shirts around, providing you with a great promotion!

  Conversely, if you come up with a *really* good tweet, you can submit it through http://twitter.threadless.com for others to vote on it. If it gets selected, it gets printed on t-shirts that others can purchase through www.threadless.com, as you can see in Figure 4-7. Gotta thank Twitter for that kind of publicity!

Integration is the key to a successful Twitter marketing strategy. You're already paying the money through your traditional marketing strategy, so why not take advantage of what you're already doing offline to promote your new Twitter username?

Speaking of paying money for a traditional strategy, you need to figure out your budget for running a Twitter marketing campaign. A Twitter marketing budget really consists of only two things:

- ✔ **Time:** In the small-business world, time is money. Map out how much time you're willing to delegate to Twitter usage. (I talk more about time management while on Twitter in Chapter 5.)

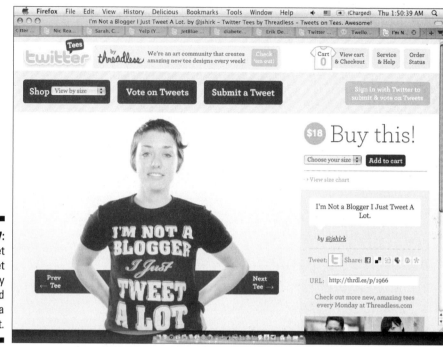

**Figure 4-7:**
You can get
your tweet
voted on by
others and
printed on a
t-shirt.

✔ **Money:** Decide how much you're willing to pay to help implement a
Twitter strategy. Use or create a budget specifically for your Twitter
marketing efforts.

# Chapter 5

# Being Productive with Your Twitter Marketing Plan

## In This Chapter

▶ Managing your time on Twitter

▶ Using Web tools for time management

▶ Making your time on Twitter productive

*I*f you want to have long-term success with Twitter (and other social media), you need to effectively manage your time and avoid burnout. If you're like me, you're a busy professional and probably have more than 20 different things to do before 8:00 a.m. and 30 things to do before noon. But if you can spare 15 to 30 minutes a day, you can get the most out of Twitter through repetition, planning, and being proactive.

This chapter takes a look at how proper planning and support can help you maximize your time on Twitter. If you follow the advice in the following pages, you can successfully manage your time and content on Twitter.

## Creating a Time-Management Strategy for Twitter

"I don't have time," many people say when they explore Twitter and other social media tools. "I'm already too busy, how am I supposed to squeeze in one more thing?"

"It's like eating an elephant," I sometimes say to these people (because I'm a little clever and more than a little weird). "You eat it one bite at a time."

Managing Twitter involves managing your time. If you look at Twitter as some big elephant that you have to eat all at the same time, you'll never get it done. But if you start small — one bite at a time — you can master the thing in less than a week.

## Avoiding Twitter overload

At times, you may become overwhelmed by all the information, content, friend requests, questions, comments, suggestions, and ideas that your followers are sharing on a consistent basis. This feeling has a name: It is called a *social media overload* or *Twitter overload.* Just don't let it get to the point of a brain hemorrhage or a heart attack! Time management and effective use of tools can help you keep your head above water.

Like with any problem, you can always spot warning signs before the worst part hits you right in the face. Bam! You fall off the edge and get overwhelmed. When you become overwhelmed, your Twitter marketing and usage will fall down the tubes, and you'll have no idea where to go from there. You'd rather not get to that point, right? In that case, watch out for these symptoms in your quest for Twitter domination:

✔ **Sleep deprivation:** You may find yourself using Twitter at times not best suited to your sleep routine. Maybe you wake up in the middle of the night with the extreme urge to tweet something absolutely ridiculous. A midnight tweet actually matters only when you have a dream you need someone to remember for you. But be honest, who really cares about your dream?

✔ **Inbox overload:** If your e-mail Inbox is overrun with Twitter requests, direct messages, and follower status updates, you need to take a step back and re-evaluate your use of your Inbox as a Twitter notification center.

You can go about silencing Inbox overload for eternity in one of two ways:

• Set up a folder to catch all your incoming Twitter e-mail announcements, and then set aside a couple of minutes every day to go through your Twitter folder. This separate folder keeps all your Twitter e-mail out of your Inbox — so you don't open your Inbox and see a gazillion messages from Twitter, giving you a nervous breakdown.

• Turn off updates in the settings of your Twitter profile. To do this, click the Settings link at the top of any page on Twitter, choose the Notices tab, and uncheck all the check boxes on the page. This stops e-mails from being sent out when new people follow you and when other Twitter users send you Direct Messages. Additionally, you can kill your subscription to the Twitter newsletter, as you can see in Figure 5-1.

Remember that you may not want to shut off all your notifications. It may be important to keep your Direct Message and Reply notifications on in order to respond to important inquiries.

✔ **Client phone-call backlog:** If you find your phone ringing constantly and voicemail messages piling up from clients upset because you're twittering rather than serving their needs, you're probably experiencing a Twitter overload. This is also the case if your spouse starts giving you the evil eye for spending more time on Twitter than together as a couple.

Make sure to set aside time to specifically to use Twitter. This will help you get work done (and possibly help you save your relationship!).

✔ **Non-stop use:** You can easily start using Twitter without stopping if you don't set barriers. There are literally millions of people you can follow, so try to keep yourself from becoming obsessed. You can burn out from information overload and follower requests.

Use your time management tools and calendar (discussed in the following section). You need to tweet on a constant — but not *too* constant — basis.

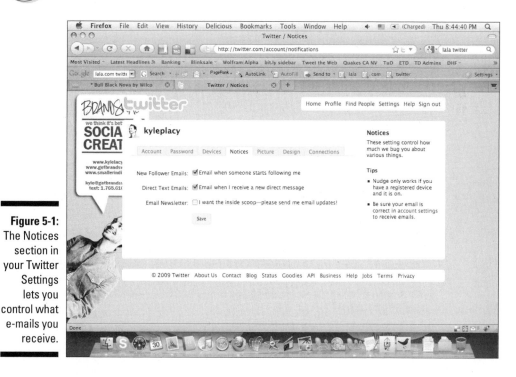

**Figure 5-1:**
The Notices section in your Twitter Settings lets you control what e-mails you receive.

## Setting aside blocks of time

To effectively manage your time, you need to block out certain parts of the day to accomplish certain tasks. The same rules apply to your Twitter and social-media usage. You can apply time blocks to any area of your business or personal life. The most important thing to remember is to stick to your schedule as closely as you can.

Think of your typical work day. What happens throughout the day? You have to pick up the kids; file a report; more than likely, do some shopping; and above all, run a business. Because you're so busy, you need to block out time in your day during which you can accomplish your Twitter marketing plan.

 The optimal amount of time in your Twitter marketing time blocks is between 15 and 30 minutes apiece. Don't set aside blocks of less than 15 minutes and never more than 30 minutes. If you start using Twitter for more than 30 minutes in the same time period, you can waste away hours with Twitter fun.

Although you may be enjoying yourself, spending endless hours on Twitter doesn't necessarily help you reach your Twitter marketing goals. Or if it helps you reach them, it is eating into the time you have previously allocated to other tasks in your business (or your life). The following list gives you tips on being productive with your Twitter time blocks:

✔ **Choose the times for two 15- to 30-minute Twitter time blocks each day.** You can choose to place the time blocks at the beginning and end of your day or during your lunch break.

✔ **Add the time blocks to your calendar.** Whether you use an electronic calendar, such as Outlook, or a written calendar, record your scheduled time blocks every day.

✔ **Respect the time block!** You wouldn't call a prospective client to reschedule a meeting because you needed to run to the store or pick up office supplies. The same rule applies for your Twitter time block.

Did your grandfather always tell you that practice makes perfect? This same principle applies to your Twitter marketing plan. Respect the time blocks that you set aside for yourself. If you don't keep to your Twitter time goals, you'll become frustrated, develop Twitter overload symptoms, and die a horrible Twitter death (well, most likely you won't die, but your spouse might want to kill you).

Make a commitment to yourself to stay on task and get your Twitter plan done in a timely manner.

# Using Third-Party Tools to Be More Productive with Twitter

You can find dozens, if not hundreds, of different Twitter applications (apps) that make you more efficient in your Twitter efforts.

As a Twitter marketer, look for an app that allows you to effectively manage multiple Twitter profiles, schedule tweets to go out at a later date and time, and measure your Twitter analytics. The following sections describe a few of the best Twitter apps currently available.

## TweetDeck

I recommend the TweetDeck (http://tweetdeck.com) application for anyone getting started with Twitter or for the people who try to use the Twitter.com Web interface and throw up their hands, saying, "I just don't get how Twitter works." Nearly everyone I know who uses TweetDeck has become a Twitter ninja.

TweetDeck runs on Adobe AIR (see the sidebar "Adobe AIR," in this chapter, for more information). You can send and receive tweets using this desktop application, so you don't have to rely on the Twitter.com Web interface. Imagine trying to watch a baseball game through a cardboard tube versus seeing the game with no obstructions. When it comes to Twitter, TweetDeck lets you see the entire game.

By using TweetDeck, you can create groups of people you want to follow, do searches for keywords and hashtags, and use any of six built-in URL shorteners, including http://bit.ly and http://tinyurl.com. (It doesn't include http://ow.ly, however.)

---

## Adobe AIR

Adobe AIR is a cross-platform application that runs on Windows, Mac, and Linux. If a program runs on Adobe AIR, and your computer runs on Windows, Mac or Linux, that program can run on your computer. When you download a program that runs on Adobe AIR, the installation application performs a check to see whether you already have Adobe AIR on your computer. If you don't have it, the installation application asks whether you want to download it. Or you can download Adobe AIR directly at www.adobe.com/products/air.

---

With a few exceptions, you should use TweetDeck for all your twittering. Send and receive tweets; send and receive direct messages; shorten URLs; and create groups of clients, competitors, industry experts, and favorite people. More specifically, TweetDeck offers the following features:

- ✔ **Groups:** When you're following more than a couple of hundred people, don't bother trying to follow all their tweets individually. For one thing, you're going to have the occasional spammer, someone who tweets about the latest little "present" his or her new puppy left, or a person who repeatedly sends the same quote about a small group of thoughtful citizens changing the world. You don't want to keep up with all that madness. So, create groups of people you want to follow, as shown in Figure 5-2.

- ✔ **URL shorteners:** TweetDeck has six URL shorteners, including `http://bit.ly`, and each of them has its pros and cons. However, TweetDeck doesn't offer `http://cli.gs` (discussed in Chapter 6), so if you want to use it, you need to go to the `http://cli.gs` Web site, shorten your URL, and then copy and paste the shortened URL into the TweetDeck What Are You Doing? text box, as shown in Figure 5-3.

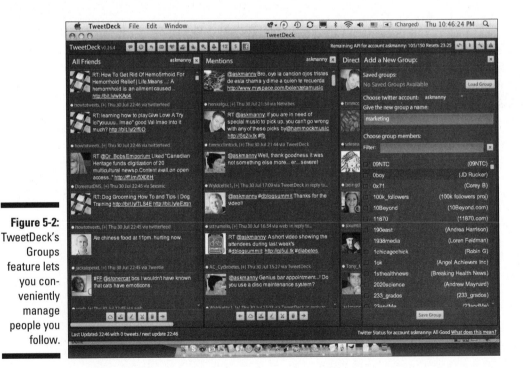

**Figure 5-2:**
TweetDeck's Groups feature lets you conveniently manage people you follow.

**Figure 5-3:**
TweetDeck supports six different URL shorteners.

✔ **Facebook status updates:** You can update your Facebook status from TweetDeck, and you can even find Facebook apps that let you feed all your tweets into your Facebook status.

Avoid pushing all your tweets into Facebook at all costs. Although you should feel free to send the occasional Facebook update by using TweetDeck, any friends you have on Facebook who are unfamiliar with Twitter can get confused with the format and abbreviations that are customary in Twitter. After all, Facebook doesn't have the 140-character (or the text only) limitation that Twitter imposes.

TweetDeck has a Facebook button that you can turn on or off before you send out status updates. You can also create a column that lets you monitor your Facebook friends' status updates as part of your TweetDeck usage.

If you think some tweets are appropriate to become your Facebook status too, the best option to selectively update your Facebook status from Twitter is to use a Facebook application called Selective Twitter Status (`http://apps.facebook.com/selectivetwitter`). After you have set it up on Facebook, only those tweets in which you add the `#fb` hashtag will appear on your Facebook status.

# HootSuite

HootSuite (http://hootsuite.com) is a Twitter tool that gathers a lot of the features of different Twitter apps and offers them on one simple Web interface. Although other apps do some of the features that HootSuite offers, I haven't found one that does everything HootSuite does.

With HootSuite, you can manage multiple Twitter accounts, let several people manage one account, schedule tweets to go out at a later time, and find out how many people clicked the links you included by using the HootSuite Ow.ly URL shortener. The latest version of HootSuite even offers you the capability to create Groups of followers, like TweetDeck.

The following list describes a few of the useful things you can do with HootSuite:

✔ Schedule tweets for specific days, such as #FollowFriday (a Twitter meme through which you share the Twitter accounts of people you feel are worth following). You can see how a Pending Tweet for #FollowFriday looks in HootSuite in Figure 5-4.

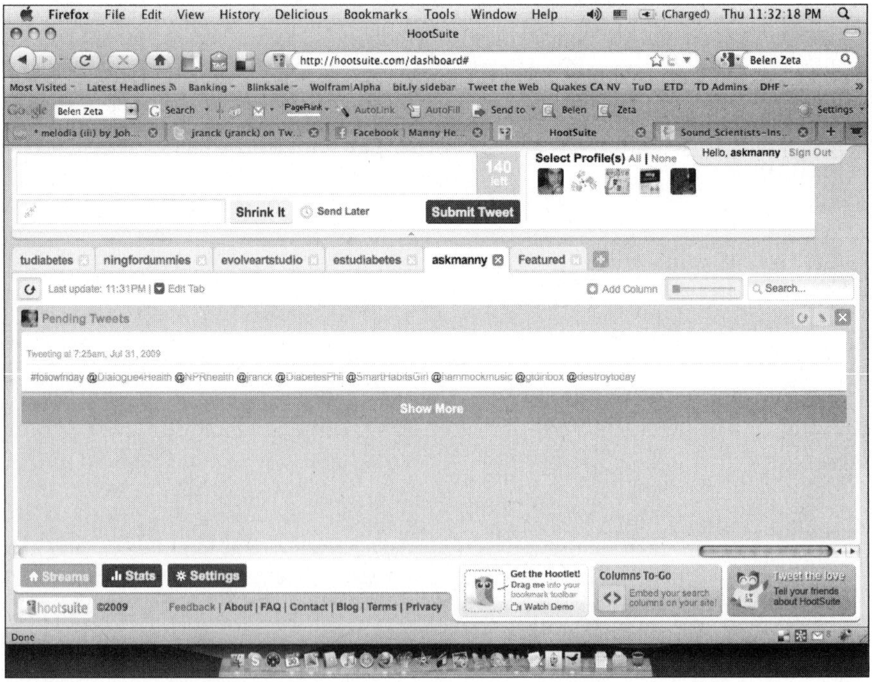

**Figure 5-4:**
HootSuite offers the convenience of scheduling tweets for a later time.

Instead of trying to remember to send out a tweet at a specific time, you can write your tweets as you have them ready, and then schedule HootSuite to send them out when needed. One cool use of this feature is scheduling tweets to congratulate customers and friends on their birthdays.

✔ Test different headlines and ideal tweeting times by creating different Ow.ly URLs for the same article and measuring which headlines and times of day get the most clicks. Use that information to write optimal headlines and schedule them to go out when the most people will pay attention.

✔ If you have clients whose Twitter accounts you are in charge of, you can manage them from the HootSuite interface, along with your own personal and business Twitter accounts, as you can see in Figure 5-5.

✔ Run a corporate customer-service Twitter account and give several employees access to it. Let them work in shifts to manage the account, forwarding the customer's tweets to the appropriate people who can manage the questions or complaints.

**Figure 5-5:**
Click the Twitter profile icon of the profile(s) you want to update underneath the Select Profiles heading on the top right of the page.

✔ As of December 2009, you can integrate Facebook Pages with HootSuite. This integration gives you the opportunity to manage more than just your Twitter account from your HootSuite dashboard! Talk about productive! To add your Pages to HootSuite, go to Settings, select Social Networks, and then click Add Social Network. You will notice an option indented underneath Facebook that says Pages.

# Ping.fm

Ping.fm (`http://ping.fm`) works a lot like HootSuite in that you can update your Twitter account from a Web site other than the main Twitter site. Ping.fm does much more than HootSuite in some respects, but it also lacks some of HootSuite's features.

Ping.fm is considered the mack daddy of all remote-posting services. It lets you post 140-character messages and send them to over 40 different social networks, including Twitter, Facebook, LinkedIn, and even a Blogger or WordPress blog.

Ping.fm can get even cooler and more useful. Say you want to send two messages, one just to Twitter and one to all your other networks through Ping.fm. By including certain trigger words, you control which network or networks your message gets sent to. You can integrate HootSuite and Ping.fm, as explained at `http://bit.ly/ping-hootsuite`, to help you post your messages to multiple networks through HootSuite.

Here's where Ping.fm gets really cool. In the following example, I used trigger words. So, the message I send to only Twitter looks this:

```
@kyleplacy: Heading to the Midwest Marble Collecting
Convention in #Findlay, #Ohio. #MidMarbCollCon
```

And the message I want to send to all my networks through Ping.fm looks like this:

```
New blog post: Day 1 at the Midwest Marble Collecting
Convention, with great photos. http://bit.ly/jxlfh
#MidMarbCollCon
```

Ping.fm sends this message to LinkedIn, Facebook, and Twitter with the hashtag, which may be confusing to some users, but the rest of the message is understandable to anyone. And because the URL shows up in all three places as a clickable link, readers are still likely to read it, even with the Twitter-speak at the end.

Ping.fm sends this message to LinkedIn, Facebook, and Twitter with the hashtag, which may be confusing to some users, but the rest of the message is understandable to anyone. And because the URL shows up in all three places as a clickable link, readers are still likely to read it, even with the Twitter-speak at the end.

# Making the Most of Your Time on Twitter

I talk about time management in the section "Devising a Time-Management Strategy for Twitter," earlier in this chapter, and if you follow my advice, you'll spend no more than 30–60 minutes per day (in two 15–30 minute blocks) on Twitter. The following sections provide some tips and advice for how to be productive during the time you spend on Twitter.

## Don't agonize over what to say

First of all, don't spend a lot of time worrying about what you're going to say. Some people refuse to tweet anything because they're afraid they'll say the wrong thing (you can't) or that nobody cares what they have to say (your followers do care).

I hate to admit it, but Twitter is a throwaway method of communication. Anything you say stays in the general timeline and on people's minds for all of ten seconds. Unless you tweet something grossly offensive or rip-roaringly funny, people aren't going to remember what you said five minutes after you tweet it, let alone what you said last week.

You don't need to make your tweets profound. Your tweets can contain abbreviations, but remember that is it extremely important to your business's image to spell words correctly and use proper grammar. Also, you don't need your tweets to always have a 50-percent click-through rate.

Falling water drops wear away stone over time — likewise, it may take weeks and maybe even months before your frequent tweets lead to increased sales and become a viable marketing strategy. Be patient, stick with it, and just have conversations with people. Let them see the real you so that they can trust you enough to buy from you.

When you talk to friends, you don't always use proper grammar, you might stumble over your words once in a while, and you've probably even said the wrong thing a time or two. Twitter is exactly the same. Your followers can forgive you for a few grammar and spelling gaffes and etiquette blunders, so don't worry too much about it. Just jump in and see what happens.

# Don't read every tweet from the people you follow

The effective Twitter marketer is following, and being followed by, thousands of people. You just can't keep up with everyone. So, accept the fact that you don't have time to read tweets from some people (okay, a lot of people).

The following list provides a few solutions to finding the people whose tweets you want to read:

- **Follow only people worth following.** Hundreds of affiliate marketers and spammers follow you, so ignore them. Find people in your industry, people in your city, and your customers. Keep your list of followers to just the people who write worthwhile tweets: This may be people who share valuable information and links, folks whom you want or need to be informed about, or even users whose tweets you love reading. You may have a relatively short list, but it's a list of people you want to follow.

- **Create groups in TweetDeck or HootSuite.** By using TweetDeck or HootSuite (described earlier in the chapter), you can create groups of people based on any number of criteria, and each group appears in its own column. Want to see what your competitors are doing? Create a group. Want to see what the people around town are talking about? Create a group. Have a thing for redheads? Create a group.

- **Save keyword searches.** Whether you use a third-party tool or Twitter itself, saving searches based on a keyword or phrase is helpful. Look for hashtag topics, keywords in your industry, or current events. Now, instead of having to scan every tweet for that elusive message about the Marble Collecting Convention, you see only the tweets related to that topic.

  To perform and save a search on Twitter, enter the keyword or phrase of interest in the Search box on the Twitter home page. Then click the Save This Search link at the top of the search results, as shown in Figure 5-6 for the search `#iranelection`. If you do this, a new link appears under the heading Saved Searches below the search box, for your convenience.

# Don't try to add value to all your tweets

Tweet whatever you want. Just try to add value when you can. *Adding value* is one of those social-media buzzwords that means you are writing about things that may help other people (even if it doesn't translate into new sales). You want to add value to their daily lives. You can add value by telling people about breaking news stories, articles in a trade journal, new blog posts, and new resources or software. You don't add value by tweeting things such as `going for a walk`, `taking the dog to the vet`, or `good night, tweeple!`

Click here to save your search

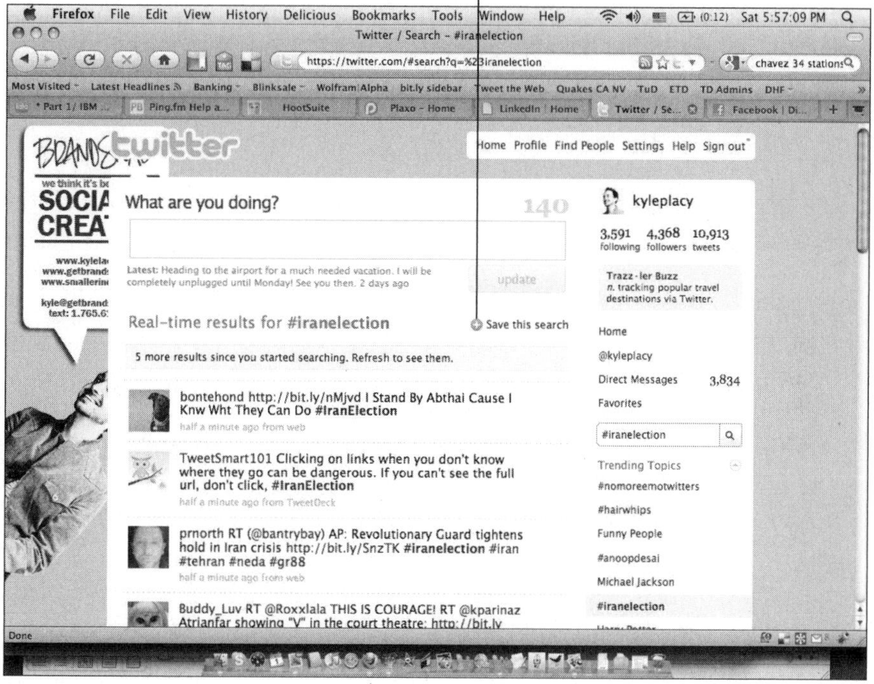

**Figure 5-6:**
Saving
searches
on Twitter
helps you
quickly
find tweets
about topics
you care
about.

Don't feel like you have to add value to every single tweet. Some people truly like those bagel posts, so feel free to throw those in whenever you feel like it, although a 100-tweet serialized epic about your bagel spread may be a little over the top.

Bottom line: Tweet what you want and feel free to be a little personal. The more you show yourself as a real person, the more likely people will buy from you. Remember, people buy from people they like. And if they like you, they're likely to buy from you.

## Do spread out your marketing tweets

If you've read other parts of this book, you may have noticed that I often tell you *not* to send marketing message after marketing message. I'm going to repeat it now: Don't send marketing message after marketing message.

Why? Because it's boring, it's considered spam, and people will quit following you. So, all your hard work goes down the digital drain.

The number of acceptable marketing tweets seems to vary from expert to expert, but a good guideline is a maximum of 1:9 ratio, though I recommend a 1:15 ratio. For each marketing message you send out, you should send out 15 messages that don't talk about your product at all. You can make those 15 tweets conversational, added-value tweets (described in the preceding section), or even 140-character love sonnets about hazelnut cream cheese on a blueberry bagel.

## *Do stick to a schedule with your tweets*

How often do you e-mail people? How often do you talk on the phone? How many days a week do you work? That's how often you should tweet.

If you work every day, including weekends, you may want to consider whether you have a good work-life balance. But if you insist that your balance is just fine, and you aren't bothered by questions such as, "Who's that person hugging mommy/daddy?" then by all means, tweet every day. If you work only during the regular work week, then tweet during that time.

Twitter is all about creating personal relationships, so if you're conducting an activity that some of your followers might be interested in, tell them about it. If you go to a festival, a party, or a conference, you can tweet what's going on because your followers may want to hear about it. These tweets can further strengthen your relationships and make you seem more real to your customers and potential customers.

# Chapter 6

# Measuring the Success of Your Marketing Plan

*B*ack in the old days of traditional media (about ten years ago), it was a footloose, carefree time. Marketing budgets were big and usually contained totals like "$????.??" or "whatever we can get," ad buys were huge, and marketers really didn't know if their ads were working.

"We're building mind share," the marketers would say. "You can't measure mind share." And then they would snicker knowingly amongst themselves, and other departments could never be sure whether they were being totally honest.

The mind share argument is one that a lot of marketers fell back on when a campaign didn't meet expectations. "At least the campaign built mind share," they would say. This was another way of saying, "The campaign helped create consumer awareness."

After a while, organizations started to hold marketers accountable for their wild spending, and so those marketers had to measure whether total sales went up after a particular campaign. If sales went up, the campaign was a success. If they didn't, it was a failure.

But marketers couldn't directly attribute a specific market, a specific commercial, or a specific time of day to a specific sale. Did the TV commercial result in that bump in sales, or was it the billboard ads? Did the radio campaign outperform the direct mail? And which of the five commercials was the one that made people interested?

One of the great things about social media is that it lets you (the marketer) measure the effectiveness of campaigns and messages, and even find out who's talking about you — and what they're saying.

# Measuring Your Advertising and Marketing Efforts

You can measure your Twitter marketing efforts in a number of different ways. Some of them are free, but others cost quite a bit of money. Regardless of the level of sophistication that you need, you can find a means to measure your marketing that fits your goals (and budget).

## Using an analytics package

You can use analytics to monitor Web site traffic and the behavior of visitors who come to your Web site. Most analytics packages work by checking the IP address of each person who visits your site. They monitor which pages people visit, how long they stay, what link they click to get there, and what part of the world they're from. Analytics can help you determine which of your tweets got customers to the site, what time of day they came to the site, and whether you're reaching your local audience.

For example, if your traffic on the Midwest Marble Collecting Convention site is coming from the Midwest, you can feel reasonably assured that your message is reaching the right people. But if most of them start coming from another part of the world, you may have a problem that you need to address (or a potential business opportunity you need to take action on).

### Selecting an analytics package

Google Analytics, Clicky, StatCounter, and Yahoo! Web Analytics are a few of my favorite analytics packages, but you can find many more options out there. Just do an online search for **free web analytics software** to find a plethora of choices. Here's a rundown of my favorites:

- ✔ **Google Analytics (www.google.com/analytics):** Most people use Google Analytics because it's free, easy to use, and conveniently integrated with the rest of Google's offerings. Google offers great reporting features, some of which you can see in Figure 6-1.

Google Analytics also allows you to build your own custom reports and filter your results by certain search criteria, such as new traffic, *referral traffic* (visits that resulted from clicking a link on another Web site), and so on.

The downside of Google Analytics is that it doesn't update your numbers in real-time (while new visitors land on your site). So, if you're a constant checker, Google Analytics may try your patience at times. But it's still the most popular analytics package available.

✔ **StatCounter (www.statcounter.com):** StatCounter is free at the basic level, but you can purchase an upgrade that gives you access to more detailed reports. The upgraded services can range in cost from $9 a month to $29 a month for different levels of pageloads. You can find out more at (www.statcounter.com/services.html).

The best thing about StatCounter is that it gives you real-time reports, so if you have a lot of traffic, you can click the Refresh button whenever you feel like it, and StatCounter recalculates everything. However, your log size when you use the basic version of StatCounter is only 500 entries. If you want to measure a bigger pool of visitors, you need to pay for the upgrade.

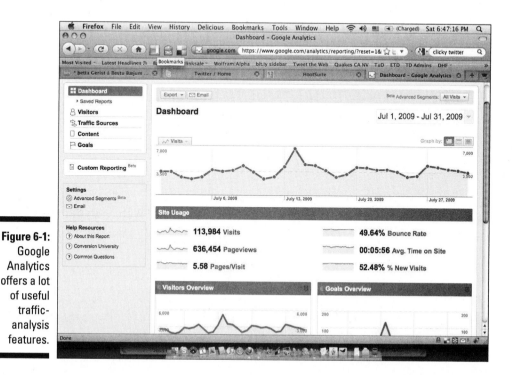

**Figure 6-1:**
Google
Analytics
offers a lot
of useful
traffic-
analysis
features.

✔ **Clicky (www.getclicky.com):** Clicky does something none of the other analytics services does today: It analyzes your Twitter traffic. Sure, other analytics packages can tell you that some of your traffic came from Twitter, but who sent most of the traffic your way? Clicky lets you drill down to the level of the data corresponding to each individual twitterer, as you can see in Figure 6-2. It's important to note that you don't receive the Twitter analytics with the free version of the program. However, some paid levels allow you to do the different page view tracking. The cost ranges from $4.99 a month to $49.99 a month.

✔ **Yahoo! Web Analytics (http://web.analytics.yahoo.com):** Yahoo! Web Analytics is a paid analytics service that's geared toward merchants and people who sell services online. It lets you see information such as where people abandon their shopping carts during the checkout process and which products visitors view the most versus how often they purchase those products. It also helps you spot whether visitors have difficulty finding certain products on your site.

Different analytics packages likely show different numbers in terms of visits, unique visitors, and page views. In simplest terms, this discrepancy is based on the mechanical traffic-counting process that each package uses. But the reality is actually more complex, going beyond the scope of this book.

**Figure 6-2:** Clicky gives you Twitter-specific traffic data, unlike any other analytics package.

To give you a simple example, different packages may count unique visitors to your site differently. Analytics packages that use cookies (a software-based approach) to count visitors may get a different number than those that count unique IP addresses (a hardware-based approach). This difference can result in different traffic numbers for the same site on the same day, depending on what package you're using. My advice? Use a couple of packages and figure out which numbers make more sense, based on the actual sales or inquiries you see.

## Installing an analytics package

You can install an analytics package on your Web site fairly easily. Each package provides you with a snippet of code that you add to your Web site. Make sure you have access to the HTML code for your Web site so that you can add the analytics snippet in a way that includes it on every page of the Web site you want to track. Follow these steps to set up analytics on your Web site:

1. **Find the part of the HTML code of your site that ends with**

```
</body>
</html>
```

2. **Copy the code snippet from the analytics package, and then paste it in your HTML right above the </body> tag.**

   If you're adding code for more than one analytics package, just paste the code for each package one after the other.

3. **If you want to track more than one page, repeat Steps 1 and 2 for all the pages that you want to track.**

You can add the code from the analytics package to your blog, as well as to Web pages that you (or your Web designer) create. If you run a blog by using Blogger (www.blogger.com) as a platform, follow these steps to add the analytics code:

1. **Go to your Blogger dashboard.**

2. **Click the Layout link.**

   The Page Elements page appears.

3. **Click the Add a Gadget button at the bottom of the page.**

4. **Click the plus sign (+) to the right of the HTML/JavaScript option, as shown in Figure 6-3.**

5. **Paste the snippet of analytics code in the Content text box.**

   Leave the Title field of the gadget box blank.

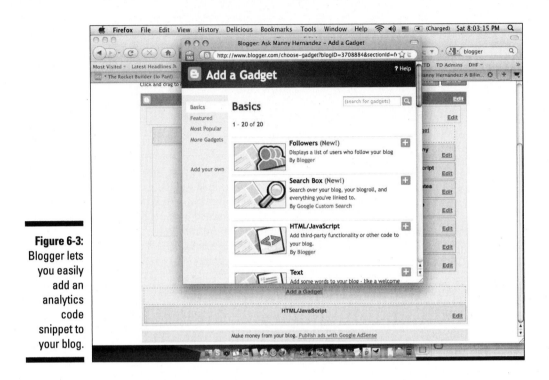

**Figure 6-3:**
Blogger lets
you easily
add an
analytics
code
snippet to
your blog.

If you host a blog by using WordPress (`http://wordpress.org`), follow these steps to add the analytics package code:

1. **Click the Theme Editor in the Appearance section of your blog editor.**

   You can find the Appearance section on the left side of your screen under comments.

2. **Click the Appearance button and then click the Editor button.**

3. **Click the Footer file of your theme.**

   You can find this file on the right-hand side of your Theme Files, more than likely under the comments section.

4. **Paste the snippet of analytics code right above the `</body>` tag.**

If you have WordPress host your blog at `http://wordpress.com`, you can't install your own analytics package.

For more details on analytics and how to make the most of them, consider checking out *Web Analytics For Dummies* by Pedro Sostre and Jennifer LeClaire (Wiley).

## *Using URL shorteners*

Not everything you tweet is going to point to a blog, let alone *your* blog. Maybe you find an interesting photo or song, or you want to refer people to another article someone else wrote. You may still want to track your URLs to see how well your tweets are performing. Many URL-shortener services offer the option to track how many clicks each link gets.

You can find a great article that compares the different URL shorteners at `http://bit.ly/z9tmw`. TweetDeck and Seesmic (TweetDeck's direct competitor) both offer numerous URL-shortener options (bit.ly, Digg, is.gd, TinyURL. com, tr.im, and twurl), but only bit.ly offers click tracking. Therefore, as a Twitter marketer who needs to track link performance, you should use bit.ly.

In addition to using bit.ly as a tool integrated into third-party tools — and even Twitter itself — you can also use it directly at `http://bit.ly`. Simply enter your long URL and click the Shorten button, as you can see in Figure 6-4. You can copy the resulting bit.ly link and use it in your tweets, your e-mail, or even on your Web site.

Enter long URL here

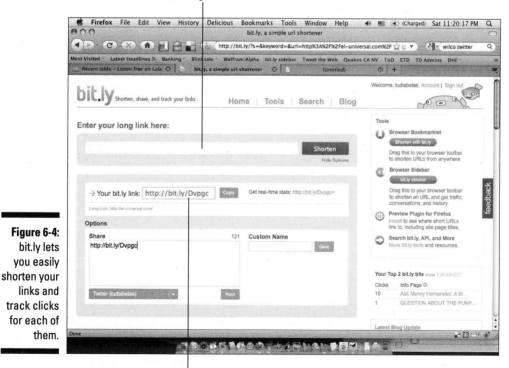

**Figure 6-4:** bit.ly lets you easily shorten your links and track clicks for each of them.

Your shortened URL

If you click the shortened link on bit.ly, you get access to detailed traffic information related to number of clicks, referring Web sites, and geographic locations of the users who clicked. You can also find out how many clicks your particular bit.ly link got compared to the total clicks on the long link. Although I've seen better and worse results, you can expect a 4-percent click-through rate (4 clicks on your bit.ly link out of 100 total clicks on that blog or content link) for a well-crafted, valuable, interesting tweet.

It's also important to remember that you need to be signed into your bit.ly account before you can enter tracking data for the link. Remember to sign into your account!

The secret to high click-through rates involves some of the principles that apply to search engine optimization: Write a descriptive and catchy headline that's relevant to most of your followers *and* have a network of people who are truly interested in hearing from you. In Chapter 7, I discuss why you need to have followers who are potential customers and/or fans.

Don't fall for one of those "build your Twitter follower count fast" programs; you just end up following other people who fell for the same thing — and you're all tweeting to each other, without any of you really listening to what the other ones have to say.

## Following the right people

Although most of marketing, including Twitter marketing, is a big numbers game, that approach isn't always successful: More leads don't always equate to more sales.

Direct mail typically has a response rate of 1 percent. So, for every 100 pieces of mail that you send out, one person responds. If you want to get 100 responses, you need to send out 10,000 pieces. If you want 1,000 responses, you need to send out 100,000 pieces, and so on.

When you use targeted direct mail, you send mail pieces only to people who are likely to buy your product, which can reduce the number of pieces you send and help improve your response rate.

Say you sell gardening tools by catalog. You want to send those catalogs to people who do gardening because they're more likely to buy your products. You probably send catalogs to everyone in a certain Zip code, assuming that they have a certain level of disposable income based on the property values in that Zip code.

However, doing a bit more research, you find out that people who do gardening are commonly either married women or retired men. You can use this information to narrow down your target. But your chosen Zip code still includes plenty of apartments: These folks probably don't garden. And a lot of married women and retired men don't garden, either.

To further enhance your list, you can consider other elements: people who fill out a survey indicating an interest in gardening, people who subscribe to a gardening magazine, and maybe even people who buy seeds from a seed catalog.

Just by defining and refining who your customers are, you can go from wanting to send out 100,000 catalogs (at, say, $2 apiece to print, plus almost $1 per catalog for sorting and mailing costs) to sending out 5,000 catalogs only to people who are likely to buy from you. Instead of getting a typical 0.5-percent response rate (500 people responding to 100,000 catalogs) while spending nearly $300,000, targeted marketing makes you more likely to get a 10-percent response rate (still 500 people, but responding to only 5,000), meaning you have to spend only $15,000.

You can boost your Twitter click-through rate by using this same philosophy. Make sure that you only follow people who consider you worth following. Don't try to boost your follower count by following anyone and everyone. Also, don't get sucked into one of those get-followers-fast programs. If you have a small group of people who are interested in you, you'll have a much higher click-through rate (and thus, higher sales) than you'd have with a Twitter "empire" of 10,000 followers who couldn't care less about your tweets.

Take it one step further, and block the people who don't add any value to your Twitter marketing efforts. The following sections discuss how to block twitterers.

### Blocking a Twitter spam account

Keep track of the people who start following you. If you have your account set up to send you New Follower e-mails, just follow these steps to block undesirable twitterers:

1. **When you receive an e-mail notification that someone has started following you, click the link in the notification e-mail to go to that person's Twitter page.**

   If you disable notifications, as I explain in Chapter 5, you have to periodically go through your list of followers by clicking the Followers link in your account, and then clicking each person's Twitter name to access his or her Twitter page.

2. **Quickly read the person's bio, read his or her past tweets, and click the link to his or her Web site to see whether they're spammy in nature.**

   Spam on Twitter looks a lot like spam sent through e-mail — get-rich-quick schemes, products that enhance certain body parts, porn, and so on.

3. **If the follower seems spammy, click the Block link below the Actions box on the right side of the twitterer's profile page.**

   Twitter prompts you to confirm whether you really want to block the person.

   You can also find the blog link in your followers list. If a follower seems to be overly spammy, click the button that looks like a gear (it's a drop-down list).

4. **Click the Block `<Twitter Username>` button to confirm.**

### Figuring out which accounts are spammy

If your new Twitter follower is following several hundred people, has fewer than a hundred followers, and has sent out absolutely no tweets, watch out. He or she is either building up a fake Twitter identity or setting up one to use with a get-followers-fast system. In either case, you probably aren't going to get much value out of this person as a follower, so block him or her. You can see an example of this kind of account in Figure 6-5.

**Figure 6-5:**
Block users who follow hundreds of people, have few followers, and send out no tweets.

### Getting Twitter involved

If you find a particularly egregious spammer, report the account by following these steps:

1. **Go to www.twitter.com/spam and follow the @spam account.**

   @spam follows you back shortly. The @spam account is Twitter's spam-reporting account.

2. **After @spam follows you, send that account a direct message that includes the spammer's username.**

   Sending a direct message to @spam gives you a way to report spammers without tipping them off that you just ratted them out.

   The Twitter authorities now block the account that was flagged for spam. If the account is verified as spam, the user is automatically deleted.

Do *not* retweet the entire message a spammer sends when DMing the @spam account. You could be flagged and deleted right along with the disgusting spammer!

## Using social-media monitoring services

I talk about social-media monitoring extensively in Chapter 12, but it's worth mentioning here, too.

In order to measure the success of your Twitter marketing efforts, it helps to know whether and where people are talking about your tweets, forwarding your links, or using those links elsewhere on the Web. You can follow that kind of activity in a few ways:

✔ **Google Alerts (www.google.com/alerts):** Have you ever Googled your own name or your company name? Everyone with Internet access has. But you probably don't want to do it every day. Google Alerts saves you some time by notifying you about new search results that contain the search terms you're interested in.

   Google Alerts sends you e-mails once a day, once a week, or when new alerts occur. Those e-mails contain links to news stories, blogs, Web sites, discussion groups, and even videos that mention your search terms. See Figure 6-6.

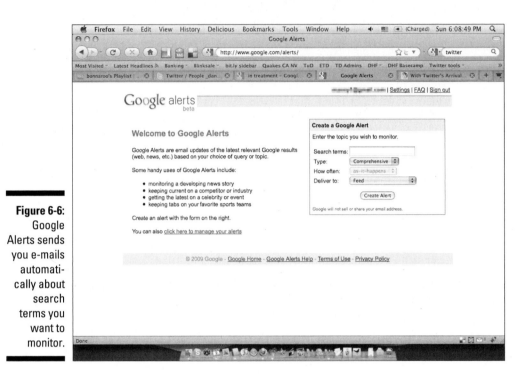

**Figure 6-6:**
Google
Alerts sends
you e-mails
automati-
cally about
search
terms you
want to
monitor.

✔ **TweetScan (http://tweetscan.com):** TweetScan is a micro-blog search service that does for Twitter what Google Alerts does for the rest of the Web. It can send you e-mails and lets you create an RSS (Really Simple Syndication) feed that contains all the results that include your keywords. These results include mentions of your company name or brand, as well as whether it appears in someone's tweets or bio. Besides Twitter, TweetScan also monitors Identi.ca and Laconi.ca, two other micro-blogging sites.

You can use the service for free directly on the TweetScan Web site, or you can pay for TweetScan to send you e-mail alerts.

✔ **HowSociable (www.howsociable.com):** Enter your brand or company name in the search box on the homepage, and then click the Measure Visibility button to see how many times (if at all) it appears on blogs, Facebook, and more than 20 outlets.

- **Radian6 (www.radian6.com):** Radian6 is a Web-based social media monitoring program that's best suited for ad agencies and businesses that manage multiple brands and clients. The service isn't free, but it's very thorough and robust in terms of its reporting features.

- **Scout Labs (www.scoutlabs.com):** A Web-based social media monitoring program geared toward small to medium-sized businesses (though a few large companies are in its list of clients). You can more easily use Scout Labs than you can Radian6, and Scout Labs automates a few more features, including *sentiment scoring* (good versus bad).

- **Cligs (http://cli.gs):** Although Cligs is a URL-shortening service, it also offers social-media monitoring. If someone retweets your shortened link, shares it on FriendFeed, or includes it in a blog post, you can find out about it through Cligs.

# Tracking and Increasing Your Influence on Twitter

You may have a new product out or a solution for a problem that has arisen, such as H1N1 flu, unemployment, or killer robots. But how can you discover whether people are truly concerned about that topic? What do you need to do to increase your influence on Twitter?

One great place to find out your overall Twitter impact is Twitalyzer (www.twitalyzer.com). It gives you an idea of your level of influence and clout in Twitter, the quality of your tweets (called signal-to-noise by Twitalyzer), how much you retweet other people's tweets, and even the rate at which you tweet. To get all this valuable information, simply enter your Twitter username in the text box to the left of the Twitalyze button and click the button, as shown in Figure 6-7.

If you set up a Twitalyzer Pro account, you can also get a good idea of your Return on Influence. *Return on Influence* is another way to monitor your return on investment when using Twitter. After you enter your Twitter username and check out your Twitalyzer stats, scroll down to the Twitalyzer Pro Reports and click the Return on Influence link.

When you have an understanding of your Twitter impact level, you can start to make the most of Twitter trends.

Enter your username here

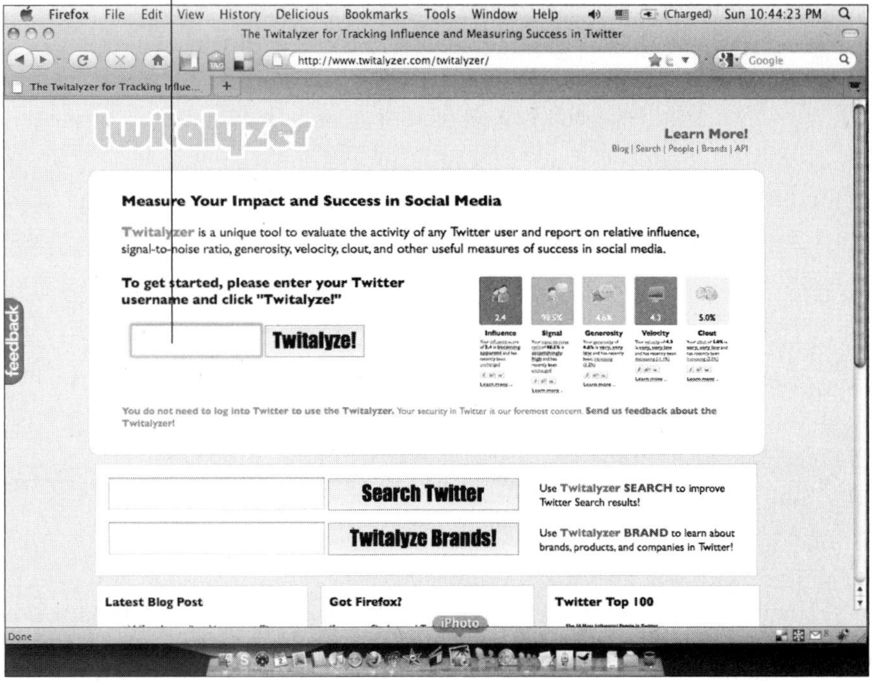

**Figure 6-7:**
You can
find out a
lot about
your Twitter
impact
through
Twitalyzer.

## Getting in on Twitter trends

*Twitter trends* are the most talked-about topics on Twitter. If you want to get in on a conversation about a local, national, or even global topic, you need to find out who's talking about what. I talk about Twitter trends extensively in Chapter 10, but you can use them use Twitter trends in order to see what is popular on Twitter. If you can create enough sensation around a specific topic (marketing your service) you can gain a lot of recognition.

For example, say a well-known computer operating system provider, Tangerine, releases a new version, 2009, that causes printers to quit working. You're a computer repair specialist (your Twitter username is @PittsburghComputers) looking for a way to boost your business. You can use Twitter trends to find the problem, fix it for several people, and boost your own business, as well, by following these steps:

1. **Do a quick search for Twitter trends by using Twitter's search feature (`http://search.twitter.com`) or one of the many Twitter trend finders on the Web that I mention in Chapter 10.**

   You start to notice that people are complaining about the same problem related to the operating system update. For example, say your search brings up tweets such as the following:

   > **kristiekreation:** I just installed the #Tangerine09 upgrade, and my printer quit working!
   >
   > **aballstudio:** The #Tangerine09 update broke my printer.
   >
   > **douglaskarr:** Does anyone know why the #Tangerine09 update would make my printer stop printing?

   You happen to know the fix consists of a quick patch that Tangerine has already released, followed by a reset of the printer preferences — all in all, a simple six-step fix.

2. **Write a blog post about the fix, giving step-by-step instructions, complete with screenshots.**

   In your blog post, be sure to include a call to action, like "If you need additional repair work, virus protection, or hardware updates, don't hesitate to contact us," with the words *contact us* linked to your Web site's Contact Us form or to your e-mail address.

3. **Tweet about your blog post and include a shortened URL link to that post.**

   For example, you might tweet

   > **PittsburghComputers:** There is a simple patch and fix to the #Tangerine09 update on my blog. http://bit.ly/ee9Zo

4. **Monitor the trend you start by using TweetDeck's Saved Search feature, Twitter's search, or Twitterfall, and respond to each and every tweet that mentions your keywords.**

   Before you know it, you're getting 100 tweets every two minutes from people all around the country who have problems with the Tangerine update. That's way more than you expected. Most of these people don't live in Pittsburgh, so they're not likely to become your customers. And although you want to help everyone, you need to focus on making money.

   Because you're a local business, you need to spend most of your time trying to follow your fellow Pittsburghers — or, at least, create a group or a saved search on your favorite Twitter application.

5. **Jump over to Nearby Tweets (`http://nearbytweets.com`), which lets you search for people who live in a specific geographic area and who are talking about a certain topic.**

   Look for people in a 20-mile radius around Pittsburgh who are talking about the `#Tangerine09 update` issue.

   You may want to respond to all of those people, whether they're following you or not. However, after a few minutes, you find yourself sending the link to your blog post that describes the fix over and over.

   Although it seems like you're helping a lot of people, those folks who are unaffected by the Tangerine 2009 issue look at you like a spammer. So, don't retweet the same content more than once.

6. **Follow all the people who result from the Nearby Tweets search and see whether they follow you back. If they do, send them a direct message with the details about the post on your blog.**

   Avoid the temptation of sending out a link to your blog post as an auto-DM (automatic direct message). I discuss the pros and cons of the auto-DM in Chapter 7, but although the idea may seem like a big timesaver, what if you forget to turn it off? Or what if a group of people follow you, but they aren't following you because of this article?

7. **Track how many times your bit.ly link gets clicked and monitor how many times it gets retweeted.**

   To keep tabs on your links, you can use a service called Retweetist, which I talk about in the following section.

If you gain a customer based on marketing through Twitter, be sure to ask him or her how he or she heard about you. If he or she heard about you on Twitter, keep track of this information: Tally up all the additional income that resulted from that tweet.

## *Tracking retweets with Retweetist*

Retweetist (`www.retweetist.com`) helps you further spot and analyze Twitter trends by sorting tweets based on the number of times they've been retweeted. As you can see in Figure 6-8, it lets you find the people who've been retweeted the most in the last 24 hours, the URLs that have been retweeted the most, and even where your links or your own messages have been retweeted.

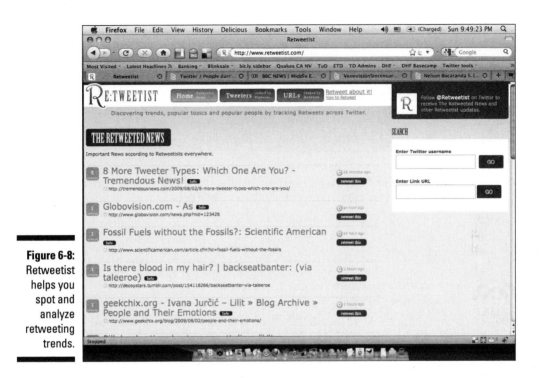

**Figure 6-8:**
Retweetist
helps you
spot and
analyze
retweeting
trends.

Being able to visualize these trends can help you, as a Twitter marketer, because you can find out who the most popular users are (regardless of their real-life popularity) so that you can get your tweets in front of them — and hope that they retweet you.

Also, Retweetist enables you to figure out what the most popular users did so that you can adapt their techniques to your own efforts. And it lets you see which of your own tweets did best: Are most of the retweeted links about 5 Ways to Solve the Tangerine09 Update or Fix the Tangerine09 Update in Six Steps?

So, how do you get retweeted more? If you want to show these influential twitterers, or the influencers in your industry or city, that you can add value to their lives, you have to start retweeting them first.

If the influencers you're targeting post interesting tweets, retweet them. If they make interesting points, respond to them thoughtfully. If they write good blog posts, write one in return, tweet about it, and include their names in the tweet. In short, make sure you're in front of them. When you become visible and valuable to them, they're more likely to retweet your stuff.

Be sure your tweets and blog posts are relevant to what the influencer and your followers do. If you're selling cosmetics, you probably won't get retweeted by a social-media celebrity, no matter how hard you work at it. Save your energies for finding the thought leaders and influencers in your industry.

# Engaging Others on Twitter

The temptation on Twitter is to get as big a following as you possibly can. For example, a site like TwitterCounter (http://twittercounter.com) shows you where you rank in the general Twitterati, based on the number of followers you have.

In the beginning of 2009, you could easily break well into the top 10,000 — usually within the 8,000's — if you had more than 3,000 followers. Now, thanks to the availability of get-followers-fast scripts and systems, you're lucky to break in the top 20,000 at all.

That's the problem with many of these get-followers-fast systems. You aren't engaged. You're following 9,999 other people who signed up through the same system. You don't care about a single one of them and probably don't pay attention to their tweets. And you know what? They don't care about you, either. So why are you following them? Why are they following you? You shouldn't, and they shouldn't.

You don't want a lot of followers if they don't do anything. If anything, you want fewer followers, but ones who actually care about you, your product, and your business. The music business has an old saying that if a band could get 1,000 committed followers willing to spend $100 per year, the band would make more than if it sold 60,000 CDs per year (because most big-label artists make $1 per CD sold).

Your business is the same way. You want to get as many committed, rabid, evangelistic customers as you can, but you don't want to spend your time chasing the hundreds of thousands of people who frankly don't give a rat's fuzzy behind about you. You'll be much more successful getting a 10-percent response rate from 1,000 followers than a 0-percent response rate from 1 million. Zero percent of 1 million is still zero.

## Balancing the follow-to-followers ratio

Your follow-to-followers ratio (FFR) (also called the Twitter Follower-Friend — or TFF — Ratio by the folks at http://tffratio.com) is a measure of your

Twitter street credibility (tweet cred?). It measures the ratio between the number of people who follow you compared to the number of people you follow (also called friends), and it's represented by either a decimal (1.0) or a ratio (1:1).

You can find your Twitter FFR by visiting TFF Ratio (`http://tffratio.com`), entering your Twitter username in the Get TFF Ratio for Twitter User text box, and clicking the Get TFF Ratio button. You can also simply divide the number of people you're following by the number of people who are following you.

In other words, if you follow a lot of people but they don't follow you back, you have a FFR of less than 1.0 (0.4:1). If you have an FFR of 10.0 or higher (1:10), TFF Ratio says you're "either a Rock Star in your field or you are an elitist and you cannot be bothered by Twitter's mindless chatter. . . ." Unless you really care about the person's tweets, I don't recommend following a lot of people with an FFR of 8 or higher.

Your ideal FFR ratio should be around 1.0 (or 1:1). That ratio means you're listening as much as you're being listened to. With an FFR around 1.0, you can think of yourself as the ideal Twitter conversation partner.

If your ratio is around 2.0 or higher, you could be a thought leader or influencer in your community or an influencer to your followers because people are interested in what you're talking about.

## Reducing your number of Twitter followers

That's right, *reduce* the number of Twitter followers. To get to your truly engaged followers, you need to lighten your load. Sure, it means you have fewer followers, but Twitter is about engagement, not an artificial measurement.

Although reducing your number of followers may create a few problems with your FFR (when you unfollow someone who's following you, he or she may unfollow you in return), believe me: It's really not *that* important. Your FFR is going to fluctuate as you get started and get things rolling, but it will eventually grow while you improve your Twitter brand.

### Unfollowing with Twitter Karma

To trim the fat and reduce unnecessary followers, follow these steps:

1. **Visit Twitter Karma (`www.dossy.org/twitter/karma`) and enter your Twitter credentials or click the Sign In with Twitter button.**

I recommend using the Sign In with Twitter button because it allows you to sign in through Twitter without revealing your Twitter password to Twitter Karma.

2. **As shown in Figure 6-9, select Last Updated from the Sort By drop-down list and select Only Following from the Show drop-down list.**

3. **Select the check boxes to the left of the usernames of the people whose last update was over 60 to 90 days ago.**

   People who haven't updated their Twitter accounts in that long probably have abandoned them and, no matter your best efforts, aren't likely to become your customers — they're quite possibly never going to sign in to Twitter again.

4. **When you're done selecting the check boxes for all the people you want to unfollow, click the Bulk Unfollow button at the bottom of the page.**

   After you click the button, Twitter Karma shows the users you decided to unfollowed.

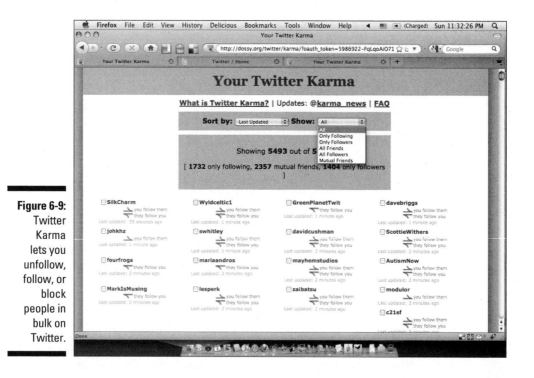

**Figure 6-9:** Twitter Karma lets you unfollow, follow, or block people in bulk on Twitter.

You can further narrow down your followers by removing people who have only a few followers:

1. **Go to Twitter Karma and log in by clicking the Sign In with Twitter button.**

   If you're already on Twitter Karma, click the Refresh button to refresh the page and pull up your network again.

2. **Select Follower Count from the Sort By drop-down list and select Only Following from the Show drop-down list.**

3. **Select the check boxes to the left of the usernames of people who have only a few followers.**

   They probably aren't very active, but you can check the profile of a twitterer who has few followers by right-clicking his or her link to visit his or her Twitter page.

4. **When you check all the boxes for users you want to unfollow, click the Bulk Unfollow button.**

   The service lets you know that you have unfollowed the users.

You need a mirror for the last follower-narrowing process. Look deeply into it, and with all the sincerity you can muster, say, "I'm good enough, I'm smart enough, and doggone it, they don't have to like me!"

Finally, remove people who have tons of followers but follow only a few people (the cewebrities) by following these steps:

1. **Go to Twitter Karma and log in by clicking the Sign In with Twitter button.**

   If you're already on Twitter Karma, click the Refresh button to refresh the page and pull up your network again.

2. **Select Follower Count from the Sort By drop-down list and select Only Following from the Show drop-down list.**

3. **Select the check boxes to the left of the usernames of the cewebrities or the people who decided to follow a small amount of people and click the Bulk Unfollow button.**

   Bulk unfollow the people who have tens of thousands of followers but follow fewer than 100 (meaning people with a TFF Ratio of 10.0 or higher).

    If you really want the latest celebrity insights, hang onto them. But remember, they're most likely not going to retweet you, buy from you, or be interested in you. They basically don't add value to your business, so why waste your time on them?

Arm yourself with patience when you're unfollowing people in bulk. Because of the way Twitter works, using Twitter Karma can be a lengthy process — but it's one worth your time.

### Unfollowing with Twitoria

You can also identify people to unfollow by using Twitoria (http://twitoria.com), but it's a little more labor intensive than Twitter Karma:

1. **Visit Twitoria, enter your Twitter username in the text box, and select a threshold of your followers' last tweets (two months ago, one month ago, two weeks ago, and so on) from the drop-down list.**

   A list of people who fit the criteria you selected appears.

2. **Right-click the name of each person who appears and select Open Link in New Window from the drop-down options to check out his or her Twitter homepage.**

   You can peruse this person's past tweets and bio to see whether you can get any indication of why you should continue to follow him or her. If you can't find one, unfollow this person on Twitter.

3. **Click the Next button on the bottom right of your screen and repeat Step 2.**

   Keep clicking the Next button until you have no more people who meet your inactivity criteria.

Unfollow people who have never tweeted, or haven't tweeted in more than two or three months, because chances are, they aren't going to start. And if they do jump back into Twitter, they'll start following people again, and they'll find you.

So, what do you do if your FFR suffers as a result of your bulk unfollowing efforts? I recommend that you stick with fewer followers who love and adore you.

If you want to be truly successful and play the numbers game, try to find more and more people who think you're great and want to pay attention to you. I discuss how to find qualified followers in Chapter 7, which can help you find followers you want as your customers, not people who are clogging up your virtual space.

# Part III
# Devising Online Strategies for Twitter Marketing Domination

The 5th Wave                    By Rich Tennant

"Before the Internet, we were only bustin' chops locally. But now, with Twitter, we're bustin' chops all over the world."

# In this part . . .

So, you've created a mind-blowing, life-altering, and business-changing marketing plan for Twitter that can increase leads and the amount of cash in your pocketbook. But you need to figure out the specific strategies that you can use to gain followers and dominate the market on Twitter.

Say it again — how do you dominate the Twitter world? How do you lead all your Twitterati to spread the word about your brand?

People who know how to qualify and measure the effectiveness of their followers have a huge marketing advantage. How do you build a network that shouts to the heavens about your product or service? Flip through this part to find out.

# Chapter 7

# Building Your Personal Twitter Tribe

*T*he problem most people have with Twitter is that they start an account, but they don't follow up with it. They add a couple of friends, post a few tweets, and then give up, saying it didn't work for them. In fact, according to some studies, as many as 9 percent of all Twitter accounts may be inactive. If you dive even further into the stats, you see that 10 percent of Twitter users produce 90 percent of the content. Still, millions of people use Twitter (at the time of this writing). And you need to get some of them to follow you.

When you use Twitter, you have an expectation that if you follow someone, that person will follow you back. This doesn't always happen, but it does a large part of the time — especially if you're a real person following real people. But if you're a spammer or you look like you're on Twitter to send nothing but commercial tweets, you don't get many follow-backs.

In this chapter, I discuss several ways that you can build your Twitter network, which can help you market and sell your product or service.

## Building Your Twitter Network

You can build your network in several ways. Depending on your attitude toward the sanctity of Twitter, you can either add people *organically* (manually following people when you find them to be a good fit for your marketing goals) or *artificially* (by letting software plug-ins and other tricks do part of the work).

Although you can use the artificial means to build up your network of followers quickly, you won't necessarily have a network of people who are interested in following you. If you use an artificial method to gain followers, you run two risks:

- ✔ People will overlook your messages in the mire of all the other artificial twitterers, sort of like having a TV commercial on a channel that shows only TV commercials.

- ✔ The only people who will follow you are other Twitter marketers and people who have systems on how to get thousands of Twitter followers quickly, like having a commercial that's seen only by other advertisers.

## Determining the best way to build your network

An organic network takes a long time to build. You find your friends and colleagues; you find people who are interested in what you have to say; and after a while, you eventually build a network of people who are truly interested in what you do. The problem is that it takes quite a while to build a network organically.

You can ramp up your network by adding a couple thousand followers a day, but you usually get those followers by using a plug-in to your browser or a Web site made up of followers who want to juice up their follower stats by following each other. You can even pay to become a VIP on some sites, which quickly boosts your follower count.

While building your organic network can take a long time, there is a bigger downside to having artificial followers: These people don't actually care about you or what you think or write.

However you choose to build your followers, keep the following points in mind:

- ✔ **Your follower/following ratio:** Twitter wants to make sure that you don't start following too many people without having many people follow you back. They do it to control spammers who hope to game the system by following tens of thousands of people at the same time, hoping that a portion of those people will follow back. So, Twitter never lets you have a difference of more than 20 percent between people you follow and people following you.

  For example, if you have 1,000 followers, you can follow 1,200 people. If you have 2,000 followers, you can follow 2,400 people. If you look at Figure 7-1, you see that @kyleplacy's Following count is 82.30 percent of his Follower count, so he could follow as many as 5,420 people before he hits a wall.

**Figure 7-1:**
You don't
need to
follow
everyone
who follows
you. In fact,
it may be a
bad idea.

✔ **Limited followers:** As a way to prevent spam, Twitter has also limited
the number of people you can follow in a single day to 2,000. So, even if
you do try to game the system through artificial means, Twitter still lets
you follow only 2,000 people per day.

## Finding friends and professional contacts

You can find your friends and colleagues on Twitter in two ways:

✔ **After you have signed in, click the Find People link at the top of the
page.** This link takes you to the Find People – Follow Them page, where
you can use the search box to find companies and groups that you want
to follow or people whom you don't have any other way to reach. When
you find the person you want to follow, click the Follow button next to
his or her name to follow that person.

When you do a search, you may end up with many names (if you're looking for John Smith, forget about it) and not know which one is the right
person. Right-click each name and select the option to open the link in a
new browser tab from the menu that appears. Then you can check out
that twitterer's bio and location to see whether this is the person you
want. If it is, click the Follow button.

If your mouse has a scroll-wheel and you're using Firefox (www. firefox.com), you can click the scroll-wheel to open a tab underneath the one you're looking at without disrupting your flow. If you're using a Mac, you can also open a new tab without a mouse by pressing ⌘ and clicking the link that you want to open in the new tab.

✔ **Import your e-mail contacts list.** You can import e-mail lists from Gmail, Yahoo!, and AOL. Just enter your username and password for the e-mail account you want to import your contacts from, and then click Continue to make Twitter find your contacts and see whether any of them are registered with Twitter. You can choose to follow people on your contacts list or not.

If you keep different e-mail accounts on Gmail, Yahoo!, and AOL, repeat the process to import your contacts list for each e-mail account. Be sure to import your e-mail contacts every three months or so because people join Twitter all the time.

Before you import your e-mail contacts into Twitter, consider importing all your various contacts into one account, and then cleaning up the contacts by getting rid of duplicates, combining multiple e-mail addresses for the same person under one name, and cleaning out the addresses of people you don't keep in touch with. You can then sync these contacts with your Outlook or Thunderbird client through a number of different shareware programs that you can find online. This good e-mail management can make your life a lot easier.

After you follow your friends, go to your Twitter homepage and click the Following link in your profile. Even if they are your friends in real life, keep your eyes open for people who don't have a photo for an avatar. If it's still the generic brown and blue o_0 symbol, right-click the person's link and open it in a new tab. Check out his or her past tweets and followers. If this person hasn't tweeted for several months, he or she has only a few followers, or it otherwise looks like an abandoned account, unfollow that person by clicking the Unfollow button and then the Remove button that appears.

## *Searching for followers based on interests and keywords*

Some applications let you find people you should follow based on your own interests, who your friends follow, and even keyword searches:

✔ **Twubble (www.crazybob.org/twubble):** This application helps you expand your Twitter "bubble" (Twubble, get it?). By clicking the Find Some Friends button and entering your Twitter name and password, Twubble examines your Friend List and finds more people you may be interested in following, as you can see in Figure 7-2.

**Figure 7-2:**
Twubble
can help
expand
your Twitter
bubble.

✔ **Twitter Grader (www.twittergrader.com):** Not only can you grade your Twitter profile (so that you can see how you rank, compared to other twitterers) on Twitter Grader, but this site can also help you find members of the Twitter elite based on a city, state, country, or even across the globe. (No one seems to call them Twelite. Sorry.) The Twitter Grader ranking takes into account factors such as the number and power of followers, the number and recency of updates, the Follower/Following Ratio, and how often your tweets get retweeted.

# Identifying industry leaders and evangelists

Nearly every industry has its leaders and evangelists. These people write the articles in the trade journals, get invited to give keynote speeches and presentations at conferences and get interviewed by media as industry experts. They write the books about their field, and everyone knows who they are. These people are the thought leaders and idea makers. You can find these leaders just by doing a simple name search on Twitter's Find People – Follow Them page and following them.

You can also build your own brand and reputation if you begin conversations with these leaders and evangelists. Retweet their stories, tweet links to their articles, and ask them questions. The following Web sites can help you find leaders in your field:

- ✔ **Twollow (www.twollow.com):** Do a search for specific keywords and automatically follow people who use those keywords in their tweets. Twollow is a great service that requires you to pay a fee after your 7-day free trial has extinguished.

  If you don't upgrade your account, Twollow will upgrade the account automatically to the Bronze package. Keep this in mind and remember to delete or upgrade.

- ✔ **Twitseeker (www.twitseeker.com):** Search tweets or profile bios for specific keywords and get a list of people you can follow. You can log in and bulk follow/unfollow the people on the list, as you can see in Figure 7-3.

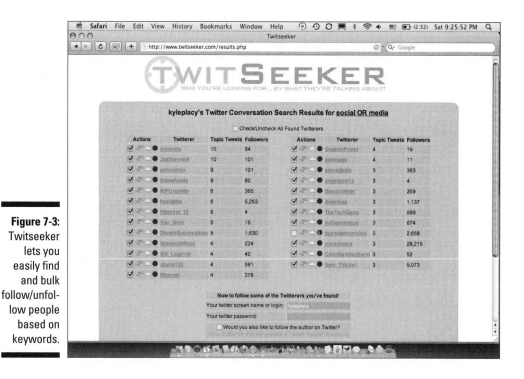

**Figure 7-3:**
Twitseeker lets you easily find and bulk follow/unfollow people based on keywords.

## Hunting down your competition

Because you're reading this book, I assume the main reason you're on Twitter is to promote your product or service to potential customers. Your competitors are on Twitter for that reason, too. So, why not keep an eye on them and see what they're saying? Hopefully, you've been keeping track of your competition anyway, and you know who the players are in your field. Do a search for them by using Twitter's Find People – Follow Them page and Search features (`http://search.twitter.com`), or some of the tools described in the section "Finding followers based on interests and key-words," earlier in this chapter.

If you're using TweetDeck (`http://tweetdeck.com`), create a group for people in your industry whom you want to keep track of, such as industry leaders, evangelists, important customers, and even your competition.

If your industry doesn't have any leaders, maybe you can become one. Build a following of people in your industry, and then blog and tweet about the issues in your industry. Several excellent books discuss how to become an expert in your field, including *Get Slightly Famous: Become a Celebrity in Your Field and Attract More Business With Less Effort,* by Steven Van Yoder (Bay Tree Publishing), *How to Position Yourself as the Obvious Expert,* by Elsom Eldridge Jr. and Mark L. Eldridge (MasterMind Publishing, LLC), or *How to Become an Expert on Anything in Two Hours,* by Gregory Harley and Maryann Karinch (AMACOM). You can find many others, too — just find the one that suits you.

## Finding the locals

You can find twitterers in your area, or even your chosen field, in a number of ways. Here are a few applications that let you find people you want to follow:

- ✔ **Twellow (www.twellow.com):** This is the Twitter Yellow Pages. Search for people by industry or name, or even use the interactive map to find people located in cities that matter to you. If you're into celebrity watch-ing, Twellow helps you find them. You can also do a search for different terms, instead of just browsing categories.

- ✔ **Twitterment (www.twitterment.com):** Twitter's regular search feature (`http://search.twitter.com`) looks only in the text of previous tweets, which isn't a great way to find people in your industry. You can find that information in the user's Twitter bio, but Twitter doesn't search bios. Twitterment searches not only the tweets, but also the bios of people you're looking for.

✔ **Nearby Tweets (www.nearbytweets.com):** This Web site lets you search for people in your chosen location as well as for keywords as a way to filter your search results. Want to find all the twitterers who sell ice cream in Cincinnati, Ohio? Nearby Tweets can do it for you.

✔ **TwitterLocal (www.twitterlocal.net):** You can download this Adobe AIR application. (TweetDeck also uses Adobe AIR, which is platform-agnostic.) You can use TwitterLocal to find out when people from your chosen area send tweets. (Remember, TwitterLocal can find people only if the local twitterers list their locations in their profiles.)

## Following #FollowFriday

Follow Friday, also called #FollowFriday, is an Internet *meme* (an idea or concept that spreads from person to person by word-of-mouth). You send out a tweet that lists people you think your followers should also follow, but you send this tweet only on a Friday. (I get rather annoyed when people #FollowFriday on any day that's not a Friday.) As part of your tweet, do not forget to include the #FollowFriday (or the shorter #FF) hashtag, as shown in the examples in Figure 7-4.

**Figure 7-4:** Here are some examples of #Follow Friday tweets.

Most people rattle off the names of a group of twitterers without saying why they think those people are worth following. But say *why* someone should be followed in your own #FollowFriday tweets. For example, the following tweet shows a #FollowFriday tweet that relays good judgment:

```
@kyleplacy Two of the better content writers on the
planet: @askmanny @edeckers
```

By creating a tweet that had two names instead of six, I allowed for the #FollowFriday to be more significant.

Of course, it's considered good manners to thank the people who listed you in their #FollowFriday tweets, or you can just list them in your next #FollowFriday tweet.

## Determining who's worth following

Not everyone is worth following. This doesn't mean these folks are bad people; they just don't provide the value you need to promote and grow your business. Maybe they tweet about subject areas that don't interest you. Maybe they have nothing but special offers, sales, and spam. Maybe they repeat the same three messages over and over in the hopes of snaring someone. When you visit a user's Twitter homepage, check out these three things to see whether someone is worth following:

- ✔ **The person's tweet-to-follower ratio:** If someone has more than a few hundred followers and absolutely no tweets, he or she is using one of those get-followers-fast programs I mention in Chapter 6. At best, this person is using Twitter incorrectly; at worst, it's a fake account used to spread spam. If the person fits this description, don't follow him or her. If someone has a lot of tweets and followers, he or she is probably a real user. Check out the next two bullets, to see whether this person is still someone worth following.

- ✔ **The person's follower-to-followed ratio:** If the person has significantly more followers than the people he or she follows (for example, someone who's followed by thousands but follows fewer than 100), this person probably won't follow you back. Don't bother following this person, unless he or she is someone you truly want to follow.

  If the person you're checking out has a lot of followers *and* a lot of tweets, he or she might be a real Twitter user. Look to see what this person tweets about. Does he or she send out a bunch of spam and commercial tweets? Or are his or her tweets conversational and useful? If it's the latter, follow that person.

- ✔ **The person's bio:** What does this person do? Look for people who share your interests, profession, or industry.

Be very wary of following twitterers whose tweets are adult in nature, given the proclivity of porn sites controlled by criminals and hackers who want to unleash viruses, Trojan horses, and spyware onto your computer. Twitter links to adult sites may take you to some of these infected sites and unleash all kinds of harmful programs onto your computer.

# Quantity Over Quality

The Twitterati have a raging debate about whether you should have a huge Twitter following or focus more on having a smaller number of loyal fans who truly care about what you have to say. Here's the lowdown on the quality versus quantity debate:

✔ **Quality:** Many Twitterati point to quality as the argument why you should have fewer people who are loyal fans, rather than thousands of followers. In other words, you're more successful with a 10-percent response rate from 1,000 followers than a 0-percent response rate from a million.

✔ **Quantity:** Other Twitterati, however, say that Twitter has an average *click-through rate* (when someone clicks a link within a tweet) of 4 percent. So, 4 out of every 100 people who receive a tweet that includes a URL actually click that URL. If you have 100 followers, 4 people will click the URL; if you have 1,000 followers, 40 will click; and 10,000 followers will equal 400 clicks.

"So," say the quantity folks, "the more followers you have, the more clicks you get. It's a numbers game."

"But you can get 400 clicks by having 800 people who actually like you," counter the quality backers.

And then the two groups stamp their little feet and threaten not to be each other's friend anymore until they can resolve their differences.

But then the cool kids come along and say it's possible — necessary, in fact — to have both. You need a lot of quality followers — as many as you can get.

## Understanding the value of quantity in the Twitterverse

In the section "Building Your Twitter Network," earlier in this chapter, I talk about how artificially building your Twitter following can give you a false sense of accomplishment — you have a lot of people following you, but not a lot of them care about what you have to say. However, having a large following does have some benefit because you have a good chance of reaching a larger number of people.

According to some informal research done by one of the social media companies I am involved with, the average Twitter click-through rate is roughly 4 percent. When you consider that direct-mail open rates are 1 to 2 percent and e-mail open-and-read rates are notoriously difficult to accurately calculate (because different people quote different rates), 4 percent is a decent response rate.

So, although you may originally look down on the idea of list building, keep in mind that a 20-percent read rate from 1,000 followers who love and adore you is half of a 4-percent read rate with 10,000 followers.

## Following the rules for building a quantity-based network

Okay, this section isn't so much about rules as the etiquette for building a large network of followers.

The most important rule is that you're expected to *earn* your followers, not get them through computer scripts and list-building Web sites. Visit people's Twitter homepages, click the people they're following, and investigate each person to see who's worth following. (See the section "Determining who's worth following," earlier in this chapter, for guidance.)

The other rule is that if you're going to follow a lot of people, you should provide value to them. Value in this context doesn't mean giving them 10 percent off their next purchase at your Web site. It means actually sharing ideas and giving them information that makes their lives better or gives them new knowledge.

## Understanding the negative side of list building

Although building a big list of people you follow can increase your odds of selling your product or service, consider a few big cons (not the big cons you usually find in prison movies, though):

✔ **You'll seem disingenuous.** People can easily spot list spammers because they're the ones following 1,500 people with only 150 followers (who are probably people who auto-follow everyone) and absolutely no tweets. Twitterers commonly block list spammers.

Blocking keeps your tweets from appearing in the other person's time-line. If enough people block you, Twitter will drop your account completely. So don't even try to play the "getting blocked" game.

✔ **You'll end up filling your list with a lot of Internet marketers and spammers.** These people's only interest is getting their message out to a lot of people, same as you. So you end up sending a message to thousands of people who ignore it, same as you ignore their messages.

✔ **While you add more followers, you'll also be following more people.** Although following a lot of people can expose you to interesting people (some of whom may turn into your customers), you may find it hard to keep up with people you really want to hear from. You can find solutions to this problem, such as creating groups on TweetDeck (`http://tweetdeck.com`), but keeping your groups in good shape can be a challenging at times.

## *Building the following that your business needs*

If you're trying to build a following for your business, you just need to find your customers. Figure out who your typical customer is, where he or she is from, what he or she likes, and so on.

For example, if you're an ice cream shop owner in Cincinnati, you want to follow only people who live in the Queen City. You don't care about people in Cleveland, Dayton, or Zanesville. Sure, they're nice people, but they aren't going to drive all the way to Cincinnati for ice cream. (Maybe you could ship it. . . .)

Similarly, if you sell poultry-feeding equipment to people all over the world but don't sell a single bolt in your hometown, you aren't as interested in people who live within 10 miles of your city (unless your business happens to be a few blocks from a major poultry farm). You want anyone and everyone who's in the poultry industry, so search for them with a tool such as Twollow or Twitseeker.

# Qualifying out of the quantified

You can add a bunch of people to your Twitter tribe, but how do you know whom you really need to reach? Pay attention to the people who engage in conversations on Twitter. Keep track of how often they tweet (if they tweet at all) and how relevant their messages are to you. Use a resource such as Twitter Karma (`www.dossy.org/twitter/karma`) to see if and when they last tweeted.

Then — and I hate to say it — drop the people who don't do anything. If you find that one-third of the people you're following have never tweeted even once, they aren't going to. If you see that several people haven't sent a tweet after their initial `trying to figure out this Twitter thing` message, they aren't going to. Stop following them and find more people who are worth following.

The people who never tweet hurt your click-through rate. Because they aren't likely using Twitter (to tweet), they are also not likely to even see your tweets and click any links you include in them, as a result. If you have 1,000 followers and 250 of them don't do anything, you are better off axing those 250 followers from your list. Your list of followers against which your click-through rate gets calculated will come down to 750, which will result in a higher click-through rate.

Yes, your click-through rate is mostly an artificial number. So, a high click-through rate doesn't guarantee success. But, if you have to prove to other people that this strategy works, you don't want to have a lower click-through rate than you actually deserve. Remember, 40 clicks out of 1,000 is less than 40 clicks out of 750: 4 percent versus 5.33 percent.

You also want to get rid of the followers who don't actually provide you with any value because they probably aren't going to be customers. These are the folks who send out nothing but spam; keep responding to every Twitter app and quiz, and then send out the results; or tweet that they've found a way to increase your follower count. No need to waste your social media efforts on them, either.

You can't follow more than 120 percent of the total number of people who follow you (in other words, if you have 100 followers, you can follow 120 people). One way to increase the number of twitterers that you can follow is to get more people to follow you. Another way is to drop the people who aren't even using Twitter so that you can engage with people who are. By dropping the people you follow who aren't following you, you reduce your following count, and you can fill it back up with quality twitterers.

# *The Pros and Cons of Auto-DMs*

*Direct messages* (also called DMs) are tweets that you send out to a follower that only he or she can see. Whereas other tweets are public to all your followers, the DM is a private message that functions like an e-mail, but with 140 characters.

An *auto*-DM is an automatic response that you can send to someone who follows you. You can set up auto-DMs by using a Web site service such as Tweet Later (www.tweetlater.com) or software packages such as TweetAdder. com (http://tweetadder.com).

However, keep in mind that sites that help automate tasks on Twitter, such as SocialToo (www.socialtoo.com), have dropped support of auto-DMs because most people don't like them. SocialToo has now even enabled people to block other services' auto-DMs. You can find my Stop Auto DM petition (shown in Figure 7-5) in the top results of a Google search for **Twitter auto DM**.

**Figure 7-5:** I started a Stop Auto DM petition in late 2008.

You may want to use the auto-DM at times, although you shouldn't have that many of those times. Here are a few reasons to use auto-DMs:

- ✔ **Time management:** If you use auto-DMs, you can save yourself a lot of time sending thank-you messages to new followers, introducing your product or service to people, and sending links to your Web site to help build your readership or Web traffic.

- ✔ **Fast and timely responses to followers:** If you like to respond to new followers, you can set up an auto-DM so that you immediately send a welcome message to each new follower. An auto-DM is one of those "set it and forget it" features of Twitter. Set it once, type in a message that includes a link to your Web site, and then just measure how many clicks you get. You can even consider changing your message and link every 30 days to measure which phrasing gets the best results.

Don't use auto-DMs too often. In fact, the reasons not to use them far outweigh the reasons to use them:

- ✔ **Brand degradation:** A lot of people may use auto-DMs, but most twitterers don't like getting them. If you send impersonal auto-DMs to people, they aren't going to respect you or your brand very much, much in the same way as they wouldn't start a conversation with a robot.

- ✔ **Looking lazy:** Although you may see auto-DMs as a way to save time, others may see you as lazy.

- ✔ **Impersonal touch:** Twitter is all about personal conversations. You can't start a personal conversation by sending a form tweet to anyone and everyone.

In short, I'm not a fan of auto-DMs. People have some valid arguments in favor of auto-DMs, but you can find a lot more made against them. If you want to be a successful Twitter marketer, don't sabotage yourself right out of the box with new followers by sending them auto-DMs.

# Chapter 8

# Leveraging Your Twitter Tribe

## In This Chapter

▶ Understanding the value of the retweet

▶ Tracking trends with TwitterCounter and Qwitter

▶ Treating your followers with respect

*Y*our Twitter tribe is your followers, an empire of people who have opted to receive your updates and content. Your followers are the most valuable thing to your business, product, or service in the Twitter world. They make up individuals who may have a need for your products or services, people in your general area, and other professionals in your industry. This chapter describes how to convince them to share your message with their friends.

Your Twitter tribe is comprised of a vast network of people connected in one simple way: They are all Twitter users. If you handle it correctly, you can use this network to produce a huge marketing push that could potentially drive visitors and (eventually) revenue to your place of business. Your tribe can build Web site traffic or send people your way who'll buy your products or services.

This chapter helps you track your followers, measure the influence of your network on your business, and encourage your followers to share your content. Remember, content is the queen bee of the Internet, and Twitter is a powerful means of sharing that content.

## The Power of the Retweet

A retweet sounds like the call a bird makes to respond to another bird. (Perhaps you heard it's popular among bluebirds and cardinals.) When you *retweet,* you tweet a message that was previously posted by another user — in other words, you're quoting another user or echoing that person's thoughts. Depending on your desktop application, to show that you're retweeting, you can use the common format RT @username, and then type or paste the original poster's message. Applications such as twhirl (www.twhirl.org) give you a choice between four different retweet formats.

People commonly retweet so that they can share content they found valuable. For example, you may see a retweet that looks like Figure 8-1.

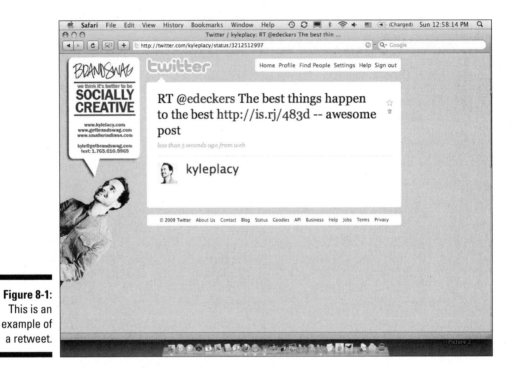

**Figure 8-1:**
This is an example of a retweet.

Figure 8-1 shows that someone loved the post by @edeckers and deemed it valuable enough to share with his or her followers. You can make retweeting work for you if you can convince your tribe to share your information with their networks. You can see some good examples of retweet worthy tweets below:

```
RT @arnteriksen: "Cheating: PR firm has interns post
positive reviews for clients" http://tinyurl.com/nebl68
(via @amandachapel)

RT @BobWarren: NEED A LAUGH? 30 Ways to Lose a Job on
Twitter http://tinyurl.com/cr4wew

RT @BarbaraJones: I know you're supposed to 'work
smarter, not harder'--anybody figure that out yet?
(no. Lol)

RT @nowsourcing: RT @TechCrunch Twitter Can Now Know
Where You Tweet http://tcrn.ch/7fU2
```

This type of sharing is *viral marketing,* which means using marketing techniques with social networks (such as Twitter) to increase brand awareness or to achieve other marketing objectives (such as product sales) through self-replicating viral processes. In layman's terms, viral marketing means that if you tell Sally about a product and she tells three of her friends, those three people could potentially tell ten people, and so on. (The idea is rather like the game Six Degrees of Kevin Bacon.) On Twitter, viral marketing takes the form of retweets.

# Discovering the art of retweeting

The art of retweeting isn't a sappy rendition of a Michael Bolton song, nor is it a Picasso painting depicting the Twitter bird. The art of retweeting involves concepts that you can apply to retweeting so that you can exponentially increase your effectiveness when you use the retweet function. I discuss the rules of retweeting in the following sections.

## Using the proper format for the retweet

You want to retweet because the world of social media and tools such as Twitter are built on the concept of content sharing. Without sharing content and adding value, you can't gain traction in the Twitter world.

As discussed previously, you indicate that you're retweeting a post by typing RT and the name of the original poster (@edeckers in Figure 8-1). User@edeckers shared a blog post of his own for other people to read.

After identifying the original twitterer, the retweet post shows the title of the blog entry posted by @edeckers; the URL (the link to the blog post); and finally, the retweeter's personal thoughts on the blog post. An alternative way to retweet is to start with your own thoughts, followed by the title of the blog entry and the link to the blog post, and close the tweet by typing via and the name of the original poster, as shown in Figure 8-2.

You can write a retweet in the right or the wrong way. Not crediting the original twitterer is an example of retweeting the wrong way. Next, there are a few rules of the retweet that I suggest you follow if you want to retweet the right way.

Example of the wrong way to retweet:

```
RT @Minervity: Fresh Web and Graphic and Development
Information and Tutorials (RSS Feed) - http://feeds.
feedburner.com/Minervity
```

**Figure 8-2:**
A properly
written
retweet
gives
credit to
the original
Twitterer.

A couple of reasons why the preceding retweet is terrible are that

- ✔ The full URL was used at the end of the retweet. You should always shorten anything that could be retweeted again.

- ✔ Too much content is stuffed into this retweet. The title of the tutorials should have been shortened for easier retweet by other people.

### Obeying the rules of the retweet

The following list describes the rules you must follow to be a successful retweeter and to write tweets that your followers can easily retweet:

- ✔ **Read before you retweet.** If you retweet everything just for the simple fact of gaining more followers, you can become annoying to the point where people may stop following you. There is no point in following a machine that only repeats what others say . . . much less, following a machine that repeats everything others say.

    An example of a non-read retweet:

    ```
    @kyleplacy: RT @arnteriksen: "I hate everything
    about Twitter."
    ```

The reason why this tweet is awful is because I actually love Twitter! The only reason I retweeted @arnteriksen's tweet is because he has a ton of followers. If you don't read the tweet before sending it out, you risk losing followers.

✔ **Leave room in your tweets for your followers to retweet.** When posting your own content, be sure to make your tweets short enough to leave room for multiple retweeters. You want to make it as easy as possible for people to share your content.

Try to keep your original tweets around 75 to 100 characters so that others can retweet your content.

✔ **Share others' content.** Retweet posts from people with whom you want to build a relationship on Twitter. This rule doesn't negate the first rule (read before you retweet), but others appreciate it when you retweet their posts. This is particularly true when you retweet a post by someone who is not a Twitter celebrity with follower figures in the five and six digits. It helps expose these folks to your followers and build up their influence on Twitter.

## Connecting with your evangelists

In the Twitter world, *evangelists* are the people who share your content the most. Twitter evangelists are valuable because they love your content, and they aren't afraid to tell people about it! Focus on your Twitter evangelists when you have content you want to share: You can now and then send them a direct message letting them know about new tweets they may be interested in.

Be sure to periodically retweet your evangelists' content with the same verve that they show toward your content.

How do you find your Twitter evangelists? Keep track of who retweets your content. If you start seeing a Twitter name popping up every so often with your content, you've found an evangelist. Be sure to thank this person for sharing your content and return the favor.

# Tracking Your Followers by Using TwitterCounter

*TwitterCounter* (http://twittercounter.com) is a Web site that allows you, the user, to generate a graph that gives you an overview of the number of followers you've earned in a specific time period. If you want to know how many users started to follow you yesterday, TwitterCounter can help you.

If you're familiar with the blog-reader counter FeedBurner (`www.feedburner.com`), you have a general idea of how TwitterCounter works. The following sections explain how you can sign up with TwitterCounter and use it to track your followers, track your competition's followers, and pinpoint the evangelists among your Twitter followers.

## Signing up for TwitterCounter

You can easily sign up to use the TwitterCounter service; just follow these steps:

1. **Open your browser and go to `http://twittercounter.com`.**

   The TwitterCounter Web site opens, displaying a random Twitter user's stats and graph.

2. **Click the Who Are You On Twitter? button in the top-right of the page.**

   The An Application Would Like to Connect to Your Account window appears. This page loads in a pop-up window.

3. **Click the Allow button.**

   This allows TwitterCounter to pull your Twitter stats automatically every time you return to the site. After you click the button, the pop-up box closes, and you are taken to your TwitterCounter Personal Settings page, as shown in Figure 8-3.

4. **Check the four check boxes on the personal settings page.**

   These check boxes are Go Directly to My Personal Statistics When I Visit TwitterCounter, Email a Weekly Update To, Automatically Follow Featured Users, and Count My ReTweets.

5. **Click the Save Settings button.**

   TwitterCounter saves your settings, and you can now click the Home tab (at the top of the page) to view your status.

TwitterCounter helps you track your Twitter stats and compare them to those of your competition. You can compare the number of followers, friends, and updates with as many as two other Twitter users, as shown in Figure 8-4. This information can help your Twitter marketing plan when it comes to tracking the success rate of your followers and your content.

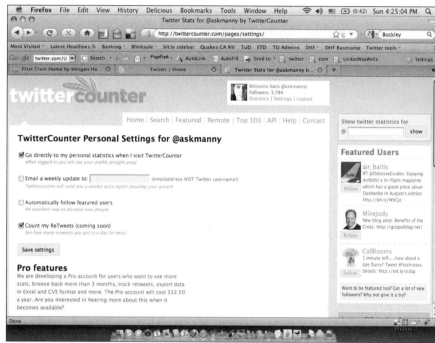

**Figure 8-3:**
The personal settings page lets you set up Twitter Counter.

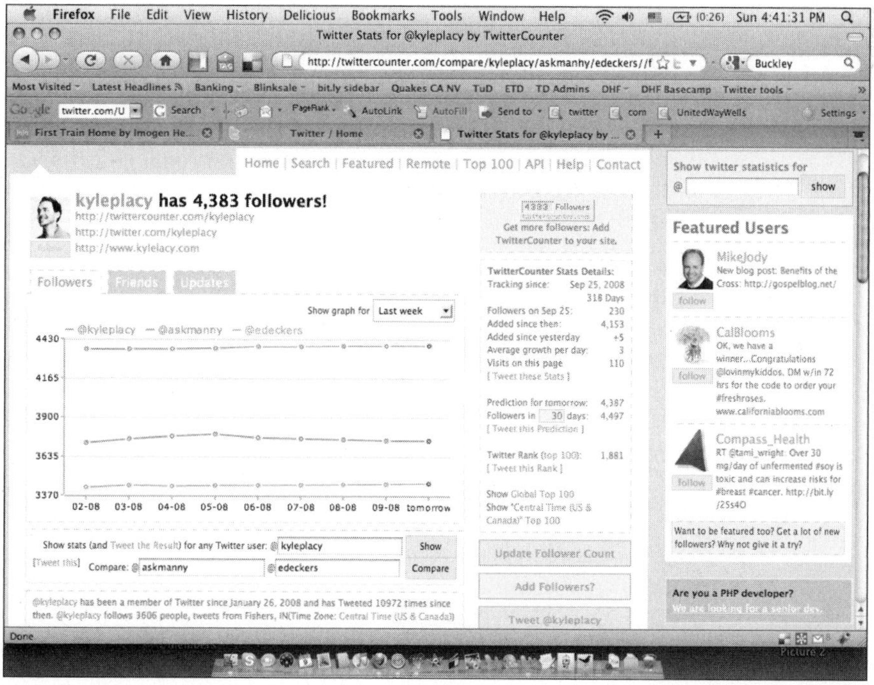

**Figure 8-4:**
Twitter user @kyleplacy compares his followers stats to @askmanny and @edeckers.

## *Viewing your follower growth on TwitterCounter*

After you sign up with TwitterCounter, you can use it to track your followers and the growth of your list of followers. The following list describes what makes TwitterCounter important to your Twitter marketing road map and how it helps you reach your goals:

✔ **Track your follower count.** You need to track how many followers you gain over different periods of time so that you can figure out what type of content your Twitter followers are most interested in as well as what kind of content will help increase your number of followers. You can view your stats and find out when you gained the most followers (although you still have to figure out why). Over a period of time, I have figured out that my followers enjoy content surrounding the topic of social media. An example of the content that is best received are quotes like this:

```
RT @kyleplacy Social media is about portability and
experiences

RT @kyleplacy 5 Tips to a More Productivity Social
Media Life http://bit.ly/2904

RT @kyleplacy Your customer is on social media and
they do not care about your ROI
```

✔ **Compare your follower growth rate to others.** TwitterCounter has a great feature that allows you to compare your growth rate to other people who use TwitterCounter. In the Compare text box below the graph on the homepage, enter a username whose follower growth rates you want to see, and then click the Compare button. A chart comparing growth rates for three different Twitter users is shown in Figure 8-4.

The reasoning behind comparing followers between certain accounts can be related to content sharing. If a competitor has more followers than your account, you need to take a look at what type of content he or she shares. You don't need to be disgruntled by being outnumbered by your competition in terms of a follower count. Remember, what is important is that your followers are communicating with you.

A competitor could have 20,000 followers, but if she doesn't communicate, she's wasting her time and you're ahead of the game!

✔ **Compare your number of updates to others.** You can also use the compare function in TwitterCounter to compare the number of updates among three different accounts. Click the Updates tab, enter the usernames in the Compare text boxes, and then click the Compare button. This helps you understand the rate at which your followers are posting on Twitter. You may find another Twitter user who is updating less and still maintaining a faster growth rate. This allows you to adjust your content strategy. You may find that some users share too much content and others share too little. It's important to find that comfortable place in the clouds. You can see the Updates charts for three different accounts in Figure 8-5.

**Figure 8-5:**
Twitter user @kyleplacy compares his updates stats to @askmanny and @edeckers.

# Adding a TwitterCounter button to your Web site

You can add a TwitterCounter button to your blog or Web site. When visitors to your site click it, they are taken to your TwitterCounter homepage. By adding a TwitterCounter button, you show in your blog (your central online content hub) how many people follow you on Twitter. If any Twitter users who are not currently following you visit your blog, thanks to the button they learn about your Twitter account and how many other people follow it. To add a TwitterCounter button to your blog or Web site, follow these steps:

1. **Click the Home button at the top of the TwitterCounter page.**

   The Home button takes you to your TwitterCounter homepage.

2. **Click the Get More Followers: Add TwitterCounter to Your Site button.**

   The button is located above your TwitterCounter stats details. As shown in the following figure, when you click the button, a new page loads, displaying different buttons and widgets that you can embed on your Web site, blog, or social network profile page (outside of Twitter).

3. **Copy the script or code, and post or embed the code into your desired site or social network.**

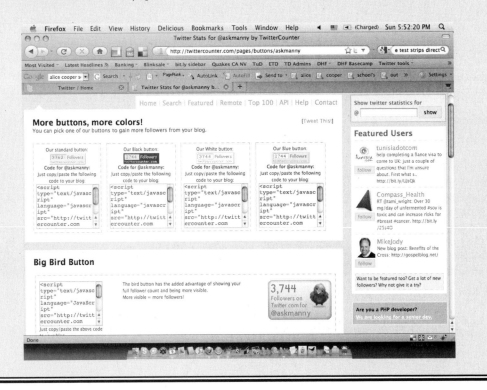

# Tracking When You Lose Followers with Qwitter

You can find plenty of tools that feed your ego and help you gain as many followers as you could possibly want, but none are quite like Qwitter (`http://useqwitter.com`). Qwitter is a service that allows you to track who has unfollowed you and guesstimate why they unfollowed you. After you sign up for Qwitter, you receive an e-mail every time an individual unfollows you.

The developers of the Qwitter service set it up to help you understand why certain individuals unfollow you. Assuming that twitterers may unfollow you as a result of a tweet you posted (there may be other reasons), Qwitter informs you who unfollowed you and what was the last tweet you posted before they stopped following your tweets. It can be quite the eye-opening experience when you have 50 to 100 people unfollow you based on one tweet.

## Signing up for Qwitter

You can get started using Qwitter fairly simply — just follow these steps:

1. **Open your browser and go to www.useqwitter.com.**

   The Qwitter login page opens, as shown in Figure 8-6.

2. **Enter your username in the Twitter Username text box.**

   Leave off the @ — for example, enter **kyleplacy**.

3. **In the Email Address text box, enter the e-mail address where you want Qwitter to send your update e-mails.**

4. **Click the Go Qwitter Go button, and you're done!**

Don't get depressed when individuals unfollow you. You may be getting quite a few e-mails from Qwitter in the next few months because you're still figuring out the best practices at marketing on the Twitter platform.

Create a separate folder in your e-mail Inbox for the Qwitter e-mails and change your e-mail account's setting so that all messages from Qwitter automatically go to that folder. You may feel like Qwitter is spamming you because of the number of notices about individuals unfollowing you, and you can more easily manage the amount of e-mail if you don't have to sift through it all in your Inbox.

**Figure 8-6:**
Find out
when peo-
ple unfollow
you on
Qwitter.

## Understanding why Qwitter is a powerful content tool

It may sound discouraging to know every time someone unfollows you because of a specific tweet or some type of content you shared, but you need to know what content generates bad responses from your Twitter followers.

If two or three individuals unfollow you after a tweet, they may not have done so because of that tweet. Don't worry when a few people unfollow you. Look for instances when a big group of people decide to stop following you.

If you see a trend in unfollowing based on the kind of content you're sharing, be very sure that you try to mix up the content. If Twitter users don't want to hear about what you're eating or what breed of dog you want to buy, take the information and use it to improve your approach to content creation. You aren't going to please everybody, but the more people who can become potential customers, the better.

Use TwitterCounter and Qwitter to keep track of your Twitter tribe, as well as the content you share. It can help you fast track your way to Twitter domination.

# Showing Your Followers That You Value Them

I say it several times elsewhere in this book, but I feel the need to say it here, too: Your followers are the most valuable thing on Twitter. They help you share content and spread news about your products and services; they also help you build thought-leadership and your ideas. You want your Twitter tribe to think the world of you and know that you'll return the favor if they share your content.

## Sharing before asking to share

The Twitter universe has an important rule: Share others' content before you ask them to share your content. Don't try to convince people to share your content without doing it first for them.

Think of it this way — say you're at a business-networking event and someone comes up to you and says, "Hey, dude, introduce me to all your friends and tell them I'm the best ever." Now, keep in mind that you have never met this person and he's already demanding that you share information about him among all your friends. What would you say? Probably no (or maybe something a little stronger).

To create a working relationship with your followers, share their content by retweeting their posts and telling your other followers about their content.

Find the top ten people on Twitter who are following you and vice-versa. Share their content as much as you can and when you can. Forge relationships with the people who have a large following on Twitter.

You'll be pleasantly surprised when they return the favor without your asking for their help. However, you can forge relationships with your followers in a better way than sharing their content outright — you just have to ask.

## Asking how you can help your followers

You can't find a better way to forge a relationship than asking how you can help your followers. If you want to build some type of content-sharing relationship with individuals on Twitter, ask how you can help them. Here are some pointers to keep in mind when you ask to help:

---

# A Twitter miracle for a single mother

Sometimes great things happen to people who are down and out. A story out of Chicago shows the power of a network where Twitter was the main source of help for a Romanian mother and her three children. The story starts with an extremely influential social media user (@armano) meeting Daniela, a mother of three from Romania. Daniela had left Romania because of an abusive husband and was trying to find support in order to help secure an apartment.

A blogger named David Armano found sympathy for Daniela and decided to write a blog post to ask for $5,000 in order to help Daniela put down a deposit and pay for her first month of rent. The blog post can be viewed at http://bit.ly/3WhVP5.

The blog was retweeted and shared hundreds of times on Twitter and was a viral sensation around the world in 24 hours. The campaign

raised $16,000 for Daniela in 48 hours. Pretty amazing, isn't it? Total strangers who were more than likely connected to David or one of his followers gave money to help a single mother from Romania get back on her feet.

The story doesn't end there. From different levels of followers and connections, Daniela was able to outfit her new apartment with furniture from Vicki Semka (http://migandtig.com) and Jerod Lazan (www.mortisetenon.com). Vicki contacted Jerod, who was happy to donate furniture to help Daniela. Keep in mind that Jerod is located in Los Angeles.

This story shows the power of using your followers for the betterment of mankind. If you have followers who respect and share content with you (thank you @armano!), the potential of viral messaging is endless! Thank you to @tkpleslie, who shared this story with me.

---

1. Create a list of the top 10 to 25 users who are following you and whom you're following.

2. Look at each user's Twitter profile, Web site, or blog, and try to find a tip that you can give each user to help in his or her Internet marketing strategy.

   For example, you can send a follower a message such as, "Hey, I love that picture on your Web site. Have you tried *(insert your advice)*?"

3. Direct message those 10 to 25 users to make contact with them.

4. If they respond with thanks, reply by asking how you can help them.

5. Do what they say.

You're creating a relationship by helping first and then asking for help second. I don't have any real rules for when you should ask someone to help you share content, but don't be annoying when you decide it's time to ask for help.

Your Twitter followers are the most important resource you have on Twitter, and the Internet, as a whole. If you present and share content in the right way, they can open doors you never dreamed possible.

# Chapter 9

# Reaching Your Customers

*W*ho are your customers? Where do they live? What do they like, buy, use, watch, read, or drive? If you keep track of your customer base, you should be able to figure out who your best customers are (those who are likely to buy more or buy more often from you) and where you can find them.

For example, if you're a marble manufacturer and sell to marble collectors, your typical customer is male, lives in a big city, and is in his 30s or 40s. If you have an ice cream shop, you know your typical customer comes from a 5-mile radius around your store. If you have a coffee shop, your typical customers may be small-business people and entrepreneurs who have business meetings during the day.

As discussed in Chapter 3, the great thing about using Twitter is that you can reach customers in a whole new way:

- ✔ You can find your exact customer, not an approximation of one.

- ✔ You can reach your customers right where they *are,* instead of advertising in places they're *likely* to be.

- ✔ You're sending your message only to people who care about marble collecting, so you don't have to waste ink and money on people who don't.

- ✔ You can create frequent — even daily — content and get that content to your customers at all hours of the day, not once a month or only during special events.

- ✔ You aren't spending thousands of dollars in print and broadcast advertising. You're spending little to no money on electronic marketing.

- ✔ People can easily share your message within their circles of influence.

In this chapter, I tell you some of the tools and techniques that you can use to find your followers, how to encourage your customers to pass your message on, and ways to direct traffic to your Web site or blog.

# Finding Your Customers on Twitter

If you want to build a following, you need to follow people first. But don't just go following as many people as you can find. That approach works for spammers, but you're better than that. You don't want to go following everyone just in the hopes that he or she might buy something from you.

You want to follow the people who are likely to buy from you, people whom you think would be interested in what you have to say, and people you're interested in. Find those people and have conversations with them. Talk about what interests them, send out links to articles that they may find useful, and retweet their articles. (For details on retweeting, see Chapter 8.)

Think of it this way: Have you ever had a friend who was involved in some multi-level marketing plan or sales club? Did he or she invite you to take a few minutes to find out a little bit more about the product or club? And did you feel like you at least owed your friend a few minutes?

Twitter is a lot like that, but without all the begrudging acceptance and feelings of guilt for saying no. Basically, if people like you because you're a good twitizen (Twitter citizen), they're more likely to pay attention to what you have to say when you send out a commercial message every now and then.

But you have to find followers first. The following sections provide a few good resources that you can use to find your future customers, as well as your competitors and industry leaders.

## Searching by subject matter on Twitter

Very honestly, the hardest part about finding your customers on Twitter is choosing which tools to use. Many search tools are available, but none of them can do all the kinds of searches you want to perform, so you need to use a few of these tools to get started.

You can dig in three main places to unearth people to follow on Twitter: people's tweets, people's bios, and people's locations. Based on tweets, you can establish an interest or a need from someone in a product or service that you offer. Similarly, the bios of Twitter users may reveal whether they are part of the industry that you serve (or the industry that you are a part of).

Ultimately, if you run a local business, knowing whether a Twitter user lives near you is critical. The following sections describe the ways to find people based on their tweets, their Twitter bio, and their location.

### Tweet searches

Search tweets for keywords and topics because people who are talking about your topics or industry issues are either in the industry itself or have a problem that you might be able to help them with. The following Web applications help you find people based on keywords in their tweets:

- **Twitter search (`http://search.twitter.com`):** Searches all tweets for your particular topic and returns tweets matching your search in chronological order. If you need to search for a particular issue, you can find all the people who are interested in it. The advanced search — `http://search.twitter.com/advanced` — enables you to exclude certain words or phrases, do a local search, and search for tweets to and from a specific person. You can see Twitter's Advanced Search options in Figure 9-1.

- **Twitterfall (`www.twitterfall.com`):** Searches for keywords and hashtags, and then automatically updates the results page, like a cascading waterfall. Twitterfall is ideal for conferences, in customer service applications, and even ongoing events such as a sporting event or an international incident, where having a live view of comments as the activity is underway can be useful to those involved in it or those following it.

- **TweetTabs (`http://tweettabs.com`):** Works just like Twitterfall, but also lets you create tabs to monitor a number of keywords.

- **CrowdEye (`www.crowdeye.com`):** A search engine that shows you not only tweets based on your keyword search, but also a time graph for when most of the tweets showed up. It even gives you some of the most popular Web links for your keywords.

- **Social Mention (`www.socialmention.com`):** More than just a Twitter search tool. Search for keywords, events, and even your own name (it's called *ego surfing,* and it's perfectly all right). See where micro-blogs, blogs, Web sites, news articles, images, videos, and even comments have mentioned your search term.

- **TweetDeck (`http://tweetdeck.com`):** Normally considered a desktop application, but TweetDeck's search function also lets you save searches for keywords and topics. They appear as an additional column (or deck) in the TweetDeck interface, which is updated automatically any time someone's tweet includes the search term.

*RSS* stands for Really Simple Syndication. It's a news feed for your favorite blogs, news sites, or even Twitter search results. Use My Yahoo! (`http://my.yahoo.com`), Google Reader (`www.google.com/reader`), or one of dozens of other RSS readers to keep up with your feeds.

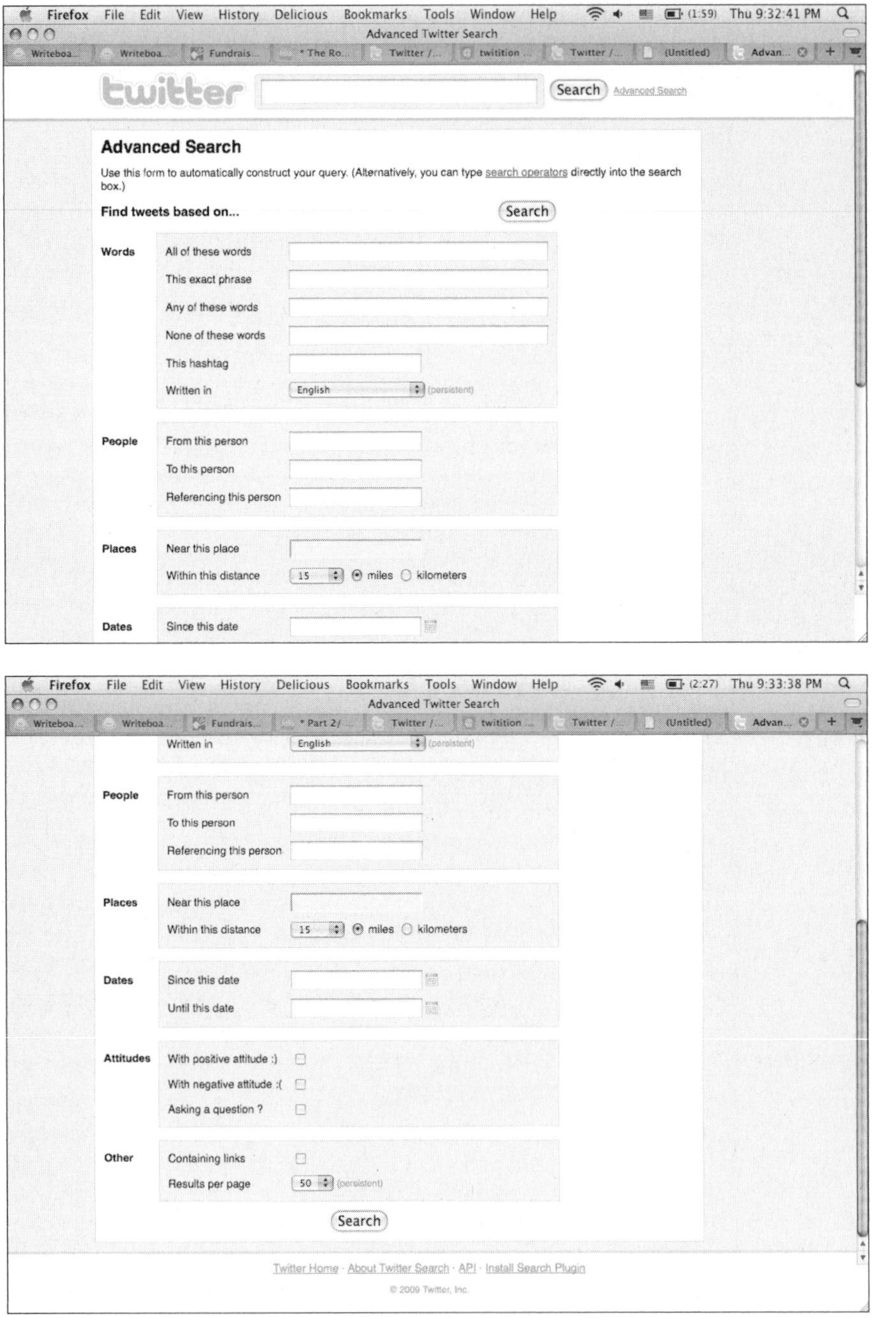

**Figure 9-1:**
Twitter
search
offers an
Advanced
Search
option that
lets you
filter your
results.

### Bio and keyword searches

If you want to find people in your industry or chosen field, you need to
search Twitter users' bio sections. However, you can't do that kind of search
in Twitter's search function, so you need to use another app to search bios. If
you sell to accountants, for example, search for **accountant** or **accounting** in
twitterers' bios, using one of these Web sites:

- ✔ **Twitterment (www.twitterment.com):** Not only enables you to search
  past tweets, but also searches Twitter bios. So, if you're looking for
  people who work in a specific industry, Twitterment can help you find
  them as long as they have included their industry as part of their bio.

- ✔ **TweepSearch (www.tweepsearch.com):** Does a quick check of all the
  Twitter bios it has currently indexed.

- ✔ **Just Tweet It (http://justtweetit.com):** A directory-based search
  that lets you register yourself under a directory almost as if it were
  the Yellow Pages of Twitter, as well as looks for other twitterers (see
  Figure 9-2). If you sell to a specific industry, such as accounting, health-
  care, or non-profit organizations, you can quickly find target customers
  using this search.

**Figure 9-2:**
Just Tweet
It offers a
directory-
based
search
broken into
categories.

- **tweepz.com (www.tweepz.com):** A more robust search engine than most of the others in this list. You can search for bios, locations, and names. Just type in the code that tells tweepz.com where to search, such as **bio: humor writer.**

- **Peoplebrowsr.com (http://my.peoplebrowsr.com):** A high-powered people searcher and Twitter browser that offers three different options: Lite, Advanced, and Business. Create *stacks* based on keywords or even bio searches. (You can think of stacks as the decks or columns offered by TweetDeck.)

### Location searches

If you have a location-specific business, such as a realty, retail store, or restaurant, you want to find twitterers who are in your area. You can search for people by city, county, and even state with the applications in the following list. You can search by map or just by typing in your city's name and selecting a radius around the area:

- **Nearby Tweets (www.nearbytweets.com):** Enables you to search for people in your area and filter the results by keywords. For example, if you're a chiropractor in Kansas City, do a search for people around Kansas City who have tweeted about a sore back or back pain.

- **Twellowhood (www.twellow.com/twellowhood):** From the makers of Twellow, a Yellow Pages–type directory that enables you to drill down to your city or town, and see how many twitterers are there.

- **Twitterholic.com (http://twitterholic.com):** The place to go if you want to find the top twitterers in your town. Visit the Web site, enter your Twitter username in the Check Out Your Twitterholic Ranking box, and click the Go button. You are presented with a plethora of Twitter stats about yourself, letting you see how you're ranked in your area, as well as who's ranked above and below you. Their names are links: Right-click on them to view their Twitterholic stats. No wonder they call the site Twitterholic!

- **Twtvite (www.twtvite.com):** The place where you can find tweetups, as shown in Figure 9-3. *Tweetups* (gatherings of local twitterers) are all the rage, and they're a great way to actually meet local twitterers face-to-face. Whether you want to find a general invitation or a meeting about a specific field, you can visit Twtvite to see whether any local tweetups are planned in your area. You can even list your own tweetup. Keep in mind that not all tweetups are listed on this site, so you may want to do a search on Twitter for the word **tweetup** and your city.

- **Tweetmondo (www.tweetmondo.com):** Enables you to log in with your Twitter info and tells you who's nearby. The more precise the location information you enter, the more precise Tweetmondo can be. If you have a storefront, you can use this tool to reach nearby customers.

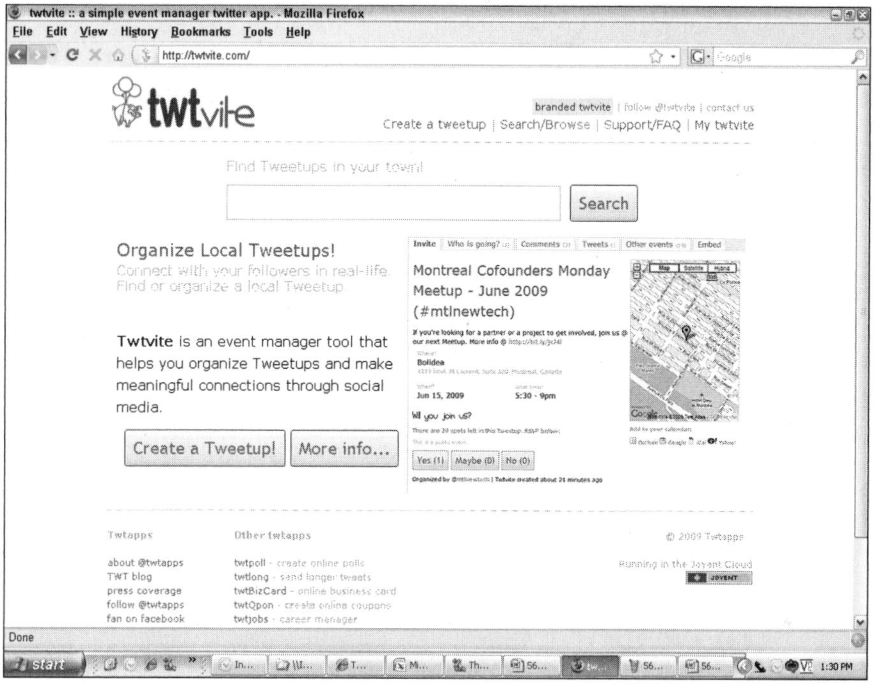

**Figure 9-3:**
Find local tweetups on Twtvite.

# Finding followers by syncing your contact list

The best and easiest way to find people to follow is to start with the people you already know. Gather up your contact lists, especially if you have them scattered around on different e-mail programs.

Unfortunately, you can't upload a .csv or .txt file from your Outlook or other e-mail program into Twitter. (.csv stands for comma-separated values files, and .txt is a text-based, tab-delimited file. You can export most e-mail address books to a .csv file and then upload the file to other e-mail programs.) If most of your e-mail addresses are in an e-mail program that sits on your hard drive, you need to take a few easy steps to find out if any of your contacts is already on Twitter.

### Exporting your e-mail contacts

Follow these steps to export e-mail contacts from Outlook:

1. **Open Outlook and then choose File⇨Import and Export.**

   The Import and Export Wizard appears.

2. **From the Choose an Action to Perform list, select Export to a File, as shown in Figure 9-4, and then click Next.**

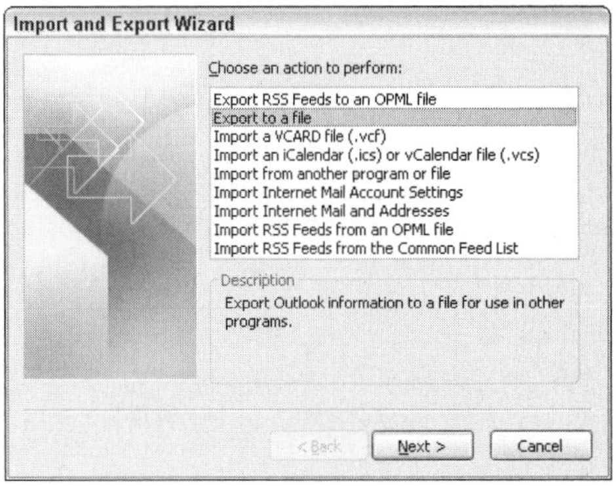

**Figure 9-4:**
The Import
and Export
Wizard.

3. **From the Create a File of Type list, select Comma Separated Values (Windows) and then click Next.**

4. **Scroll down the list of folders and select Contacts as the folder you want to export from. Then click Next.**

   By default, you are presented with a hidden folder when you can save your Contacts.

5. **Click the Browse button, and in the Browse dialog box that appears, select where you want to save the file.**

   Save the file in a place where it's easy to find, such as on the desktop.

6. **Enter a name for the file in the File Name text box.**

   Give the file an obvious name, such as `contacts.csv`.

7. **Click OK to close the dialog box.**

   The file you selected appears in the Save Exported File text box, as shown in Figure 9-5.

8. **Click Next and then click Finish.**

   You're done!

To export e-mail contacts from Apple Mail, follow the steps on this page from the Apple Web site at `http://bit.ly/vCardExport`.

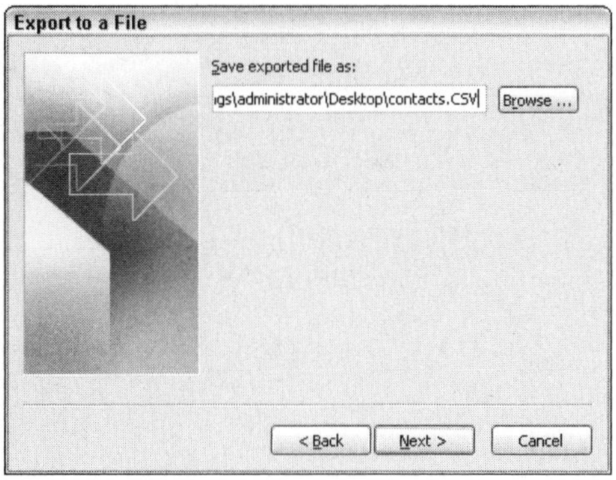

**Figure 9-5:**
Choose
where to
save your
exported
contacts
file.

## Uploading your contacts to Gmail, Yahoo!, or AOL

After you export your contacts to a `.csv` file or a vCard, follow these steps to upload the contacts to your Gmail, Yahoo!, or AOL e-mail account, and then upload the contacts to Twitter:

1. **Create a Gmail, Yahoo!, or AOL e-mail account, or log in if you already have one.**

   You can easily create a Gmail or Yahoo! e-mail account — just go to `http://mail.google.com` or `http://mail.yahoo.com`, and look for a Sign Up link or button. If you use AOL, you should already have an AOL e-mail account.

2. **Import your contacts from the `.csv` or vCard file.**

   In Gmail:

   *1. Click Contacts in the navigation on the left.*

   Your list of contacts appears.

   *2. Click Import in the upper-right corner of the window.*

   The next page lets you select the `.csv` or vCard file to upload, as shown in Figure 9-6.

   *3. Click the Browse button and find the file on your desktop. Click OK/ Open.*

   At this point, you're ready to import your contacts.

   *4. Click the Import button.*

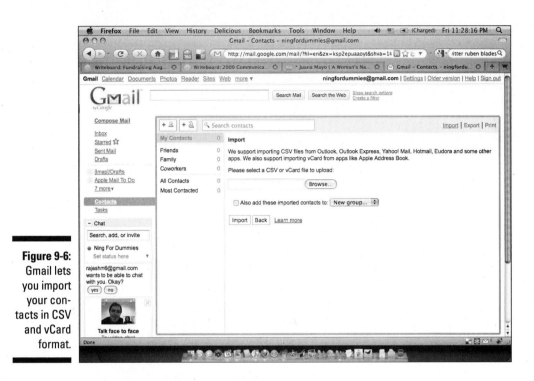

**Figure 9-6:**
Gmail lets you import your contacts in CSV and vCard format.

In Yahoo! Mail

1. *Click the Contacts link in the menu on the left side of the page.*

   This loads all your Yahoo! Mail contacts in a new tab on the right side of the page.

2. *Click the Tools button at the top of the window and select Import.*

   This lets you set up Yahoo! Mail to import your contacts in multiple formats.

3. *Select the type of file you want to import, click the Browse button to find the file on your computer, and click the Import Now button.*

   At this point, all your contacts are imported into Yahoo! Mail.

4. *Click the Tools menu again and select Clean Up Duplicates to eliminate any duplicate e-mail addresses.*

In AOL

1. *Click the Contacts link in the menu on the left side of the page.*

   As with Yahoo! Mail, AOL loads all your contacts on the right side of the page.

*2. Click the Import button at the top of the window.*

This lets you choose between `.csv` and `.txt` files with your contacts.

*3. Select the type of file you want to import, click the Browse button to find the file, and then click the Import button.*

You're all set with your contacts loaded in AOL mail.

**3. Log in to your Twitter account and click the Find People link.**

This page lets you find current Twitter users by searching for them by keyword/name and importing your contacts from Gmail, Yahoo! or AOL; inviting them by e-mail; or choosing among users suggested by Twitter.

**4. Click the Find on Other Networks tab.**

The Find on Other Networks page opens, as shown in Figure 9-7.

**5. Click the Gmail, Yahoo!, or AOL button.**

You're prompted to enter your e-mail address and password for your account so Twitter can import your contacts from your e-mail contact list.

**6. Enter your e-mail address in the Your Email text box, enter your password in the Email Password text box, and click the Continue button.**

Twitter doesn't store your login credentials, so it's safe to enter this private data.

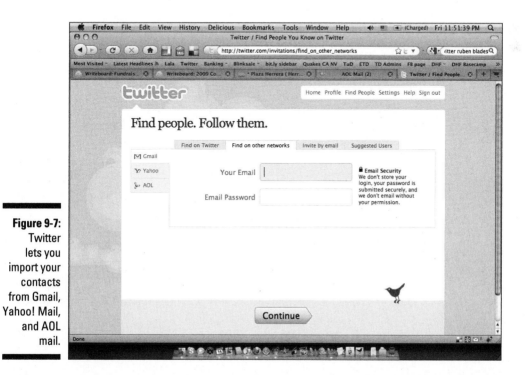

**Figure 9-7:**
Twitter lets you import your contacts from Gmail, Yahoo! Mail, and AOL mail.

7. **Select the check boxes next to the names of people you want to follow, uncheck the boxes next to people you don't, and click the Follow button.**

   This adds the people you selected to your Following list.

   Now you're following those people. Depending on their settings, they get e-mail notifications that you're following them, and hopefully, they'll follow you back.

# Empowering Current Customers to Spread the Message

Hopefully, your customers are also your fans. Hopefully, you're providing the best customer service and greatest value so that your customers want to tell all their friends about you. And hopefully, you're making it possible for your customers to do just that.

## Spreading a message to friends of friends of friends

Retweeting isn't just a way to spread your message to other people (although that's a big part of it). When someone retweets a message, it's a sign of respect, implying that the poster wrote something funny, wise, useful, or otherwise valuable. When you write something worth sharing, your followers retweet your message to their followers. And if one of your friends retweets to his or her friends, your message can reach thousands — and even tens of thousands — of twitterers with just a few clicks. Figure 9-8 shows how a retweet can spread through friends and friends of friends.

The messages shown in Figure 9-8 build from each preceding message. @chrisbaskind sent the original message and @Kim retweeted it. Then @JeanneMale retweeted @Kim's retweet and @askmanny (the user closest to the top of the Twitter timeline) retweeted @JeanneMale's retweet. Each of them has placed the letters RT in front of the username whose message they've retweeted. This kind of retweet chain is called *viral marketing,* and it's the way most Internet memes start.

In this example, if each of the people who retweeted the message in Figure 9-8 has 100 followers, this message could potentially reach 1 million people (if everyone who receives it retweets it).

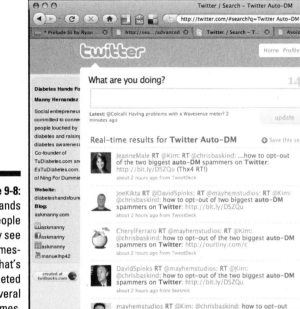

**Figure 9-8:**
Thousands
of people
may see
a mes-
sage that's
retweeted
several
times.

I discuss how to measure clicks and retweets in Chapter 6. Pay particular attention to the section on tracking retweets with Retweetist (www.
retweetist.com).

It's considered proper Twitter etiquette to give retweeting credit to as many
people as you can. But if you find you're running out of space, give the credit
to the person who *started* the message, not the person from whom you got it.

## Understanding viral marketing on Twitter

*Viral marketing* is basically marketing techniques that spread from person to
person to person. The 1980s shampoo commercial that said "and they told
two friends, and they told two friends, and so on, and so on, and so on" illustrates the concept of viral marketing. You tell a few people, they tell a few
people, and it grows from there.

Viral marketing techniques commonly spread YouTube videos, games, Flash
movies, ads, blogs, and Web sites, to name a few.

A few examples of successful online and offline viral marketing campaigns include

- **Ponzi schemes:** You get recruited, then you recruit your friends, and they recruit theirs, until the whole thing collapses, and the creator goes to jail.

- **Mystery Science Theater 3000:** Producers encouraged viewers to video-tape the show and pass the tapes on to friends.

- **Hotmail:** Microsoft made Hotmail popular by putting a small ad for — what else? — Hotmail in the e-mail footer of each message. Every time a Hotmail user sent an e-mail message, the tiny ad for the free e-mail program went with it.

- **HomeStar Runner:** These Flash movies have been an Internet hit for several years, thanks to a presence on iTunes as well as friends sharing videos with their friends.

- **Will It Blend? videos:** These videos feature Tom Dickson of Blendtec, a heavy-duty blender manufacturer trying to blend various items, including a tiki torch, an iPhone, an Olympus digital camera, and several action figures, including a Chuck Norris figure. (The result? Everything blends . . . except Chuck Norris.)

In all cases, users and fans made these videos, schemes, and e-mail programs popular by telling their friends about the items, who then told their friends. Thanks to tools such as Twitter, you can easily forward new information and viral campaigns on to your friends, who then pass them on to their friends through retweeting.

## Creating your own viral marketing campaign

You can't always create a successful viral marketing campaign, no matter how hard you try. Many attempted campaigns have fallen flat on their faces. Many that started out as a cute little video for a few family members and friends turned out to be huge successes. Typically, commercial marketing campaigns don't fare well, unless done properly. The Blendtec Will It Blend? videos are an example of a commercial marketing campaign that made it big, despite the commercial nature of the videos.

So, what creates a successful viral marketing campaign? Although following these tips can't guarantee viral marketing success, just remember, chance favors the prepared mind:

- ✔ **Create a clear, easy-to-remember marketing message.** Have one benefit or idea that you can sum up in a single tag line (for example, Murphy's Marbles — So durable, diamonds can't cut 'em).

- ✔ **Create a Web site for your product or service.** Get an easy-to-remember URL, such as `www.murphysmarbles.com`.

- ✔ **Put sharable items on your site and allow others to share those items, too.** Create your own videos and encourage others to upload and share those videos by including Email This buttons and offering embed codes for blogs.

- ✔ **Upload your videos to YouTube, Vimeo, and other video-sharing sites.** Create a publication schedule. Instead of uploading them all at the same time, trickle them in every week or two to build anticipation.

- ✔ **Send out links to your videos through Twitter, your blog, your e-mail newsletter, and anything else you can get your virtual hands on.** Remember to use a URL shortener when you link out to your videos so you can track the performance of each channel you use to get the word out about your videos.

- ✔ **Create some offline collateral, as well.** Hand out business cards that include your URL and tag line to every potential customer, and give several of your business cards to friends and family. Encourage them to hand your cards out to their friends, too. If your budget allows for it, get your business name, URL, and tag line printed on t-shirts and hats, and give them to people who'll wear them in public.

# Driving Traffic to Your Web Site or Blog

In other chapters, I discuss the importance of creating interesting, valuable content, so I don't need to say it again. But, assuming that you've done that, how do you get people to your blog or Web site?

First, keep in mind that a blog and Web site are two different things. A Web site is generally static and unchanging, so if you want to get people to visit it, you need to change it once in a while and offer something new and of value (for example, a special offer or downloadable coupon). A blog, on the other hand, changes every time you publish a new post. It's a little like a newspaper, with every blog post like a new issue, and you can let people know that a new issue is on their newsstands now.

The following sections describe two ways to share updates to your blog (or Web site): by hand and automatically.

## *Publishing blog feeds by hand*

You can easily share by hand with your Twitter followers when you update your blog. Copy the URL of your latest post, shorten the URL with one of the many URL shorteners, and send out a tweet that includes the shortened URL. TweetDeck has several built-in URL shorteners, and they all have their own Web sites, as well. I discuss Cligs (`http://cl.igs`) in Chapter 6, but a few others are bit.ly (`http://bit.ly`), is.gd (`http://is.gd`), and TinyURL.com (`http://tinyurl.com`).

A typical format for tweeting about a new blog post is to type **New post:**, copy and paste the blog headline, and paste the shortened URL, as shown in Figure 9-9. The **Please RT** at the end encourages your followers to retweet the message to their followers.

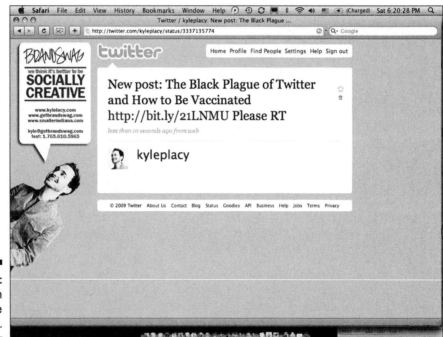

**Figure 9-9:**
Tweet when you update your blog.

## Automating your blog feed

You can use a few programs to automatically send out tweets when you update your blog, but the most popular ones are Twitterfeed (http://twitterfeed.com) and Ping.fm (www.ping.fm).

Twitterfeed works by visiting your blog at set intervals, from every 30 minutes to every 24 hours, to see whether you have any new posts. It then posts the headline and URL to your Twitter feed (hence the name). So, when you create a new blog post, you don't need to do anything else. It's all done for you.

Ping.fm sends out a 140-character message to different social networks, including Twitter, Facebook, LinkedIn, Iconi.ca, Laconica, FriendFeed, and even your blog. In fact, Ping.fm can post to nearly 40 social networks, if you're on that many (but I recommend that you use only two, maybe three, tops). However, you have to write each message and shorten each URL manually.

But — this is the really cool part — you can feed your Twitterfeed, uh, feed into Ping.fm. When you set up a Twitterfeed account, tell it to send your posts to your Ping.fm account, rather than your Twitter account. Then make sure you have all your social networking tools set up on your Ping.fm, as explained in Chapter 5.

## Retweeting to add value

The underlying theme of much of the advice in this book is value, value, value. Make sure your tweets are valuable to your followers and their followers. Write interesting tweets, forward helpful articles you've read, and write useful blog posts and tweet them. In the same vein, make sure that your retweets follow the same rules. If someone says something you think is particularly useful, retweet it. If you have room in the message, add a short comment.

Retweeting is not only a way to pass on valuable information, but it also gives a little Twitter-love to the original writer. It's a way of saying, "I think what you have to say is valuable." Any twitterer with a pulse gets a little thrill to see his or her name preceded by an RT and the message he or she wrote. Retweeting is a little virtual validation of the poster's thoughts and ideas, and it inspires people to repeat the behavior so that they can get the same thrill again.

Occasionally, you run into problems when you don't have enough room to give proper retweet credit to the original poster. If that happens, it's perfectly acceptable to edit the original message in order to get the person's @username and URL (if he or she has one) to fit. Make edits such as changing *two* or *to* to *2, with* becomes *w/,* and *people* becomes *ppl*. Every little bit helps as long as you can get your message across.

## Encouraging your followers to retweet

Anyone who's used Twitter for a few days is already familiar with the concept of retweeting. However, that doesn't mean a follower is going to do it. You need to make it easy and convenient for your followers to retweet your messages.

Here are the best ways to get people to retweet your content:

- ✔ **Keep your messages short.** Leave at least 14 characters for your user-name and the RT flag. Leave at least 20–30 characters of space at the end of every Tweet if you want several people to retweet.

- ✔ **Use hashtags.** You can get people to see your message who don't normally follow you.

- ✔ **Be sure to include a URL.** A URL makes your content more valuable than just some clever quote. Use a URL shortener to save space.

- ✔ **Tweet relevant content.** Be interesting, clever, and have something important or valuable to say.

- ✔ **Ask your followers to retweet.** Include the phrase **please RT** at the end of the message.

- ✔ **Don't use too many usernames and URLs.** People are less likely to retweet tweets that have too many @names and URLs. Too many @ names means less space to add your own words when you retweet, and multiple URLs dissolve the focus of the tweet: Which URL should people click? The original URL is the only one that should be included in a tweet or a retweet.

- ✔ **Use Retweetist (`www.retweetist.com`) to find the people who retweet most often.** Follow those twitterers and provide them value (by retweeting their stuff), and they may eventually retweet your tweets, too. Just make sure you follow the other suggestions in this bulleted list.

# Understanding What Etiquette Has to Do with Twitter Marketing

The rules of Twitter etiquette and procedure apply to marketing, possibly more so than they do for regular users. Remember, as a marketer, you're like someone who crashed a party. No one will complain as long as you behave. But if you step over the line, you'll get tossed out by security guys with large muscles and tight black t-shirts.

On Twitter, you need to engage in the conversation before you start market-ing. Let people see that you're a real person who's interested in other real people. If you only hammer people over and over with the same messages about buying your product and taking 10 percent off today only, the twitterers will shun you. But, if you become someone who provides good information and only occasionally sends out an "oh, by the way, this is what I do for a living" message, people more willingly accept the marketing when you send it.

Depending on whom you ask, your ratio of marketing to non-marketing mes-sages can be 1 marketing message to every 5, 10, or even 15 non-marketing messages. Remember, if people think you're a good Twitter citizen, they're more likely to pay attention to your marketing message.

And although spacing out your marketing messages this much can seem like a real pain, just remember that you can use tools to help make your Twitter life easier. (See Chapter 5 for more on these types of tools.) Use what's avail-able to you, create some good content, and form some solid relationships with other twitterers.

# Chapter 10

# Creating Quality Content on Twitter

*I* base everything discussed in earlier chapters on one simple idea: People are interested in what you have to say. If you aren't interesting, if you don't have quality content, if you don't provide value, then people are going to ignore you. If you want people to pay attention to you and, as a result, visit your Web site and buy your product or service, then you need to have quality content in your tweets.

This chapter digs into the art of creating content that your followers will want to read.

# Generating Quality Content

Quality content is one of those things you can't really define, but you know it when you see it. *Quality content* is basically content that provides some value or interest to the people who read it. (You thought I was going to say "has quality," didn't you?) Quality content has to be something people actually want to read in the first place. Forget whether you're laid-back or exciting, funny or dramatic, erudite or obtuse. You need to be interesting. If you aren't interesting, people will quit paying attention to you.

Being interesting on Twitter doesn't just mean having something clever and witty to say, although that doesn't hurt. Being interesting actually means you write things that aren't just commercial in nature. If you're only tweeting about your latest coupon or sale, then you're going to bore your readers to tears. If you're only sending out links to your latest blog post, you're providing valuable content, but you're nothing more than a news feed. If you're tweeting what you had for breakfast that morning, or that you're taking the dog out for a walk, then you're being personal — but maybe a little too much. To be a quality twitterer, you need to strike an effective balance between tweeting about what matters to you, what matters to your followers, and what matters to your brand or product.

## Tweeting about what matters to you

Your tweets start with you. This is *your* form of communication, *your* words, and *your* ideas. So, if you really do want to tweet rhapsodic about the hazelnut cream cheese you had on your bagel this morning, so be it. If you want to make clever remarks while you're watching a TV show, that's fine, too.

In fact, you need to tweet about things in your own life. You want to look like a real person, even if you're tweeting as your company, because everyone knows a real person hides behind those tweets, and they want to get to know you. If they know and like you, they'll buy from you.

So, tweet about things such as the lunch meeting you had with fellow twitterers, the conference you just attended, or even something clever your kids said. Personal tweets help foster and grow personal relationships with fellow twitterers, which can lead to all sorts of opportunities for you. Plus, it's a great way to embarrass your kids when they get older.

You can also use Twitter to announce your victories in life, such as job offers, marriage proposals, book-publishing deals, and any other events you want to celebrate with your friends.

## Tweeting about what matters to your brand

What matters to your brand is pretty much the same thing that matters to you — or, at least, it should be. If you're an entrepreneur or own a small business, then the line between you and your brand tends to be a little blurry. You want people to identify you with your company. So, feel free to have a joint business/personal Twitter account. I know several people who do. I do it myself. But if you work for a larger business, you want to separate the two.

## Be careful what you tweet

Be careful not to send tweets that may cause you problems with work or endanger you, your family, or your property. For example, avoid tweeting about when you're out of town or how much you hate your job.

One twitterer tweeted that he was going with his family on vacation. When he returned, he found that someone had broken into his house and stolen a lot of valuable items.

Another twitterer, who's now Twitter-famous, sent out this tweet: `Cisco just offered me a job! Now I have to weigh the utility of a fatty paycheck against the daily commute to San Jose and hating the work.` The tweet was seen by someone who actually worked at Cisco, and he responded: `Who is the hiring manager? I'm sure they would love to know that you will hate the work. We here at Cisco are versed in the web.` The original twitterer responded by taking her tweets private, but the damage was done. Cisco withdrew the job offer (actually, an internship), although the twitterer had actually already turned it down. Imagine what would have happened if she had been going for a promotion and big pay raise? And what might happen if her name becomes known to the next hiring manager who interviews her? (You can read more about this story at `www.msnbc.msn.com/id/29901380`.)

Treat your brand or company like a person when it comes to Twitter. If you have business victories, tweet about them. If something funny happens at work, tweet about it. You may need to be very vague and refer to "a client" — rather than a particular person, or his or her username — but unless it's inappropriate, illegal, or proprietary, you can share information *about* your business with people.

Having said that, don't tweet trade secrets, inside information, or financial information with your followers. You can get into some pretty big legal trouble.

In Chapter 11, I talk more about the importance of not bombarding followers with commercials. Send out commercial messages only about 1 out of every 15 other messages. Remember, a balance of tweets doesn't mean one-third personal, one-third about your followers, and one-third about your business.

## *Conversing with your followers*

Believe it or not, your followers aren't sitting and staring at their computers, waiting eagerly to see what you're going to tweet next. Their eyes aren't bloodshot from lack of sleep, backs sore from trying to lean closer to the monitor so that they can rock back, roaring with laughter at your latest witticism, or scramble for their credit cards at your next special offer.

Your followers are people with their own lives and interests. And very honestly, they aren't waiting for your tweets. Chances are, they forgot they're even following you.

So, if you truly want to stand out, find out what your followers are talking about. You can do this one of two ways: Read each tweet that they send out or see what everyone's talking about.

If you truly want to show people that you're interested in what they have to say, respond to their tweets. Have an actual conversation with them. If someone sends a tweet out that he or she just came back from lunch at your favorite restaurant, reply that you were just there last week, or say that it's your favorite place, or ask what he or she had. Sure, it seems tiny and unimportant, but to the person you just tweeted, he or she gets a little thrill of recognition that someone just read his or her tweet. So, make sure you do it publicly.

Respond to several of your followers, making sure to respond with a kind word, big idea, or clever response to something they've said. Even if you respond to only five people a day, you get a reputation as someone who's involved and in touch with your followers, and that impression can start to make a difference in how you're seen in your circle of twitterers. It shouldn't be hard for you to find at least five tweets you are genuinely interested in from your followers that you can respond or add something to.

Of course, responding to people on Twitter (actually reading tweets, to select which ones to respond to) can be pretty time-consuming, especially if you have a lot of followers — or, more importantly, if you want to see what people are talking about the most. To most easily find topics people are talking about, just pay attention to the latest Twitter trends, discussed in the section "Keeping Up with Trends on Twitter," later in this chapter.

# Developing Your Story on Twitter

From a traditional marketing standpoint, advertising and design are created to tell a story. Every brand from here to Timbuktu (they did a great job at brand development) is around to tell a story. The end goal is that the story will be told over and over again until the masses know about the brand.

Your story is the lifeblood of your brand. There are some fine points to creating your story, and no, you are not going to write an autobiography (unless that is what you are trying to sell by using Twitter). The following sections delve into how you tell your story.

## Developing your brand story

Nothing is more exciting than developing your brand story for the masses to communicate. You love the idea, products, services, and people. Your story is how you go about your daily routine and help the people involved in your brand. So how do you develop your story? Here are some tips to help you along the way:

- ✔ **Share customer success stories.** Your brand is your stories. If you have customer success stories, it is important to share these stories on Twitter. Better yet, get your customers to share them on Twitter.

- ✔ **Share your company history.** How did you get started? Many people (your tribe) would love to know about the history of your company. If you are new to the scene or a new business owner, share stories about your past career.

- ✔ **Share your personal opinion.** Your personal opinion on topics can be a brand story builder. Just make sure you don't fall in love with your opinions too much. Remember that the customer is always right.

## Developing content

How do you develop content that caters to the needs of your Twitter followers? How do you tell the customer story and share your information with the masses? It is important to answer these questions and build your story out of your customer's thoughts, needs, and desires.

The content you share will help drive users to your site where the sale will (potentially) be made. Because of this, content is one of the more important aspects of Twitter marketing when you're developing your following and is potentially your lead-generation tool.

Your main source of content is your blog or Web site. It is important to have a central location where your followers can gather and communicate with you or your brand.

A blog can be a great resource to send followers to on a daily basis. You can think of Twitter as a content taste test: You are whetting the appetite of many followers throughout the world with the main goal of acquiring some of your followers as clients or customers.

The following list provides tips you need to consider when you're developing your content strategy for Twitter:

- ✔ **Share information based upon a blog post or newsletter.** You are sharing information on Twitter in order to gain trusted clients and potential customers. Remember to use a URL shortener to share content from your Web site.

- ✔ **Share little details about your daily routine.** Remember not to overstep yourself in this area. However, many people enjoy hearing about a movie, a dinner, or something fun going on in your life. Show some personality in your thoughts and opinions.

- ✔ **Share news about your clients.** Write about your clients, plain and simple. Write and share information, press releases, other blog posts, or e-newsletters from your clients.

- ✔ **Share info about your industry.** It's important to build thought leadership in your industry. Subscribe to industry newsletters, competitors' blogs, and industry content. One way to follow your industry is to keep up with trends on Twitter, which I discuss next.

# Keeping Up with Trends on Twitter

When you get a bunch of people together, they're eventually going to start talking about the same topics. They're talking about politics, current events, sports, or that funny video they saw on YouTube. So, what if you feel passionate about a particular topic? How can you keep track of it and what other people are saying about it? Can you follow all the tweets about this topic?

Sure you can. Just use Twitter trends.

## Understanding Twitter trends

*Twitter trends* are discussion trends on Twitter. These are the topics that people are talking about with some frequency. Everyone's been discussing a Twitter trend, only not necessarily with each other. Twitter actually keeps track of what people are talking about and counts keywords.

Twitter Trending Topics are shown on your Twitter homepage, below the Search box, as you see in Figure 10-1.

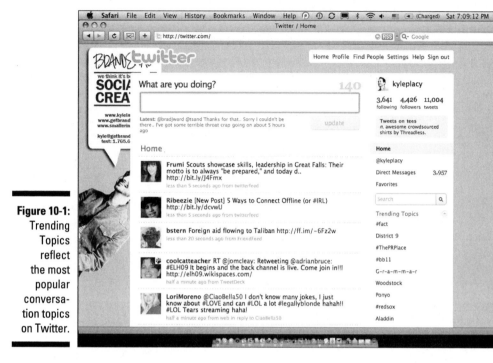

**Figure 10-1:**
Trending
Topics
reflect
the most
popular
conversa-
tion topics
on Twitter.

You can also go to the Twitter search page (http://search.twitter.com) to see the most popular topics of the day. You can go to other Web sites, such as http://hashtags.org, to get not only a numerical count of the topic discussion, but also a graphical representation. You can choose to display trends for right now, today, this week, and this month, as shown in Figure 10-2.

Twitter trends can help you as a marketer because they enable you to identify any problems people might have that you can solve, see what opportunities are coming up, or figure out whether you want to be part of any conversations. A good marketer keeps his or her finger on the pulse of potential customers. Twitter trends are a great way to quickly and easily monitor that pulse.

## Monitoring Twitter trends

You can monitor Twitter trends in a couple of different ways — by keywords and hashtags. Because search engines can index and search all text, that means they can index and search tweets, as well. Services such as Twitter and Google make it possible to search for any keywords you might want, whether you look for a brand or company name, an idea, a song, or even a specific word. Some Web sites monitor Twitter trends and let you see regular updates to not only the latest trends, but also the latest stats surrounding those trends.

Of course, the downside is that you sometimes see words such as *could, might,* and *many* trend just because they're part of normal language usage.

Looking for specific keywords can sometimes be a drag. People may talk about a person, but you could end up looking for several variations of that person's name before you finally find all the conversations you want. For example, say that you want to find tweets about George Washington. Do you search for *George Washington* or *GeorgeWashington?* What about looking for meatless chili recipes? You could look for *meatlesschili, meatless chili,* or even *vegetarian chili* and *vegetarianchili.* Needless to say, variations in wording can make it very difficult to track trends, which is why people use hashtags, as described next.

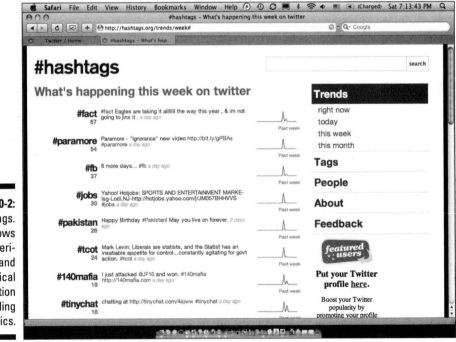

**Figure 10-2:**
Hashtags.
org shows
numeri-
cal and
graphical
information
for trending
topics.

# The Art of the Hashtag

*Hashtags* allow Twitter users to tag their tweets in a way that can help give a bit more context to your tweets or designate them as being part of a particular conversation currently underway. You can use hashtags — also called #hashtags — to build a temporary community, create a buzz, or start a discussion around a particular topic. While you talk about that issue, other people will start to talk about it, too.

## Understanding tags

To understand what a hashtag is, you first need to start with what a regular tag is. A *tag* is a classification system, a keyword or keywords given to a piece of information or an item, such as a file, photo, document, Web site, or blog post. Tags help describe and even summarize all the items in a collection. This collection process allows you to search for and browse only those items that have a particular keyword or keywords in common.

Say that you have to take inventory of your canned goods. You have three cans of green beans, three cans of tomato soup, two cans of red beans, and two cans of corn chowder. Here's how you might tag each can:

- ✔ **By its main ingredient:** Beans, tomatoes, and corn
- ✔ **By the main purpose or use of the food:** Soup and vegetables
- ✔ **By its actual contents:** Tomato soup, green beans, and so on
- ✔ **By the food's possible uses:** Chili, casserole, and so on
- ✔ **By the color of the food:** Red, yellow, and green
- ✔ **By the food's consistency:** Liquid and solid
- ✔ **By how the food grows:** Pod, vine, and stalk

Then, when you want to do a search for all yellow foods, you pull out all the cans that have that tag. You can do the same procedure to find all foods grown on a vine, all foods that are soup, or any other way you want to classify your cans.

Here's a more realistic example (although if you're the kind of person to tag your canned goods, I won't judge you). Say that you go on vacation to Washington, D.C., with your kids, Bobby and Susie. You take a vacation photo of your kids standing in front of the Lincoln Memorial, so you might tag the photo with *vacation, children, Bobby, Susie, Lincoln Memorial, Washington, D.C.* Then, you take another photo of the kids in front of the Starbucks in Georgetown, and you tag it with *vacation, children, Bobby, Susie, Washington, D.C., Starbucks, Georgetown.* Then, when you want to view the photos of your kids, you do a search for any photo tagged with *children, Bobby,* or *Susie.* Every photo you've tagged with those keywords shows up, including the vacation photos, their Little League games, and their birthday parties. Or, if you want to view any photo from any vacation, you search for the *vacation* tag to bring up all the photos that you took on your vacations. And if you want to see any photos from any time you've been to Washington, D.C., you search for *Washington, D.C.*

The tag creator defines these tags, so they don't need to follow any rhyme or reason. You can create a weird tagging system that only you and your closest circle of canned food–tagging friends understand. Of course, no one else can search or view your items, so you want to use tags that are useful to other people — or, at least, easy to figure out.

Thanks to tagging, you can search, group, and browse these photos without having to search through all your photos and pull out the ones you want.

Now, imagine if everyone tagged his or her photos and made them available for sharing. You can search, browse, and see what other people are doing with their photos, which helps you determine whether they're leading more exciting lives than you. (They're not; I checked.)

You can upload your photos to a photo sharing site, such as Flickr (`www.flickr.com`) or Picasa (`http://picasa.google.com`), and search for a particular tag or group of photos. Say you want to find all photos related to Washington, D.C., or see what other people did on their vacation. Just type the terms into the Search box and click the Search button, and the site presents you with all the photos that have those tags. You can see how a tagged photo looks on Flickr, in Figure 10-3: All the tags applied to this photo are listed below the Tags heading on the right.

Bookmarking tagging sites such as delicious (`http://delicious.com`) allow you to save and tag Web sites that you want to share with other people. You can show other users of delicious what sites you think are interesting *and* why. Then, when people are searching for a particular Web site, they can go to delicious and see what other people have deemed important to know about things such as trips to Washington, D.C., or why anyone would ever make chili with corn in it.

**Figure 10-3:**
Flickr is a
photo-
sharing site
that lets you
tag photos.

# Understanding hashtags

The *hashtag* allows you to tag your tweets by designating them with just one character, the pound sign (#). Because space is at a premium in a tweet, you don't want to waste it with extra characters such as **tag:**, by surrounding the tags with brackets, or by writing your tweets in all capital letters. (Writing a tweet in all capital letters doesn't add extra characters, but it is considered shouting.)

So, you tag things by placing # right in front of whatever keywords you're using. You can find Twitter hashtags for cities, states, countries, current events, brands, sports teams, or anything else you can think of. As discussed in Chapter 2, hashtags are a great way to create groupings and generate popularity around a particular keyword or topic.

The # symbol also carries a lot of meaning around it. It's basically a message to other twitterers that you're talking about this topic, and if they want to talk about it with you, they should use this hashtag in all their tweets; otherwise, you may not know they've tweeted about it (if you are not following them). It may be hard to believe you can put all that into one little #, but you can. For example, Figure 10-4 shows a tweet that includes three hashtags.

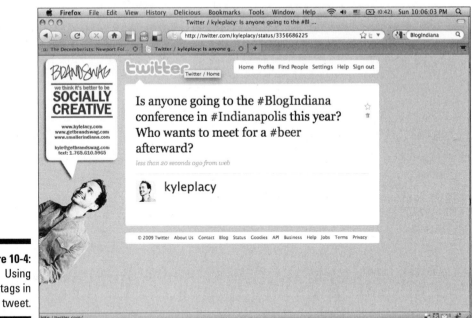

**Figure 10-4:**
Using
hashtags in
a tweet.

In Figure 10-4, the poster tagged `BlogIndiana`, `Indianapolis`, and `beer`. *BlogIndiana* is a blogging conference held in the Hoosier state, *Indianapolis* is a major Midwestern city, and the poster tagged *beer* just because it sounded good in the moment.

## Making the best use of hashtags

You can't really use a hashtag in a wrong way. You can tag anything you want. The question is, will people follow suit?

One of the best ways to use a hashtag is to see what other people are talking about and use their tags, rather than create your own. Otherwise, you run into the problem of having too many hashtags in a single tweet. You don't want to waste characters by having hashtags that are three variations of one idea. For example

```
#BlogIndiana #BlogIN #BlogIndiana2009 #BlogIN2009
```

would take up too much space on a single tweet (49 characters, in fact), so use the most common hashtag and ignore the others. Many event organizers decide on the hashtags that they want twitterers (those attending and those following the event remotely) to use before the event even begins and ask people to use those hashtags in their tweets. Of course, you also want to remind people from time to time to use the correct hashtags.

Make sure your hashtags are one word, even if it's a two- or three-word idea. If you create a hashtag that says #blog Indiana, the word "blog" is the only word that's actually tagged. If you're worried that people can't read the word, then capitalize the first letter of each word: #BlogIndiana, #MichaelJackson, #PortlandOregon. But separate the hashtags if each word could also stand on its own: For example, you can use #Philadelphia #Phillies or #PhiladelphiaPhillies, but #Coca #Cola instead of #CocaCola would probably not be as useful.

You can also create your own hashtag if you can't find an appropriate hashtag created by somebody else. But make sure your hashtag is both as short as possible and as understandable as possible. If you pick #BI09 for BlogIndiana, your followers might be confused. Although you can use BI09 to name a file folder on your own computer, you don't necessarily want to inflict it on other people. People will either completely ignore a hard-to-understand hashtag or complain about it, which creates the kind of traffic you don't want.

One of the least effective ways to use hashtags is to tag common words, such as *car, computer,* or *lunch.* Although you can probably get some people to use those kinds of tags when talking about your topic, you'll have a real problem getting people to follow those tags. Save your hashtag energy to create ones that twitterers most likely will follow.

Don't start a hashtag for your own company or product. If you do, you'll look like you're trying to create a movement yourself. At worst, other twitterers will accuse you of *astroturfing* (creating an artificial grassroots movement). At best, you'll just look desperate and sad.

It's generally expected that hashtags come at the end of a tweet, sort of like the second verb in a German sentence, as shown in Figure 10-5. There's nothing grammatical about them.

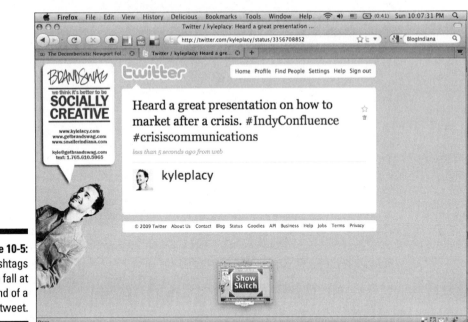

**Figure 10-5:**
Hashtags
often fall at
the end of a
tweet.

Sometimes, you can work a hashtag into a normal tweet and make it sound natural and conversational, as shown in Figure 10-6.

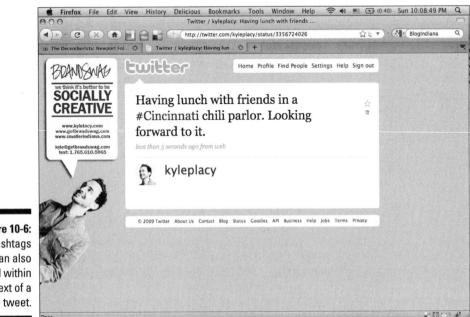

**Figure 10-6:**
Hashtags
can also
fall within
the text of a
tweet.

# Tracking the hashtag

Sometimes, you need to track hashtags — for example, if you want to see whether twitterers are mentioning your company, brand, or event. People talk about you and your company, though probably not as much as celebrity deaths or charges of election tampering. (While I was writing this book, Michael Jackson, Farrah Fawcett, and Ed McMahon died; and Iranians protested the presidential elections, accusing President Ahmadinejad of rigging the election. So, those events were all major topics of discussion on Twitter.)

The following Web sites enable you to track hashtags:

- **#hashtags (http://hashtags.org):** A site that lets you see not only what's trending that day, week, or month, but gives you a graphical representation of the frequency of tweets on the topic, who's using hashtags, and even a count of how many times a hashtag is used. You have to follow @hashtags to have your hashtags tracked. Otherwise, the #hashtags site's application doesn't pick up the hashtags.

- **Happn.in (www.happn.in):** Find the trends that are being widely talked about in your city. Right now, Happn.in tracks fewer than 100 cities around the world, but if yours is one of them, you can see what the top Twitter trends are in your city. This site is great for local marketers and businesses who want to stay on top of what's happening in their city.

- **HashTweeps (www.hashtweeps.com):** Type in the hashtag for which you want to search and click the Search button, and HashTweeps shows you the people who've been talking about that issue. You can use this site to see who's been talking about a particular problem in your industry, and then start following them so that you can join the discussion.

- **Twitterfall (www.twitterfall.com):** A Twitter search site that searches for your hashtags and keywords (it can search for non-hashtagged items, too). It displays the tweets that it finds in a cascading waterfall fashion.

- **monitter (www.monitter.com):** This site looks like an Adobe AIR application, like TweetDeck, but it operates like Twitterfall. You can search for several different keywords and keep them grouped in columns, instead of just running them all in one column. You can even tell monitter to search around a specific city if you're interested in seeing people within a specific area talking about your topic.

- **Twitter Search (http://search.twitter.com):** Twitter's own search function not only lets you search for keywords and hashtags, but it also keeps track of what's trending the most that day.

- **What the Trend?** (**www.whatthetrend.com**): This site follows search trends, as well as gives a brief explanation of why a particular topic is trending that day.

- **Trendistic** (**http://trendistic.com**): This site tracks hashtags, letting you visually select timeframes for which it shows the tweets that contain the hashtag you are searching for, as you can see in Figure 10-7.

- **TweetDeck** (**http://tweetdeck.com**): This desktop application lets you do searches for people or keywords, and create groups of users whom you want to follow.

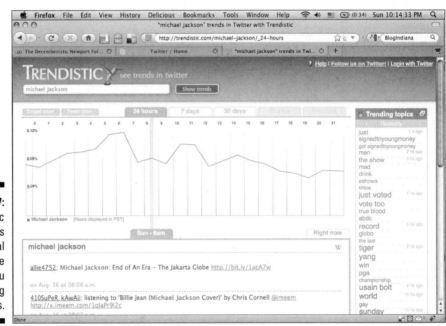

**Figure 10-7:** Trendistic provides a visual interface to let you see hashtag trends.

# Part IV

# Implementing Twitter Strategies for Offline Marketing Domination

The 5th Wave                    By Rich Tennant

Honey — is one of your Twitter friends an elephant herder from India?

## In this part . . .

Marketing experts all agree on one thing: Marketing is all about integration. You need to combine your offline and online marketing communication to put your brand right in your customers' faces. (Okay, maybe that sounds a little extreme, but I stand by the concept.)

How do you incorporate your offline marketing strategies — such as public relations, brochures, events, and everything in between — to push your brand message through Twitter? How do you use Twitter for offline domination? You can get ahead of your competition by using Twitter to effectively defeat them in front of your customers! I don't know about you, but defeating competitors sounds pretty good.

Ready your pencil and take notes. And while you read the chapters in this part, remember three things: integration, integration, integration.

# Chapter 11

# Promoting to Attract Sales Leads

. . . . . . . . . . . . . . . . . . . . . . . . . . . . . . . . . . . . . . .

. . . . . . . . . . . . . . . . . . . . . . . . . . . . . . . . . . . . . . .

*I*f you skipped right to this chapter — and I don't blame you, it's my favorite — you're hopefully already familiar enough with Twitter that you can jump right into this topic. If not, go back and read Chapters 1 and 2, which talk about setting up Twitter and getting started. Go ahead, I'll wait for you.

If you stuck around or you're back, I should tell you a little secret: Attracting sales leads on Twitter isn't easy. In fact, it can be rather difficult. Sure, the technology is easy. Thanks to some wickedly smart people out there, you can use Twitter, automate and track your tweets, and manage different profiles in a snap. But now you're dealing with persuasion and marketing. Here's another secret: People hate being interrupted, and they love conversations.

In this chapter, I discuss why interruption marketing doesn't work on Twitter. I then go on to cover how you can use keyword searches and discussion to market yourself or your company. Included in this discussion is also the topic of promoting your followers and unique content by using tweets.

# Avoiding Interruption Marketing Tactics on Twitter

*Interruption marketing* is the kind of advertising that involves the commercial that interrupts your favorite TV show or your favorite radio station, the tele-marketing call that interrupts your dinner, or the billboard that interrupts your view of the scenery. But people are so used to seeing interruption marketing everywhere, they tune it out, change the channel, or purposely ignore it. So, interruption marketers do it more frequently and in more places, which people tune out even more. And so on and so on.

Enter *permission-based marketing,* in which consumers give marketers permission to get in touch with them. For example, consumers sign up for their favorite restaurant's text club and e-mail newsletter. They become fans of a company or product on Facebook. They follow their favorite corporate brand on Twitter.

Many Twitter marketers use the old interruption-based marketing model, and they can't understand why they aren't reaping the thousands of followers. But these marketers don't seem to realize that people are fickle, they hate being interrupted, and they absolutely hate being tricked.

If you want to succeed on Twitter, be honest and don't bug people. In other words

- ✔ **Don't lie.** If you send out a tweet where you link out to an affiliate make-money-fast Web site, but you make it sound like you want people to see a cool video they can't miss, you will lose the trust of everyone who clicks on that link, and word will spread about your deception.

- ✔ **Don't spam.** Similarly, if you send out nothing but commercial messages, such as the ones shown in Figure 11-1, Twitter users will unfollow, block, and report you as a spammer, and Twitter can shut down your account.

**Figure 11-1:**
Twitter spam gets very old very quickly.

If you get tired of spam tweets from people, or you get followed by someone who sends out content that you don't want to read, visit that person's page on Twitter. Click the Block This Person button (on the right side of each Twitter profile page, above the avatar) to block that person from ever seeing your tweets or following you.

To report spammers to Twitter, follow these steps:

1. **Go to `http://twitter.com/spam` and follow @spam.**

   `@spam` automatically follows you back.

2. **To report a spammer, send @spam a direct message (DM) that includes the name of the spammer.**

   Twitter checks out the reported spammer and removes the account, if necessary. As shown in Figure 11-2, by sending a DM, you can preserve your anonymity and prevent reprisal.

Anyone can send out hundreds of thousands of spam e-mails and get one or two people to sign up, making the spam campaign "worth the effort." But I hope you don't want to do that kind of marketing. Rather, you want to be persuasive and find people who actually want to buy your product and who like your company enough to tell their friends about it.

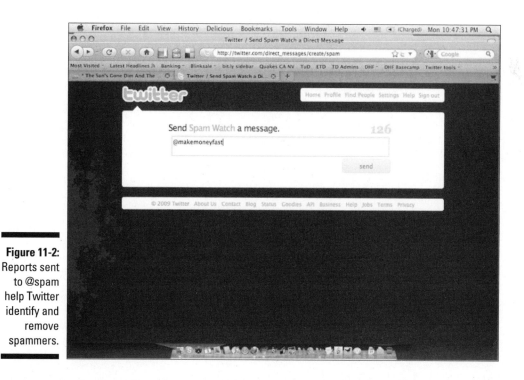

**Figure 11-2:**
Reports sent to @spam help Twitter identify and remove spammers.

## No spam, please

If you're the kind of person who wants to send out spam tweets and use dishonest tricks to get people to come to your Web site, this book isn't for you. Although some people oppose the commercialization of social media, that commercialization is happening. I'm writing this book to show people the right way to market your product or service through Twitter, which can hopefully be done while maintaining the integrity of Twitter, specifically (and social media, in general) before social media becomes as spam-ridden as e-mail.

I intend this book — and this chapter, especially — for people who want to use Twitter as a way to support their other marketing efforts through the noble art of selling, not those who want to use it to bludgeon people with oily, shady get-rich-quick schemes.

I have to warn you, this road isn't going to be easy. You need to have a passion about what you're selling. You need to love it. Because that love and passion, not some gimmick or trick, will capture people's interest in you and what you have to offer.

To get started, you need to lay the groundwork for permission-based marketing and figure out how you want to talk about what you do. A good place to lay the groundwork is with keywords, which you can read about in the following section.

# Making the Most of Twitter Keywords

*Keywords* are the words that people use when they are searching for something on the Web. They're the one, two, or maybe three words that describe the topics prevalent in your industry, which help define your business. Customers find you by using keywords, whether they know it or not — they talk about those keywords, ask questions related to them, or search for them.

## Developing your business keywords

If you work in the windshield wiper market, your keywords might be *clean windshields, thunderstorms,* and of course, *windshield wipers.* If you're in real estate in Portland, Oregon, you'd have the keywords *home sales, mortgage,* and *#Portland, #Oregon.* If you specialize in travel to Liechtenstein, your keywords are *vacation* and *#Liechtenstein.*

The # is a *hashtag* that you put in front of a location or keyword to help people on Twitter find the term in searches, as well as tell other people. For more about hashtags, see Chapter 2.

To develop your keywords, you need to figure out what it is you do. Hopefully, you know what you do already, but you need to figure out how to explain it in a single sentence. For example

- ✔ I sell heavy-duty windshield wipers.
- ✔ I sell homes in Portland, Oregon.
- ✔ I help people plan trips to Liechtenstein.

You've probably heard the term *elevator pitch*, which comes from the idea that you're on an elevator with a potential client, and you have about ten seconds to explain what you and your company do. So, you need a single sentence about your business that can *fully* explain what you do and show the person what he or she gets out of it by buying from you. Here are some example elevator pitches:

- ✔ I can reduce your risk of an accident by 20 percent by keeping your windshield clean with a special windshield wiper.
- ✔ I help new home owners in Portland save 20 percent on their first homes.
- ✔ I can save business travelers 25 percent on their next flight to Liechtenstein.

Now, compare the preceding two bulleted lists and find the differences. First, the elevator pitches include stronger benefits: Reduce accident risk, save money on a home, or save money on a trip. Second, the elevator pitches are very specific. They're not just selling products, selling homes, or planning vacations; they're reducing mortality and saving money.

The benefits don't have to speak to everyone, and you shouldn't try to chase down anyone and everyone. Improving visibility in the rain might not matter to some people, but to people such as truck drivers and traveling salespeople, visibility while driving can be lifesaving. Saving 20 percent on a first home isn't important to anyone who's already a homeowner, but a 20-something who just got married and is looking to buy a home may see these savings as crucial. And for people who don't want to leave the country for vacation, Liechtenstein is just a country they've never heard of. But for fans of the landlocked principality, 25-percent savings can make them take notice.

To develop your elevator pitches — and you may have one or two, depending on whom you meet — run through an imaginary conversation with a new potential client:

> You: Hi, I'm Sue, I plan vacations. What do you do?
>
> Client: Hi, I'm Vincent. I sell windshield wipers to small landlocked countries in Western Europe.
>
> You: Fascinating. What's the biggest problem you face in your travels, Vince?
>
> Client: I never have enough time to plan my sales trips, so I wait until the last minute, which means I end up paying more than I wanted.
>
> You: Well, I run a small travel agency, and *I can save business travelers 25 percent on their next flight to Liechtenstein.*

Notice the use of the elevator pitch in the preceding dialogue? See how that information all fit in the conversation, nice and neat? By developing that elevator pitch, you can zero in on the client's problem and present him with the exact solution he needs.

Figure 11-3 shows what happens if that same message appeared on Twitter.

The Twitter exchange in Figure 11-3 illustrates a couple of important points:

- ✔ @LiechtTravels responded only to @WiperMagic's immediate need. She didn't blast out a lot of tweets, such as Save money on your next flight to Liechtenstein. Visit LiechtensteinTravels.com for a quote. She participated in regular conversations and just happened to find @WiperMagic's message through a search for his keywords. (Yeah, none of that appears in this exchange, but trust me. I have a whole back story written for these two, involving their eventual meeting and elopement to Belgium, and I'm in talks with a movie studio for the rights.)

- ✔ Notice @LiechtTravels asked @WiperMagic to DM her for more information. A DM request helps keep the conversation private and spares their other followers from seeing every word on Twitter.

So, if you haven't done so already, figure out your keywords and work on your elevator speech. Determine what you do and what your customers want, and then figure out how to tell them you can help them get what they want.

# Finding people who are talking about your keywords

After you figure out your keywords, you need to figure out who is talking about them.

### Twitter search

Twitter has two types of searches:

- ✔ **Find People:** You can click the Find People link at the top of the Twitter homepage — or any Twitter page, for that matter. Type in a keyword and see whether anyone is using that word in his or her username.

- ✔ **Twitter's search tool (`http://search.twitter.com`):** Twitter doesn't have a link to this search tool, so you have to type the address in your browser's address bar directly. Use Twitter's search tool to search for keywords and hashtags in people's conversations.

The search bar in the middle of your profile gives you the ability to search for Twitter keywords. This may be an easier path to take if you are using the Web version of Twitter. If you don't see the Twitter Search box, scroll up to the top of your page and click the Home link. It's on the middle-right side after the page loads.

When you find someone who's talking about a keyword you are targeting, right-click the username and open his or her profile in a new tab on your browser. Check out the user's past tweets and see whether he or she is someone worth following. If so, click the Follow button, and you're set. When the user sees you have started following him or her, that person may choose to check out your profile to see if you're worth following back.

### Twitter trends

You can use Twitter trends to see what the most important topics of discussion are on Twitter at that time. The more popular the topic, the higher in the Twitter trends list the word appears, as shown in Figure 11-4.

If you sell a product or service that's popular at the moment — say, software technical support when a new version of Windows or Mac OS comes out — you'd be wise to explore Twitter trends so that you can see who's talking about the issue and what they're saying about it. You can pick up common threads of discussion and start tailoring your tweets and blog posts about the topic.

The most popular topics

**Figure 11-4:**
Twitter
trends
(below the
Search box)
show the
most
popular
topics of
the day.

## Other search tools

I discuss search tools a little more extensively in Chapter 9, but here's a quick list of some of the most useful keyword search tools:

- ✔ Twitterment (www.twitterment.com), TweepSearch (www.tweep search.com), and tweepz (www.tweepz.com) enable you to search user bios for your keywords.

- ✔ Nearby Tweets (www.nearbytweets.com) enables you to both search for twitterers in a chosen location, such as your hometown, as well as specify keywords. You can use this search to find locally based customers, which may be really helpful if your business is local, as in the case of real estate, restaurants, cleaning services, and so on.

Use one or more of these search tools to find people who are talking about your chosen keywords. Follow those people and start a conversation.

# Promoting Your Niche by Using Tweets

Some forms of traditional advertising allow you to target the people most likely to be interested in your product or service. For example:

- ✔ Send a postcard from your landscaping service to people whose homes are of a certain value or located in a specific neighborhood.
- ✔ Send coupons for your restaurant to every home within a five-mile radius.
- ✔ Place an ad in a manufacturer's trade journal touting your latest offering.
- ✔ Send an e-mail newsletter to everyone you've done business with over the last three years.

By using social media — especially Twitter — you can do this kind of targeting much more easily. In the preceding sections, I talk about how to find those people who may be interested in your products or services. Now, you need to write messages that appeal directly to those people.

But you have to overcome a major hurdle — everyone is being hit with thousands of advertising messages online and offline every day, according to experts. And the people you want to reach through Twitter are also being bombarded by people just like you wanting to get their attention. To avoid turning off and losing potential customers, try the techniques described in the following sections.

## Writing about sales and deals

Tweeting about sales and deals is a little tricky. If you have a special offer or deal that you want to present to customers, that's fine. However, as I discuss in Chapter 9, keep your messages at a ratio of about 1 marketing message per 10 or even 15 non-commercial messages. If you send out commercial tweets more often than that, people will think you're just trying to spam them and react accordingly (unfollowing you, blocking you, or reporting you to @spam).

You need to find that special balance and make sure you're actually partici-pating in conversations with people.

### How to tweet about sales and deals

Write about sales, special offers, deals, and coupons very carefully so that you keep a balance and avoid going overboard (thus getting people to unfol-low you or worse, to report you as a spammer). While still sharing details about a special offer every 10 to 15 tweets, you can keep a balance in one of two ways:

- Write a few tweets and write fewer special offers. With this approach, it will take you longer to present your followers with all the offers you may have to share.

- Write a lot of tweets so you can share the number of special offers you have to offer in a shorter period of time.

Needless to say, the second choice in the preceding list is your better option. Write a lot of solid, valuable, useful, personal tweets and every 10 to 15 tweets you can add a marketing tweet: You don't want people to think you're on Twitter only to sell to them. (Even if you actually are on Twitter only for the marketing opportunities, at least try to make it *look* like you're trying to be a real person.)

Also, make sure your messages look natural. Messages like the one shown in Figure 11-5 look too commercial, so people can easily tell you're advertising.

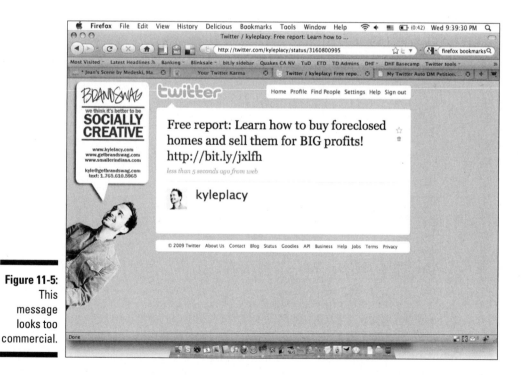

**Figure 11-5:**
This message looks too commercial.

Instead, try to make your messages flow a little more naturally and conversationally, as shown in Figure 11-6.

Admittedly, it's a fine line between being tricky and being, well, market-y. In the section "Avoiding Interruption Marketing Tactics," earlier in this chapter, I said that you shouldn't lie to people. If you're tweeting that you bought and sold a foreclosed home in three weeks, make sure you *actually did it.* Be truthful. If you didn't do something, don't make it sound like you did.

When you are tweeting, even if it has been ten or more tweets since you last shared a marketing message, avoid sounding like you have all the answers on how to make easy money with little or no work or how to cure an incurable disease. Those are sure ways to end up treated like a spammer.

### When to write about sales and deals

Try to write tweets about sales and deals in response to someone else's tweets. I talk about how to find tweets about your keywords in Chapter 9. When you find those tweets, send a personalized response to the user, not a canned one. For example, in response to a tweet by @minipeg1, where he says he is trying to decide which shooter marbles to buy for his upcoming tournament, you could direct the tweet shown in Figure 11-7.

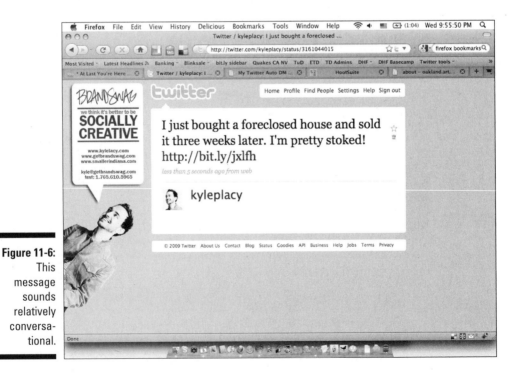

**Figure 11-6:** This message sounds relatively conversational.

**Figure 11-7:**
Make your
Twitter
marketing
responses
personal.

The reply to @minipeg1's original statement included his username and the response was geared directly to him and his tweet. This reply is also personal from the sender: *I* did a review on *my* blog. So, @minipeg1 knows @Brandswag was thinking about him, specifically, and that he might find checking out this blog useful.

As I discuss in the section "Avoiding Interruption Marketing Tactics," earlier in this chapter, this interaction is an example of permission-based marketing. @minipeg1 gave @Brandswag permission to contact him by following him on Twitter. So, @Brandswag responded appropriately by sending him a link to an article that can help him solve his immediate problem, instead of just sending out tweet after tweet about special offers and coupons that may or may not be what he wants (which is interruption marketing).

## Writing about your services proactively

There is no doubt that you must reply to tweets pertaining to problems in connection with your products or services. However, this is a rather reactive approach to using Twitter (though it may help you protect and improve your image among your customers).

*Being proactive* means keeping an eye on upcoming trends and events in your industry, creating content to educate people about what's coming, and writing articles related to what you know, have found out yourself, and can usefully explain. (See the section "Promoting Your Content Through Discussion," later in this chapter, for more information about blogs.)

### How to write proactively

If you know the Midwest Marble Collection Convention is coming up in three months, write a couple of quick blog posts, such as Five Marble-Friendly Hotels and Five Favorite Restaurants for Marble Collectors. Do a recap of last year's tournament and review this year's entrants. Discuss some of the issues people will be talking about at the convention this year. You can link to these entries in some of your tweets as the convention approaches.

Additionally, here are a few ways to be proactive in your specific industry:

- ✔ **Keep an eye on the trade journals and the leaders in your industry.** Find out what they're talking about and discuss those issues on your own blog. Chances are the major voices in your industry are looking at the important issues before they even become issues. Forward the leaders' articles to your followers, in addition to your own articles.

- ✔ **Keep up to date in the allied and related industries.** If you're writing about marble manufacturing, you may see an article in *Glass Blowers Digest* about how glass blowers are having problems getting their hands on raw materials, or *Sand and Aggregate Monthly* might include an article about a severe shortage in this year's sand harvest. You know these issues will trickle down to the marble manufacturing industry. Write about these upcoming trends in your blog and promote them on Twitter.

If you keep your ear to the ground for trends in your industry and related industries and share your insights, you'll become the visionary in your industry. Pretty soon, the industry leaders will be contacting you to invite you to coffee so that they can pick your brain!

Don't do these two big things: wait until it's too late to share a very useful tip (such as reviewing the top five restaurants on the next-to-last day of the conference) or do nothing at all. Nothing kills proaction like procrastination.

### When to write proactively

Figure out when people are getting ready to talk about new or upcoming issues. If you've just heard about an issue, write about it immediately. Maybe you're the first to write about it. If you can offer a preview of an upcoming conference or event, start talking about it at least a month in advance, before people start making travel plans.

Whatever you do, start writing about upcoming events or issues sooner rather than later. You can become the go-to resource for anything related to that issue. And if your followers pass your information on to their followers, hopefully they'll give you the credit, which can help you gather some new followers.

# Promoting Your Content Through Discussion

This section deviates from the Twitter topic a little bit and touches on another area that goes hand-in-hand with Twitter: blogging. Because Twitter is also called *micro-blogging*, it's only appropriate that I discuss them together.

Blogging offers you a great way to allow other people to read your ideas so that you can establish yourself as an expert in that industry. You may find blogging especially useful in B2B (business-to-business) sales because you want to establish yourself as a solution to your customers' problems.

I don't go into the how's or why's of blogging in this book. You can find several good books about blogging (such as *Blogging For Dummies,* 2nd Edition, by Susannah Gardner and Shane Birley [Wiley]) that can help you get started with blogging.

Make blogging a part of your Twitter marketing plan. Use your blog to promote ideas and solutions that you know about. Then use Twitter to promote your blog. Because you've already created a network of people in your industry, now you need the content to pass on to them. Remember, the more they see, the more they'll understand you're the expert in that area. And when they have a problem, they're going to call the expert.

People love lists. Just love 'em. (That's why *For Dummies* books include the Part of Tens, with chapters that give top-ten lists.) When you write your blog posts, try to create numbered lists — your readers will love it.

Don't believe me? Create your blog post, and send out two different tweets, one with the numbers in the headline (such as `5 Marble Friendly Restaurants for #MidMarbCollCon`) and one without (for example, `Review of Marble Friendly Restaurants for #MidMarbCollCon`). Give each tweet its own separate shortened URL so that you can track the resulting number of followers who click the links. You can see an example of a list kind of tweet in Figure 11-8.

**Figure 11-8:**
Lists make
for great
content
people love
to read.

# When and where to promote:
# Promoting the right way

You can find a couple of schools of thought on when and where to promote. One says there's no wrong way to promote, as long as you don't over-promote. The other maintains that you should promote/post only at certain, ideal times. Whichever school you belong to, follow these steps to promote your business:

1. **Create and publish your blog post.**

   Make sure you use your keywords appropriately — in the title, inside some hyperlinks, and throughout the text at a ratio of 1 keyword per 100 to 150 words. You don't need to get overly mathematical: Simply avoid overusing keywords and be natural about the way you write.

2. **Copy the URL of the new post and switch over to TweetDeck (described in Chapter 5), paste your URL in the URL shortening window, and click the Shorten button.**

   Make sure you have a URL shortener selected.

Alternatively, copy the new post's URL and go to your favorite URL shortener's Web site. Shorten your URL and then switch over to TweetDeck and paste the new, shorter URL in the message window.

3. **Type** New post: **followed by the headline of your blog post.**

   Copy and paste the blog post title into TweetDeck. Play a bit more with the post headline to make it descriptive. You want to summarize the article in just a few words and keep the whole tweet to around 110 characters. That will make it easier for others to retweet it.

Tweet about your blog posts at these ideal times:

✔ **Sunday evenings:** It turns out that a lot of people spend Sunday evenings on the couch, laptop on their laps or PDA in their hands, watching TV. They tweet, play on Facebook, and just cruise the Web.

✔ **Weekdays in the morning or after lunchtime:** Another time to tweet is whenever your customers are likely to be in front of the computer. If your customers can use social media during the workday, then post your tweet sometime during the day, either in the morning or right after lunch.

✔ **Weekdays after dinnertime:** If your customers tend to be in the B2C (business-to-consumer) realm, they probably can't use Twitter at work. So, set your blog posts to publish in the late afternoon, but tweet the new post information after dinner time.

✔ **Near the middle of the week:** Closer to the middle of the week more people are using Twitter, so if you want to maximize the exposure of a tweet (or a series of tweets) that you could share on any day, save them for Wednesday.

# The value of thought leadership in B2B sales

B2B sales — any sales, actually — are all about solving problems. B2B sales differ from B2C (business-to-consumer) sales in that consumers often make impulse purchases, even for higher-priced items, whether they solve a problem or not. B2B customers typically don't make impulse buys. So, you have to gear your blog posts to solve problems that may arise for your group of customers (see the section "Writing about your services proactively," earlier in this chapter) for one simple reason: search engines.

People no longer surf the Internet; they search it. Web users surfed 12 to 15 years ago when the Internet offered only thousands of Web sites. You could have a conversation with your friends about "that site with the dancing baby," and everyone knew what you were talking about. Now, thousands of sites are created every hour. Back then, you could click a link that went from one site to another, to another, before finally landing on the page you really wanted. And if you found something interesting along the way, your life was the better for it.

Nowadays, Web users fire up Google, Yahoo! or other search engines to see what they can find. (People mostly use Google. According to a Hitwise.com survey, more than 70 percent of Americans use Google, so optimize your blogs, Web sites, and even tweets for Google.)

Search terms and keywords are getting longer and more complex. You can no longer search for **marbles** without getting 10,100,000 possible pages or **marble manufacturing** without getting 4,970,000 pages (most of which are about the building material). Instead, people are searching by inputting questions such as **how are marbles made?** or **how do I hold and shoot a marble?**

This explosive growth seen in the Web both helps and hinders thought leaders when they want to communicate. On the positive side, you can be specific about very small issues within a very small niche and create a lot of content about that niche. On the negative side, you have to be specific about very small issues within a very small niche and create a lot of content about that niche. However, because many blog posts can run around 300, 200, and (in a few cases) even 100 words, you can easily generate this content.

Then, when a potential customer has a question — such as "How do they play marbles in Taiwan?" — your blog post that explains the rules and general play of the game will show up near the top of the search engine results. If your blog posts appear in enough of these searches, you will eventually become recognized as one of the thought leaders for that niche.

When you have some free time, create a few how-to articles about problems in your industry and post those articles to your blog. Tweet the links when you post them (but try not to flood your followers with ten new posts within minutes). Also, feel free to send the links out again when you answer a question or solve a problem for a follower.

# Chapter 12

# Improving Your Customer Service

**Y**ou can't deny that social media has changed everything. But one particular aspect of the business world that has seen this change in the face is customer service. Customers can now speak more easily with each other and spread the word about good companies, but by the same token, they can also tell each other about bad experiences with great ease. Any company that is unable to adjust to this will not even know what hit it and, one by one, will start losing customers.

Welcome to the world of Customer Service 2.0, where Twitter can be one of your most powerful allies. In this chapter, I discuss how to turn Twitter into a tool to help you improve your customer service.

## Can I Help? Twitter Customer Service from Comcast

If there's such a thing as a customer service celebrity, Frank Eliason is it. He's the Director of Digital Care for Comcast, the huge cable company. (He's @ComcastCares. Go ahead and follow him. He'll follow you back.) Frank's job is to provide customer service to Comcast customers by watching out for them on Twitter.

He reads tweets that contain the words Comcast, #Comcast, and sometimes Comcrap. When they come across his desktop, he responds to each and every one of them, as shown in Figure 12-1.

**Figure 12-1:**
@Comcast
Cares
responds
to every
customer
complaint or
problem.

The response from the customer is usually one of pleasant surprise, followed by a summary of the problem. The customer describes the situation, and Frank gets on the job. He can usually solve the customer's problem — or, at least, refer him or her to the correct department. More often than not, Frank calls the department himself and arranges to get the problem fixed.

Frank has been offering Twitter customer care only since April 2008, but he already has seven people working for him: @ComcastBill, @ComcastBonnie, @ComcastSteve, @ComcastGeorge, @ComcastSherri, @ComcastMelissa, and @ComcastDete. Together, the team monitors all complaints about Comcast and handles problems for the hundreds of thousands of Comcast customers.

The Digital Care reps can walk disgruntled customers through their problems and help them find solutions; get their account numbers and troubleshoot the problems; get phone numbers and call them personally to fix the problems; or, in some cases, alert the correct department and have a technician sent out to their homes. And here's the really cool thing: Regardless of how angry the customer is, the Digital Care for Comcast response is always positive, as shown in Figure 12-2.

Needless to say, a lot of people are talking about Comcast Customer Service. Many magazine articles have been written about Frank and his Digital Care department. Bloggers have waxed rhapsodic about the attention they received.

And social media geeks like me tell clients this little bedtime story to help them dream of a happy day when they can solve their clients' problems in 140 characters or less.

@ComcastCares has gotten so popular that many Comcast customers tweet Frank, instead of calling the customer service number and waiting for several minutes for an operator to help them. Also, some @ComcastCares fans often do some troubleshooting for Frank while he's on vacation.

I talk elsewhere in this book about having raving fans and evangelists for a company or brand, and the following that Frank has built provides a perfect example. Comcast has often had a bad reputation for being a giant corporation that doesn't care about its customers. But efforts such as Frank's have helped turn that reputation around. Many journalists and bloggers say that they notice a huge improvement in Comcast responsiveness and care. And Frank Eliason and his team have played an important role in that turnaround — in 140 characters or less.

You can read more about Frank on the *Business Week* Web site at www.businessweek.com/managing/content/jan2009/ca20090113_373506.htm.

**Figure 12-2:**
@Comcast Cares responds to all customers the same way.

# Empowering Your Customer Service

Comcast's Frank Eliason was successful in his efforts to provide great customer service on Twitter for two simple reasons:

- ✔ His employers let him do it.
- ✔ He stuck with it.

These are the two biggest reasons that any company successfully uses Twitter. Although you need to do many other things to ensure your Twitter customer service success (and different social media pros tell you different things that you need to do), I guarantee that if you don't have the understanding, approval, and backing of your boss, and you don't stick with it, you're guaranteed to fail.

If you're the boss, flip through this book to try to understand the what, how, and why of using Twitter in your business. If you still don't get it, just start repeating, "Because the book told me to, because the book told me to," over and over until you at least understand that you have to do it, whether you get it or not.

The following sections help you determine how to best use Twitter for customer service if you run a customer service department, if you have customer service reps (CSRs) working for you, or if you own a small business. First, I cover what Twitter customer service efforts can do for your business, and then help you determine how you can use Twitter to improve your customer service.

## Discovering why you should use Twitter for customer service

Remember, Twitter is just a tool. It doesn't give you a whole new way of doing business — it just provides a new method of communication. It combines texting, chat, and e-mail. And if your customer service representatives are already proficient at texting, chat, and e-mail, they'll be whizzes at Twitter.

Adding Twitter to your customer service repertoire makes sense for these reasons:

- ✔ **You save money and training time.** Twitter is free. You can use it easily. It takes only an hour (at most) to sign up for a Twitter account, download TweetDeck (it's free from `http://tweetdeck.com`), and give your customer service rep instructions on how to use TweetDeck and Twitter.

✔ **You improve customer service output.** Say you have customer service people who have a lot of time between calls — you can put them on Twitter duty (twuty?) so that they can handle customer problems on Twitter in their downtime. You've improved your customer service output without adding staff.

✔ **Your customer service reps save time.** Think back to the last time you, as the customer, had to make a customer service call. How much of that conversation was spent waiting for the CSR to search for your account information? In a Twitter conversation, you often have a gap between a tweet and its response. The other person may be doing something else or needed to step away from his or her computer. Twitterers expect these gaps. Your CSR could spend that downtime looking up account information, making notes on the customer file, or contacting the appropriate department.

✔ **You save the customer's time.** How many minutes a year do people spend on the phone waiting for "the next available operator"? If you have a major emergency — say, the cable went out, just before the Weird Al Yankovic video marathon — you have to wait on hold. But what if you have a minor problem that you're too busy to deal with at the moment? Do you really want to wait for 20 minutes for a minor problem?

✔ **You improve the customer's mood.** Speaking to a CSR who helps solve the problem can improve a customer's disposition. Lo-o-o-o-o-ng wait times don't. If you can resolve a customer's problem in less time than that individual would have spent waiting to speak to a real person (face-to-face or on the phone), you'll end up with a happier customer.

✔ **You leave a public record of customer service.** The public can see the Twitter stream. People are talking about your company and your brand. One of the stories they're frequently telling is about your customer service or (hopefully not the) complete lack thereof. When people search for your company, you want the good stories to outweigh the bad ones. And a good story could include a Twitter conversation between you and a customer you just helped.

✔ **You improve your reputation.** The people who tweeted about being unhappy with your business usually turn around and tweet that they're happy again after what your customer service people did for them. And if they're popular, that happy little story may get retweeted a few times, spreading that success story beyond just the original customer's followers.

So, how would you use Twitter for customer service? For example, say you own a company called My Eye, a high-performance eyeglasses-frame manufacturer. You sell ergonomic glasses to computer programmers, and you find the following tweet: "Really upset today. @myeyecares glasses just broke, and I have to use my old glasses to see." The conversation shown in Figures 12-3 and 12-4 could easily ensue.

**Figure 12-3:**
An example
of a
customer
service rep
helping a
customer on
Twitter.

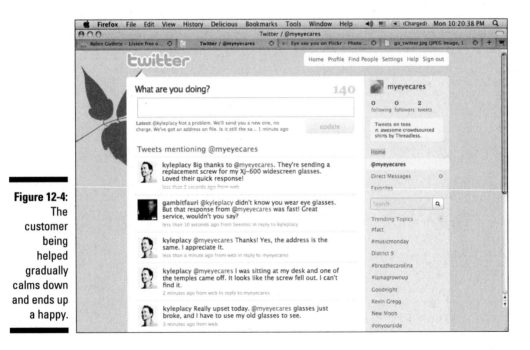

**Figure 12-4:**
The
customer
being
helped
gradually
calms down
and ends up
a happy.

The interaction in Figure 12-4 is an example of a great customer service experience for several reasons:

✔ In a five-minute Twitter conversation, @MyEyeCares was able to solve @KylePLacy's problem. Solving this problem could have easily taken a 10- or 15-minute phone conversation. Also, because @MyEyeCares is able to solve this particular issue faster, the company is able to deal with more customer inquiries in the same time, thus improving customer service output.

✔ @KylePLacy received an immediate response. He didn't have to wait for "the next available representative" for ten minutes, so he was hopefully in a much better mood when he received the tweet from @MyEyeCares than he would have been talking to a CSR over the phone. This immediate response also adds to Like Eye's reputation for providing prompt service.

✔ @MyEyeCares was able to look up the customer's address during the downtime of the conversation. @KylePLacy didn't have to wait on the phone while the rep did an address search, and he didn't have to repeat his address to the rep. The result? A less frustrated customer.

✔ This problem-solving session is a public conversation, so potential customers can find it on search engines and/or see it in their Twitter streams. Anyone following @MyEyeCares can see that the company solved another problem. Anyone following @KylePLacy (as can be seen in Figure 12-4) can see his half of the conversation, wonder what's going on, and then search for the conversation. (TweetDeck and other Web-based apps have a function that lets you follow an entire conversation, even if you aren't following the parties.)

✔ My Eye got a little branding push out of this. @KylePLacy tweeted his happiness to all his followers. And, depending on how many people follow him, that tweet could have just reached anywhere from a couple hundred to a few thousand people. For example, if @KylePLacy has 6,000 followers, My Eye just got a free bit of advertising to 6,000 people, including a link to the business's Web site. And, as every marketer knows, an unsolicited testimonial from a satisfied customer carries a lot more weight and credibility than a paid advertisement.

## Determining who should use Twitter for customer service

Not everyone is cut out for customer service. You probably know a few people who aren't. They just don't have the right temperament for dealing with people who want to give your business money. (Of course, they probably don't work in customer service, in the first place.)

The most obvious place to find a Twitter CSR is in your customer service department. Find out who's friendly and able to multitask, and who has the aptitude to use the technology. You want this person to start using Twitter for customer service.

I discuss corporate reputation management in more depth in Chapter 13, but here are a few tips and rules to remember when choosing CSRs to handle your Twitter customer service:

- ✔ **Train your best, friendliest employees in how to properly use Twitter and social media.** Proper use may include not abusing Twitter and other social media networks by using them for personal posts. Of course, you need to be a little flexible and not go overboard if a CSR makes a personal comment, but at the same time, your CSR shouldn't play Facebook games at work.

- ✔ **Also, train them in how to communicate with the public.** Although CSRs usually don't have a problem with communication, keep in mind that people can easily forget they're in public when they're online. Even if a customer's a jerk, the CSR can't be. You can find many stories repeated in blogs and mainstream media when a CSR flies off the virtual handle at a customer. As rude as a customer might be, company employees must know better because people spread the news of an employee meltdown like a virus.

- ✔ **Have your employees use their own names, instead of just using the company name.** Although Frank Eliason is known as @ComcastCares, employees who work for him use their own names.

   People buy from people they like. And although your CSRs aren't selling anything, if customers can put a friendly face and name to your company, they're likely to continue to buy from you.

- ✔ **Act above board in all things, tell the truth, and be fair to your customers.** Remember, you provide customer service through Twitter for the public to see. If you say you're going to do something, do it. If you fail to deliver on your promises, now everyone knows about both the original problem *and* your failure.

## Responding to public complaints on Twitter

Some people in your company may start feeling a little nervous at this point (usually, they're in the Legal department). You may be thinking, do you really want your company's screw-ups on the Internet for everyone to see? Don't worry: Your screw-ups are already online. (Check out `http://customer-circus.com`, `www.measuredup.com`, and `www.my3cents.com`, for examples.) Every major and minor mistake you make has the potential to show up in a tweet or blog post. The billing department's error leads to angry tweets, the video of a sleeping cable installer appears on YouTube, and someone will devote an entire blog post to his broken eyeglasses.

The question isn't whether people talk about you — because they do, and they have a place to do it. The question is whether you have a way to respond and help resolve the problem just as publicly as the customers can complain.

Don't assume you can keep complaints and problems from going public. You have to assume that every gaffe and error could become a public issue. In many cases, your CSR team needs to become a mini-crisis response team. How they respond determines how far customers' issues travel. (See Chapter 13 for more on using Twitter for crisis management.)

Fix customers' problems quickly and to their satisfaction to make them not only stop complaining, but also maybe even sing the company's praises. I can't count how many times I've seen blog posts about problems with products that the bloggers later updated with the resolutions to the problems, saying they're now very happy with the companies again.

---

# When you shouldn't use Twitter for customer service

Many of your customers' problems are ones that you can't or shouldn't discuss on Twitter, such as issues with a customer's account, billing problems, personnel issues, or any kind of information that anybody (customer or staff member) could find embarrassing or in which you would need to release private, personal information.

Also, avoid using Twitter if it's your only foray into social media. If you have only a Web site that you haven't updated in five years, you don't have a blog, and your Facebook page is one your 14-year-old nephew set up for you so that you can play Mafia Wars, then you don't want to start out with Twitter. First, update your Web site (and put a blog on it), and made it look like you've joined the 21st century.

If you're not monitoring the social media realm for your brand or company name, you shouldn't be on Twitter, either. Otherwise, you miss the important tweets from customers who need your help. You're better off not having a Twitter presence at all than to miss tweets from people who know you're on there. It's equivalent to not picking up your office phone during business hours.

---

Avoid getting into angry debates and discussions on Twitter. Not only does it embarrass you and your company, but it also lives forever on the Internet for anyone to find. If you find yourself getting testy, take several minutes to cool off (remember the time gap between tweets; no one will think anything of it), and then get in touch with the person by phone.

# Practicing the Art of Listening

You may remember grade-school lessons about how to carefully listen to people. CSRs get trained in this skill, too. Listen to the customer: Don't simply think about what you're going to say when he or she stops talking. Focus your attention on your customer, and don't get distracted by other things going on.

You start listening with the first message from a customer. Messages typically come to you on Twitter in two ways:

- The customer knows you're there and sends you a tweet directly in the hopes that you'll see it and answer it.

- The customer's angry and wants everyone to know about it, as well as whose fault it is (even if it wasn't really yours).

Either way, you need to respond with a friendly, "What can I do for you?" or "How can I help you?" Start the conversation off on a positive note, instead of getting defensive and escalating it into a Twitter shouting match before you even identify the problem.

## Understanding why it's important to listen on Twitter

You need to listen to your customers on Twitter because that's where people are talking. Twitter has over 4 million users worldwide, and it's the most popular micro-blogging tool. Although it doesn't have the same reach as Facebook or MySpace, it's still in the mainstream, and millions of people are using it.

So, are you customers using Twitter? Take a look at your ideal customer, the person who spends the most money with your company. Can you identify a pattern among the top spenders for your business? Are they technology users? Are they social-media users?

Do a quick Find People search on Twitter to figure out whether you can find any of those ideal customers. (If you can, be sure to follow them.) If they're on Twitter, chances are more people like them are also twitterers. (See Chapter 11 for information on how to gather those potential customers.)

Then, take it a step further. Export your customer database to a Gmail, Yahoo!, or AOL mail account (create a special account just for this step, if you need to), and then import it into Twitter so that you can see how many of your current customers are using Twitter. (See Chapter 9 for more in-depth instructions on uploading your contact list.) Let your customers know you're on Twitter, too, and proactively ask them whether they need any help or have any questions.

## Using an RSS feed to track your brand

I talk in Chapter 10 about using certain Web sites and desktop applications to follow different Twitter trends, topics, and even your brand. By using applications and sites such as Twitter Search, Twitterfall, TweetTabs, and even TweetDeck, you can easily check the pulse on the conversations happening about you and your brand.

But sometimes the tweets about your brand disappear from the screen because there are only so many tweets that the application you are using can hold, and you can't recover them easily, if at all. For example, the Twitterfall page holds anywhere from 10 to 20 tweets, depending on the size of your browser window, and after those tweets disappear from the screen, they're nearly impossible to recover.

In this kind of situation, an RSS reader can really make a difference. RSS stands for Really Simple Syndication, and you can use this monitoring tool to keep up with different content feeds. Your Twitter stream on TweetDeck or other Twitter apps is a type of RSS feed. Using an RSS reader, you can combine different feeds from different newspapers, blogs, social networks, and even Facebook.

So, you can convert your Twitter searches for tweets about your brand or company to an RSS feed, which you can access from any RSS reader. (See the next section for more on choosing an RSS reader.)

Using RSS feeds gives you a number of different advantages. You can

- ✓ **Be away from your desk.** One of the problems with Twitter is that if you step away from it, you can miss something. You can always create narrow, specific searches that don't get populated very frequently and thus don't get lost on your regular Twitter feed. But sometimes, you still lose search results if you have to reboot your computer. An RSS feed doesn't depend on your computer being on, so you don't have to worry about information getting lost while you (or your computer) are sleeping.

✔ **Share the feed with other people.** If you have other people in your department, send them the URL of the saved feed, and they can import it into their RSS feed reader. You can also easily get to the feed if you often work on more than one computer. Just keep your RSS feeds in one location in an easy-to-access spot, such as Google Reader, so that you can see your feeds anywhere.

✔ **Easily access old tweets.** Even after you read a tweet, the RSS feed still keeps it in place. Just scroll back to the tweet you're looking for to display it.

## *Investigating popular RSS readers*

You can find a number of different RSS readers available, whether you use a Mac, Windows, or Linux computer, or even just want to keep it online. Here's a review of a few of the more popular ones:

✔ **Google Reader (`www.google.com/reader`):** Google already owns everything, so why not own an RSS feed reader? As shown in Figure 12-5, you can add feeds to your iGoogle homepage or add them to the separate reader, which keeps all your feeds in a single location, showing you only the ones that you haven't read. (Don't worry, you can still pull up feed items you've already read.)

✔ **My Yahoo! (`http://my.yahoo.com`):** My Yahoo! is a great news aggregator, which is sort of like a newspaper that you build. As you can see in Figure 12-6, it's compact, without a lot of wasted space, so you can squeeze more feeds onto one screen. You can also create tabs ("pages") for different types of content. Create tabs for Brand mentions, Industry news, Company updates, or whatever you want.

✔ **NewsGator (`www.newsgator.com`):** Pull up RSS feeds on a Mac, Windows, your Web browser, or a mobile device, or even have feeds sent to your e-mail address. You can benefit from this last delivery method if you have a Legal department that requires you to save this kind of information. Drop all the e-mails into their own folder after you read them, and you can keep them as long as you need.

NewsGator allows you to download and use a variety of applications for your computer. FeedDemon, NetNewsWire, NetNewsWire for the iPhone, NewsGator Go!, and NewsGator Inbox are just a few of the services it offers for RSS subscription. These applications are part of the NewsGator RSS Reader Suite, and they are free to any user. NewsGator does offer Enterprise models, which are a paid service. Find out more about the upscale NewsGator services at `www.newsgator.com/business/enterpriseserver/default.aspx`.

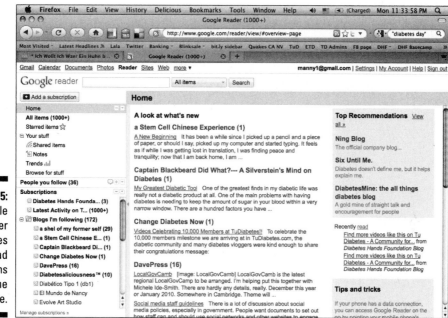

**Figure 12-5:**
Google
Reader
enables
you to read
many items
in one
place.

**Figure 12-6:**
My Yahoo!
aggregates
items of all
types for
you.

✔ **NewsFox (https://addons.mozilla.org/en-US/firefox/addon/ 629):** This is a plug-in for your Firefox Web browser. Firefox actually has several RSS plug-ins, but NewsFox is one of the more popular ones. You can read feeds offline, group your feeds, and subscribe to a new feed with one click.

✔ **Bloglines (www.bloglines.com):** This Web-based reader has an e-mail-like interface. It stores your feeds on its server so that you can access them from any computer.

✔ **Liferea (http://liferea.sourceforge.net):** This is a Linux-based RSS reader, and one of the easier ones to use. Liferea stores your feeds in its own cache, so you can read them offline. However, you can read the feeds from only one computer.

# Using Twitter for Customer Service for a Small Business

If you're wondering how you, as a small-business owner, can use Twitter for customer service, read the preceding sections in this chapter — but when you read *your staff* or *customer service representative,* substitute *you.* (I actually tried just reusing those sections, making the replacements for you, but my editor said no.)

As a small-business owner, you have a big limitation, and that's time. If you're like most entrepreneurs, you're already busy enough trying to prospect for new customers, sell your product or service, keep the books, market the company, and now do all the other stuff I tell you about in this book.

Running your business can be very time consuming, and although I can easily say, "Well, you should make time for *this* because it's really important," you know that everything you do is important, so it's hard to prioritize. Here are a few things that you can do to provide excellent customer service on Twitter — and social media, in general — and possibly even save yourself some time:

✔ **Recruit your loyal customers.** Ask some of your best customers — you know, the ones who refer people to you, who are glad to hear from you, and whom you consider friends — if they'd be willing to lend their expertise. Maybe a customer has a problem that other loyal customers may have experienced before. If you helped one of your loyal customers with this problem in the past, when someone else poses that question, that customer can answer it for you.

✔ **Write blog posts about your customers' most frequently asked questions or most common problems.** If you see some of the same issues over and over, write a detailed blog post that explains what the problem is, how to fix it, and how to prevent it in the future. Then, write a very short tweet about it that includes a URL to the article, and save that tweet in a word processing file in which you store your most commonly used responses. Whenever you get that question, copy and paste that response in a reply, and then send it to the customer.

When you send out commonly used responses that include a shortened URL, be sure to use the link from a URL shortener such as bit.ly (`www.bit.ly`). (See Chapter 6 for more information about URL shorteners.) Keep track of the number of times you send this tweet, and then track how many times twitterers have clicked the link. For a little variety, and if you have the time, use a different URL each time so that you can see what kind of traffic patterns each link gets. You may start to see a pattern in click-through rates that can help you figure out a new social-media or customer service strategy.

✔ **Write blog posts about issues that might become problems.** If you identify an issue that may become a problem later on for your customers, write a blog post that addresses the issue. Don't cover it up and hope it doesn't blow up; otherwise, you'll end up with much bigger problems (and a lot more wasted time). Promote the post to your customers through Twitter, e-mail, and any other communication you normally use with them. Try to head off most of the problems before they become problems.

✔ **Put someone else in charge of customer service.** If you have someone in your business who can also handle this kind of problem, have him or her manage the Twitter side of customer service, while you deal with phone calls and in-person visits. If you don't currently have anyone else who can take some of your customer service workload, consider hiring someone to handle some of your customer service issues. Try to determine whether you could make up for the expense by spending all that reclaimed time in getting more sales.

# Offering Actionable Advice on Twitter

Customer service is more than just a sympathetic ear and vague promises that you'll take care of the problem. When you use Twitter for customer service, you need to remember that your messages are public, so whenever possible, try to give advice that others might also find useful. For example, if you give advice on how to fix a computer problem, don't just put the information in a direct message that only the person who asked the question sees. Send your recommendation out as a general tweet in case other people have the same problem (now or in the future).

Also, don't just offer commiserations and sympathy to your customers, although you should do that. Be sure to actually help them solve their problems. Customers would rather have their problems fixed than find out that you feel bad for them. If you have the space, do both. If not, fix the problem first, offer well-wishes later. Figure 12-7 shows this fix-then-sympathize tweet approach.

Be sure to thank people in your tweets. After you solve their problems, thank them for being customers and thank them for using Twitter. Thanking customers for reaching out to your through Twitter also encourages other people to use Twitter in the future, which is good for you!

## Handling customer issues, concerns, cares, or problems

What are some of the issues your customers are typically going to tweet about? You can answer this question pretty easily by considering what they call and e-mail you about now. Usually, customers have issues because something's broken, they don't know how to work something, they have a question about their bill, or they feel they're not getting the satisfaction they expected from your product, service, or company.

**Figure 12-7:**
Fix the problem and then offer condolences.

You can deal with all these issues pretty easily. If something's broken, tell customers how you're going to fix it or explain how they can fix it. If they can't figure out how to use something, send them a link to a blog post that explains the steps they need to follow. If they have a question about their bills, ask them to send you a direct message (you should follow them when you see they're customers) and get all the important details that way (don't ask them for private information, limit yourself to getting their e-mail or account number). If they aren't satisfied, find out why and help them fix the problem.

# Big businesses that use Twitter for customer service

Blogger Jacob Jegher wrote in March 2009 about several banks that use Twitter for their customer service. Banks aren't well-known for their rapid change, so this move is quite an interesting bit of news. Here are a few of Jegher's examples:

✔ **@Ask_WellsFargo:** Wells Fargo bank shares one Twitter account among several employees and answers questions about products and customer service issues.

✔ **@1stMarinerBank:** A small regional bank in Baltimore, Maryland, has a CSR run the account. The CSR has conversations outside of banking, too, such as inquiring about local tweetups.

✔ **@Wachovia:** Wachovia bank answers customer service questions, provides directions to branches, and tweets news about its mergers and acquisitions.

Other notable companies that use Twitter for their customer service include the following:

✔ **@JetBlue:** Jet Blue tweets updates about flight delays, answers customer questions, and sends airline news.

✔ **@HomeDepot:** Someone from Home Depot's PR department is occasionally joined by a couple of people from the CSR team to answer questions and offer assistance to people who need it.

✔ **@MyStarbucksIdea:** This is a place to discuss ideas generated on @MyStarbucksIdea, gather opinions from followers about ideas submitted, and even refer customer questions and complaints to the right department.

✔ **@PopeyesChicken:** This chicken place posts news, provides directions to stores, and wants to know if you wonder how blue M&Ms would taste in your mashed potatoes.

✔ **@HRBlock:** The company answers customer questions, offers help, and gives out CSR e-mails to customers who need additional help.

What shouldn't you tweet about? Any financial, medical, personal, or legal information can be potentially risky to expose through Twitter, so don't discuss that kind of information publicly. In other words, don't tweet bank balances, test results, credit card information, or the results of your client's parole hearing over Twitter.

## Remembering to say yes

Customer service is more than just a buzzword — it's actually providing assistance to customers so that they stay happy. I can give you a bunch of great advice about how to use Twitter to help serve your customers, how to devise strategies to establish the greatest reach, and how small businesses can use Twitter to drive success. But none of that advice gets you very far if you don't use one simple word: *yes.*

Basically, if you can't or won't fix your customers' problems, you're actually better off staying away from Twitter completely. Remember, angry customers communicate quickly. Twice-angered customers communicate twice as quickly and twice as loudly. (Don't believe me? Take a look at `http://customer circus.com`, which started out when Bob Garfield, host of NPR's *On The Media,* created a Web site called Comcast Must Die, boldly declaring what he thought of the cable giant and what should happen to it. Luckily, Comcast took the complaints to heart and turned its customer service around.)

If you can't provide the customer service that your customers have come to expect thanks to the advent of social media, tuck yourself away and try to make yourself as invisible as possible — because you're going to get hammered pretty soon. Putting yourself out on Twitter just makes you that much more vulnerable to angry rants from customers about how poorly your business has treated them. Not to worry. Pretty soon, your company will shut down, and all the angry people will go away.

Or you could just provide better customer service. Need help? Check out *Customer Service For Dummies,* 3rd Edition, by Karen Leland and Keith Bailey (Wiley).

# Chapter 13

# Relating to the Public

*P*ublic relations is in some ways becoming both easier *and* more difficult. It's more difficult because as more newspapers are consolidating
or closing down completely, and TV and radio stations are shedding their
local stories in favor of the more cheaply produced national ones, people are
turning away from traditional media for their news. And as public relations
becomes more popular and sophisticated, more PR pros are competing for
fewer column inches and air time.

At the same time, the public is starting to get its news and information online —
from blogs, alternative news sites, YouTube, online TV and radio, and online
sites for print newspapers. Thanks to search engines and social media tools
like Twitter, Facebook, and blogs, you can reach the public yourself and skip
the media middle man.

# Managing Your Reputation

Your reputation is one of the most important factors in running a successful
business. It's how your customers and potential customers perceive you. If
you have a reputation for bad customer service, people will avoid you. If you
have a reputation for great value, people will seek you out.

How you act online is just as important. Do you provide useful, helpful information, or are you an Internet troll who flames everyone who slightly disagrees
with you? The helpful people get new business and referrals from clients and
social-networking friends. Everyone avoids and refuses to do business with the
trolls, regardless of the quality of their products or their prices.

I know a couple of Internet trolls on different social networks, and unfortunately, they have damaged their reputations beyond repair. Everyone just rolls their eyes whenever they show up online, and no one will have anything to do with them. The problem for these trolls is that information on the Internet lasts forever, and their rambling speeches, insults, and diatribes show up whenever someone looks for them by using a search engine.

The general rule for personal reputation management is this: Don't say anything online that you wouldn't say in front of your mother or want printed on the front page of _The Wall Street Journal._

## Following some general guidelines

The following list provides a few rules to remember when it comes to managing your corporate reputation:

- ✔ **Train your best, friendliest employees in how to properly use Twitter and other social media.** Some people just seem to have a personality for this kind of work and take to it easily.

- ✔ **Also, train those employees in how to communicate with the public.** Not everyone can — or should — communicate with the public. Train your employees in how to deal with the public so that you don't run into a situation where you have to clean up after them when they mismanage a conflict with a customer.

- ✔ **Have your employees use their own names, instead of posing as the company.** Using their own names keeps them a little more honest and friendlier. They may take more care to be polite if they know that not only their current employer, but also future employers, can see what they do.

- ✔ **Act above-board in all things, tell the truth, and be fair to your customers.** If you don't, people will talk about it, and you'll have to spend too much time trying to repair the damage (if you can pick up the broken pieces — sometimes you can't).

## Monitoring what other folks are saying

It can be a tough thing to let go, but a big lesson you need to take to heart is that you are no longer able (nor is it in your best interest) to control the message about your company in social media at large, and Twitter specifically. This may not sound like too big of a deal if people are praising you or your products and services. But it may be a tough pill to swallow when others are badmouthing you.

This section deals with what to do (and not do) when people are talking about you and your products, whether they are saying good or bad things about them.

### Some evangelists are communicating with others on our behalf. Should we stop them?

Suppose you run across fans who are communicating with others on your behalf. Should you try to stop them? Absolutely not! These people are your evangelists, your raving fans, your — and this is important — paying customers and repeat business. These people are doing a lot of your PR work for you. They're answering questions that new customers may have, they're promoting your brand for you, and they're working as an extension of your PR department.

This may seem like a common-sense question, and a common-sense answer, but I've been asked this many times. You have to resist the urge to control all content that is about you, even if it's in your favor. If people are talking about you, answering questions for you, or posting information on your behalf, you actually want to encourage them to keep doing it. Think about it this way: Not only are you getting some great press and marketing, but you're also getting it for free. Most marketing and PR people would give their weight in gold to get this kind of coverage and fan loyalty, so don't risk damaging it by trying to control it.

### Someone is talking badly about us. Should we stop them?

Say you discover that people aren't just talking about you, they're bashing you. Should you step in and try to stop them? Again, the answer is absolutely not! Leave them alone — you'll only make the problems worse and create a Streisand Effect if you try to hush them up. (The *Streisand Effect* is named for Barbra Streisand, who, citing privacy concerns, sued Pictopia.com for $50 million to have the aerial photo of her house removed from the publicly available photograph collection of 12,000 California coastal homes. Because of the publicity surrounding the case, more than 420,000 people visited the site to view the photo.)

If you try to stop people from talking badly about you, they'll simply spread the word of your silencing efforts. Then they'll have two stories to tell: the original complaint and the story of you trying to cover it up. Instead, look at these complaints as an opportunity to resolve the complainer's problem in a public forum. By solving the problem publicly, you show off your customer-service prowess and willingness to address people's issues with your product or company.

"But people will see the complaint on our Web site and think we do a bad job," is the response I often hear and is the biggest reason many corporations don't enter the social media realm. I'm not naming any names or departments

> **kyleplacy:** *cough* *LEGAL* *cough*

but you need to realize that people are going to talk about you, regardless of whether you have a Web site with a comments section, a Facebook page, or Twitter.

If anything, you *want* these people to make complaints on your Web site. For one thing, they'll expend all their energy venting their frustrations at you and not to the world in general. They'll complain and rant, feel that someone has heard them (make sure you are actually listening, please), and then go on about their business.

"But what about the people who visit the site? The complainers won't come back to say we resolved their problem for them," the *cough* unnamed department says.

 Who says you can't say it yourself? When you respond to a complaint, do it publicly. Be sure to address the complaint in a professional manner, offer a solution, and then follow through. Don't take it private or deal with it via e-mail. The person made a public complaint for everyone else to see, so you need to have a public solution. By solving the problem publicly, you can show off your customer service prowess and willingness to solve people's problems.

Then when other people see that you have addressed the problem, you look like you care about your customers and will do whatever is necessary to keep them happy. (***Note:*** It actually helps if you really *do* care about your customers and want to keep them happy.)

# Using Reputation Management Services on Twitter

Managing your reputation is crucial, whether it's in print or online. Where other people are talking about you is just as important, probably more so, than what they're saying. Some places get more traffic than others, some people have a bigger social media presence than others, and some people have more influence than others. Short of joining every social network out there, and reading everything people say in the hopes of finding something about you, there are much easier ways to find out who's saying what.

You can do a Twitter search (http://search.twitter.com) and a Google blog search (http://blogsearch.google.com) a few times a day, every day, or you can monitor your reputation through a free or paid automated service, as described in the following sections.

# *Free reputation management services*

You can find several free reputation management services online. If you're a small business or an entrepreneur, these services will usually give you what you need. But if you're a larger corporation, or an entrepreneur who has a lot of accounts and brands to monitor, you may want to consider one of the paid ones (which I discuss in the next section).

If you're looking for a free service, check out one of the following reputation management services:

- ✔ **TweetScan (www.tweetscan.com):** This service e-mails you whenever people use your keywords, company name, or brand in their tweets or even their bios. It scans Twitter, identi.ca, Laconi.ca, and several other micro-blogging sites. You can view the results of your search directly on TweetScan (as shown in Figure 13-1) or choose to receive notifications by e-mail or RSS feed.

- ✔ **Twitalyzer (www.twitalyzer.com):** This Web app evaluates your activity and gives you a score in terms of your influence and clout on Twitter, the quality of your tweets, how much you retweet other people's tweets, and even the rate at which you tweet.

**Figure 13-1:**
TweetScan
search
results help
you monitor
comments
about your
products.

A particularly useful feature (found in the professional version) is the Return on Influence, which tells you how many people clicked a particular URL in a tweet. (Note that you need to use the bit.ly [`http://bit.ly`] URL shortener for this feature to work.)

✔ **Google Alerts (`www.google.com/alerts`):** Go to the Google Alerts site; enter your company name, brand, or other industry keywords in the Search Terms text box; and save it as a Comprehensive alert type. You then receive daily notifications of all news articles, Web sites, blogs, videos, and groups that mention your keywords.

✔ **HowSociable (`http://howsociable.com`):** Enter your brand or company name in the text box and click the Measure Visibility button to see how many times (if at all) it appears as a search result on Google; in a blog; or on Flickr, Facebook, or MySpace.

## Paid reputation management services

Although you can find very good free reputation management services, they sometimes can't handle the more in-depth reporting that a corporation or an agency that deals with multiple accounts needs. You can use these services to see who's asking and answering questions about your products, who's complaining, and who's praising you. Then help the complainers, answer the questions, and give a little love to the people who are praising you.

Some of the best reputation management services that you can buy include the following:

✔ **Radian6 (`www.radian6.com`):** A Flash-based social-media monitoring program geared toward ad agencies and businesses that manage multiple brands and clients. Radian6 is a better choice for larger companies and brands because it's a very time-consuming and complicated program that may need one or two people to look after it full time.

✔ **Scout Labs (`www.scoutlabs.com`):** A Web-based social-media monitoring program geared toward small to medium-sized businesses (see Figure 13-2). You can more easily use the program than Radian6, and it automates a few more features, including *sentiment scoring* (measuring good versus bad sentiments).

✔ **Vocus (`www.vocus.com`):** This Web-based PR suite lets you manage and monitor communications with journalists, government officials, and other key audiences like thought leaders and industry big shots. You can manage your communication with these folks and then get reports on the effectiveness of your efforts.

**Figure 13-2:**
Get in-depth
reporting
with Scout
Labs.

# Promoting Live Events on Twitter

You promote live events just like you deal with every other aspect of social-media marketing and public relations. You have a product (an event) that you want people to buy (with their time and possibly the price of a ticket). You need to promote it to get people to come to it, and then to pay attention to it while it's going on.

## Promoting your event

Twitter offers you one more tool in your promotional toolbox. If you already work with newspapers, radio and TV stations, and other media outlets, you're more than ready to tackle Twitter to promote your events.

First, read the section in Chapter 9 about creating your own viral marketing campaign. Some of those same ideas apply to promoting your event on Twitter. When you're promoting an event on Twitter, use the following tactics:

✔ **Create a clear, easy-to-remember slogan.** For example,

> ```
> Roll into the Midwest Marble Collecting Convention,
> July 16–18, 2010.
> ```

✔ **Create a Web site for the event.** Get an easy-to-remember URL, such as

> ```
> www.midwestmarbleconvention.com
> ```

✔ **Put shared items on your site and allow others to do the same.** Share pictures and videos from last year's convention and ask others to post their own pictures and videos from the event. Offer buttons on your site to make it easy for others to share items through e-mail and by embedding them on their blogs.

✔ **Upload your videos to YouTube, Vimeo, and other video-sharing sites.** Create a publication schedule. Instead of uploading all your videos at the same time, trickle them out every week or two so that you can build anticipation. Send out links to the videos through Twitter, your blog, your e-mail newsletter, and anything else you can find.

✔ **Encourage people to follow you, and send out an occasional reminder tweet that you're going to be live tweeting (as described in the next section) and live blogging during the event.** Encourage the attendees to tweet during the event, too. Remind everyone about the use of a pre-selected hashtag, to make it easy to follow all tweets about the event.

## Live tweeting your event

*Live tweeting* is basically just tweeting while you're at an event or game, or even just watching TV and tweeting about what you see, hear, and think.

Be sure to use hashtags so that people who are monitoring those topics can easily find your tweets about the event. Your hashtags also remind other twitterers to use the same keywords when they talk about the event. You can see an example of a hashtag-based conversation about an event in Figure 13-3.

The weird tag #sessj in Figure 13-3 is short for Search Engine Strategies San Jose. Spelling out the entire hashtag — #SearchEngineStrategies SanJose — would take up 29 characters, too much space in a single tweet. So, the organizers of the convention established #sessj as the hashtag to use when tweeting about the convention.

**Figure 13-3:**
Live tweets
related to
the SES
San Jose
Conference.

Establish what hashtags you plan to use before these events. Then communicate those hashtags to the attendees and online attendees so that everyone uses the same tags, thus avoiding any confusion. If the organizers are monitoring #sessj, but a few people are using #sessanjose, the event's Twitter stream will miss the #sessanjose tweets.

## Monitoring live tweets at an event

I talk about different ways to monitor keyword-based discussions in Chapter 9, but here are some techniques that are particularly helpful for monitoring live tweets at events and seminars:

- ✔ **Use a Twitter search site such as Twitterfall (www.twitterfall.com) or Twitter's search feature (http://search.twitter.com), or a desktop app such as TweetDeck.** Set the app to search for chosen keywords and hashtags. Project the screen of tweets onto a centrally located wall at the event so that people can follow along.

✔ **At breakout sessions in a conference, use hashtags to post questions and items for discussion during the presentation.** You can suggest a session-specific hashtag in addition to the conference hashtag, so it's easier to follow the tweets that pertain to the session.

Encourage Twitter usage by giving priority to tweeted questions (just don't ignore the people who don't carry a PDA or have a wireless laptop). You can monitor the event or session hashtags to hear from people who couldn't come to the event and are watching it online.

✔ **Encourage people to tweet about the big ideas they hear about at the convention.** Using hashtags can create discussion among people who have not attended the conference or people who might not otherwise be interested in attending.

✔ **Post photos from the event at TwitPic (`www.twitpic.com`) by using a cell phone, or a digital camera and wireless laptop.** When you send in a photo to TwitPic, it generates its own URL for that photo and sends it to the general Twitter stream.

# Setting the Proper Tone in Your Twitter Communications

When e-mail first came out, people quickly realized that you can't convey emotions and underlying meaning easily. Because you can't hear the tone of the sender's voice in an e-mail, you tend to read your own emotions into the message, rather than try to figure out what the other person meant. Now, imagine trying to do that with a 140-character message.

Sure, you can use emoticons such as ;-) and :) to let the reader know you're making a joke or you're happy. But if you're marketing on Twitter, you should be certain that what you are about to tweet does not lend itself to confusion before using emoticons in it. Conveying the wrong tone in a tweet can ruin your credibility and make you look unprofessional.

## Maintaining a professional tone

If you are using Twitter for marketing, you have to take several things into consideration. I have discussed the importance of balancing your tweets so you don't overwhelm (and lose) your followers as a result of posting too many marketing tweets.

# Keep your cool and avoid the news

Try to avoid angry outbursts on Twitter because they might end up making the news. In early 2009, a major dustup occurred between a (Canadian) *National Post* reporter and a marketing professional after the reporter made an angry phone call because he felt the marketer had snubbed him on a story he was working on. So, she tweeted her frustration, without naming the reporter, and he saw it. The two held a rather public, profanity-laden airing of the grievances on Twitter. Or, at least, the reporter did — the marketer maintained her cool and never rose to the reporter's bait. The exchange made the international news and was discussed *ad nauseum* on many tech and gossip blogs. The reporter was embarrassed enough to delete his tweets from his Twitter page as a result.

Use a professional tone in all your tweets, whether they're messages to all 5,000 of your followers or direct messages to your friends. Keep in mind that twitterers can very easily forward messages on to others — that's the magic of Twitter — and you can find these forwarded messages on search engines.

I have also mentioned that you should attempt to be casual and personal in your tweets, as a way to interact with your potential customers on a one-to-one basis. This includes providing your followers with useful information, even if it doesn't translate into a sale.

However, whether you are tweeting about a discount or sharing useful information about your niche to benefit your followers, always maintain a professional tone. Here are some thoughts to help you be professional while you are personal on Twitter:

- ✔ **Don't do something on Twitter you wouldn't do in person.** If you think about it, Twitter is a very personal medium. This lets you approach potential customers in unique ways. But ask yourself if you would make fun of a funny accent by a customer. Most likely you wouldn't, so don't mock other Twitter users about their typos, broken links, or anything they may find offensive. Simply put, don't do something on Twitter that you wouldn't do in person.

- ✔ **Always read carefully and look for the information in the tweets about your products or company.** Buried below a nasty complaint by an upset customer may be an opportunity to improve your product, your service, and your company's image. Make the most of it, by being attentive and reading carefully, showing empathy and understanding.

- ✔ **Avoid making negative remarks about interactions with customers.** Even if you just had the worst exchange with a customer in history, don't tweet something like "Just got off the phone with the most annoying customer! I hate this job!" If you decide to tweet about your exchange, look for a positive spin: "Just assisted another customer on the phone."

# Keeping it real: Transparency and authenticity

While you spend time in the social-networking realm, you hear the words *transparency* and *authenticity* a lot. Here's what these terms mean within the context of a social network:

- **Transparency:** Being clear and forthright in your communications. Social-media and marketing professional Beth Harte differentiated transparency from being *translucent* (clear professional communication, but no personal information) and *opaque* (one-way conversations, using typical PR and marketing techniques).

  In your tweets, updates, and blog posts, reveal as much information as you feel you need to. Don't hide behind the corporate veil on Twitter. As long as you aren't breaking any laws or rules, or doing anything illegal, people expect transparency. And if you don't deliver it, they'll stop following you, at best. At worst, they'll tell the whole world that you are a fake.

  For example, suppose your company's latest software release has some serious flaws, and people begin tweeting complaints and asking what you're going to do about it. The non-transparent company would send out meaningless messages that say, "Thank you for bringing the problem to our attention. We'll let you know when we've resolved the issue." The transparent company would tweet, "We've heard about the latest bug. Two of our developers are working on it, and they'll have a fix in 24 hours or less."

  One of the masters at transparency is Zappos, an online shoe store recently acquired by Amazon.com. In Figure 13-4, you can see an exchange between a customer who is experiencing an issue with his order and a customer service representative from Zappos writing from @Zappos_Service.

- **Authenticity:** Being truthful and honest. Don't set up fake accounts under fake names. Don't make stuff up. Don't lie. If you have to keep things a secret for corporate security, you're better off saying so than lying about it.

  For example, say that you want to launch a new product and create some buzz about it on Twitter. The inauthentic company would create five Twitter accounts, all with fake names; amass as many followers as possible; and then start pumping out different tweets from each account as a way to trick people into thinking a lot of folks are interested in the product. The authentic company would set up a single account, follow the advice in Chapter 9, and list the company's information in the account's bio.

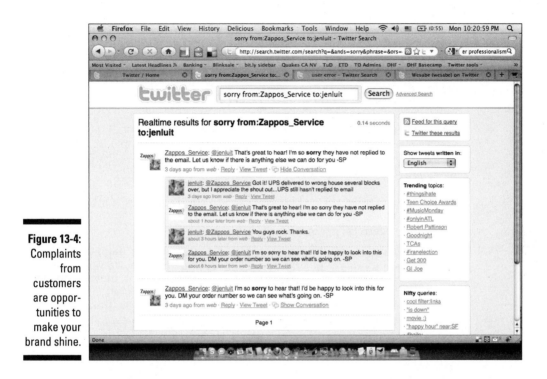

**Figure 13-4:**
Complaints
from
customers
are oppor-
tunities to
make your
brand shine.

# Doing Media Relations with Twitter

Of course, no chapter on public relations is complete without talking about media relations, providing information and story ideas to journalists to help them do their job. And in an effort to keep up with the rest of the world, many journalists are also using Twitter and other social media tools, which means your PR efforts can also reach them. In fact, MediaOnTwitter (www. mediaontwitter.com) has a resource for all journalists who are using Twitter. You can use it to follow certain journalists and send them your story ideas, as shown in Figure 13-5.

Does this mean that journalists have embraced Twitter as their only source of story ideas? That they're sitting in front of their computers, staring eagerly at TweetDeck, hoping someone will send them their next story idea before deadline? No, it doesn't. Journalists are using Twitter like everyone else. They're communicating with friends and colleagues, finding interesting articles to read, and following people who might have something important to say.

These journalists are *not* waiting for you to tell them how they can "get followers fast" or how they can make money in their sleep, or waiting for yet one more pitch on why your poly-resin marbles will revolutionize the world of marble manufacturing. So, if you don't want to get unfollowed, blocked, or reported as spam, don't do any of those things.

## Pitching a story to journalists

You want to treat journalists like customers, and treat them the way I tell you about in Chapter 9. Communicate with them as regular people first. Don't bombard them with commercial messages or press releases. Provide information that is of value so they see you as a resource.

Prior to the Internet, this is how you used to pitch a story to a journalist.

1. **Write a generic press release.**

2. **Send it to every editor and journalist on your PR list and tell the client you sent a release to over 200 media people. Brag about the fact that you got ink and air time in a few different outlets.**

   Try not to think about the fact that 97% of the recipients trashed your release the first time they saw it, because it didn't appeal to them.

3. **Repeat these steps.**

**Figure 13-5:**
Media
OnTwitter
lists all
journalists
using
Twitter.

Here's how you pitch a story to a journalist now:

1. **Research each journalist you would like to see writing about your company, your product, or you.**

   Find out what they write about, read their last few stories, and determine whether your story idea would appeal to them.

2. **Do *not* send them a press release. Instead, write them individual, personalized e-mails that explain why you think the story would be a good fit for them. Tell them if they would like some background information, refer to your Web site and/or offer to send them a press release.**

   For example, "I read your story a couple of months ago about the Milwaukee Marble Championships, and was wondering if you would be interested in doing a story about the Midwest Marble Collecting Convention."

3. **If they ask for more information, send them what they asked for.**

4. **Repeat these steps as needed until you get the coverage you desired.**

5. **Pat yourself on the back for not wasting your time and energy on the other 182 journalists who never would have responded in the first place.**

   Remind yourself that by not bugging journalists with something that doesn't affect them, you're more likely to get a good response from them when you do send them something with this approach.

## *Finding someone to write about your product*

Very few traditional journalists write about products. They just don't do product reviews. However, there are plenty of people who will write about your product: bloggers.

Blogging has become the latest way for people to find news and information, as well as become newsmakers and thought leaders themselves. Rather than beating their heads against old media walls, people have established themselves as leaders and experts in a particular niche or industry, with some great success.

CASE STUDY

---

# Motrin and moms

Do not try and force something on moms of the world. Motrin made the mistake of releasing an online video advertisement that degraded the concept of "babywearing." Babywearing (according to Wikipedia) is the practice of wearing or carrying a baby or child in a sling or other form of carrier. Apparently Motrin made a misstep with the mothers of the world when it shouted out against slings or against slinging in general.

There was a huge backlash on Twitter and other social networking sites about the ad. Moms from every corner of the Earth flooded Twitter with tweets about Motrin and the misstep that had just occurred. The hashtag #motrin-moms shot up to one of the top trends of the week, and the debate continued.

There were only two things missing from the conversation: the PR firm (TAXI) and the company that produces Motrin (Johnson & Johnson). What did we learn from this outburst? Always listen to the masses after launching a campaign. Always.

---

I've talked before about how Twitter — all social media, in fact — is about sharing. Another word for this is *user generated content (UGC),* where the readers and the Web site visitors, not the journalists, create the content. What you may find interesting is that traditional media is becoming less and less trusted by the general public. According to the 2009 The State of the News Media report, no media outlet ranked higher than 30% in "believing all or most" of what that outlet said. You can find the study at

```
www.stateofthemedia.org/2009/narrative_overview_
        publicattitudes.php?cat=3&media=1
```

This means that UGC has become a great source for certain types of information that people find valuable. I'm not saying that bloggers are going to replace mainstream media for important news and current events. But some bloggers are filling a niche with reviews of certain types of products.

A lot of these bloggers are called *Mommy Bloggers* because they are moms who write about family life and occasionally review products for kids and families. These bloggers sometimes have a readership of just a few thousand people in a month, but the manufacturers understand that a positive review from a blogger with a small audience that actually cares about this person's opinion is often more effective and profitable than a review from a newspaper writer with a substantially larger audience.

The manufacturer also understands that a review on a blog will stay online forever, easily found by search engines, which adds to their online presence. A newspaper is recycled or wrapped around old fish by the end of the day, a TV show is forgotten before the credits roll, and a trade journal is usually buried under a whole pile of them, put there by someone who promises to get to them when he or she has the time.

So if you want to get your product reviewed by these bloggers, first go back and read the previous section on how to pitch to journalists. Then wherever you see the word "journalist," replace it with "blogger."

Keep in mind that I think of bloggers as journalists. Maybe not professional journalists, but citizen journalists. There's still some animosity and jealousy that exists between the dead tree and broadcast journalists and the new electronic media, and I'll avoid that whole discussion except to say that good, credible bloggers are quickly becoming an accepted source of news and information as well as mainstream media.

## Using virtual press centers

If you're in media relations, you need to set up your blog to function as your press center. Post all press releases to your blog for a couple of reasons:

- ✔ It helps with search engine placement.
- ✔ It lets you easily refer people to updated information.

Then rather than e-mailing or faxing press releases, you can post them on your blog and send out notifications via Twitter. Use a product like GroupTweet (www.grouptweet.com) and create a group of journalists on Twitter to send a tweet only to them without sending it out to everyone else.

CASE STUDY

---

## The Air Force and rumor control

A witness reported the crash of Air Force C-17 — the president's plane! CNN picked up on the story, splashing the news and images all over the news network. Seventeen minutes later, the Air Force used Twitter to counter that the story was not true. An hour later, CNN retracted the story from the network.

The Air Force used Twitter as a communication medium in order to offer a quick response. A couple of days later, there really was an F22 crash. The Air Force had to balance the need for quickly reporting the incident with the importance of alerting the families of the crash victims.

The key to victory in quick crisis control is issuing statements and *not* being silent. The rumor mill can spread through the likes of Twitter and Facebook. Twitter and social networking can be a wonderful place to spread information but can also be detrimental to crisis control and a brand.

# Using Twitter for crisis communications

Crisis communication is basically regular PR, but people tend to use more expletives during the event. During an emergency, whether it's a public health scare or a product recall, or your CEO just absconded with millions of dollars, this is a time when controlling the message is important, and timing is crucial.

You can't just send out a press release, do a few interviews with the mainstream media, and assume you've done your job. People are talking with each other about what's going on, and these opinions are making it into the general conversation.

Although you can't (and shouldn't) try to stifle the conversation, you can be a big part of it, and you can try to steer it in a positive (or at least less negative) direction.

Here are a few steps you can take during a crisis to monitor and communicate with Twitter:

1. **Set up a laptop running TweetDeck or Twitterfall.com with an LCD projector to show the message windows on the wall for employees responding to the crisis to see. If it's just you, skip the projector.**

2. **Make sure all staff members responding to the crisis have their own Twitter accounts and followers.**

    You should have set this up *way* beforehand. Be sure to follow people in your particular industry or community. If you have staff using private Twitter accounts to communicate internally, make sure you have at least one account that's public.

3. **Establish #hashtags about the incident.**

    Make sure all employees tweeting about the crisis use them. Let the media and concerned parties know about them.

4. **When you find a piece of information that's wrong, correct it and refer people to the source for correct information.**

5. **Post media updates to your blog, and send out tweets when they're up.**

6. **Answer questions on Twitter and refer people to your blog for additional information.**

# Chapter 14

# Building Thought Leadership on Twitter

## In This Chapter

▶ Discovering why you should be a thought leader

▶ Writing an effective Twitter bio

▶ Becoming a thought leader in your industry

*B*eing a *thought leader* means you're recognized by others as having innovative ideas. People are interested in what you have to say. They follow your tweets, read your blog posts, and buy your books. You get invited to speak at industry events — and often get paid to do it.

Being a thought leader doesn't mean you're going to be famous. You might be *vertically famous:* You're the dominant name in your industry, the rock star of your niche, the one name that everyone whispers in hushed tones whenever you're at a conference. But you're just another regular person whenever you go to the store, and your spouse's friends just smile politely and say "that's nice" whenever you try to explain what you do.

In the social-media world, you call these Web celebrities *cewebrities.* (This term comes across better in writing — when you say "cewebrities" out loud, it sounds like baby talk.) Each industry has cewebrities and thought leaders. Take any industry (it could be the poultry production business, political polling, or carbide-tipped saw-blade manufacturing), and you can find people who have earned the respect and envy of their colleagues.

You too can become a cewebrity! It all starts on Twitter and with your blog.

Don't limit your thought leadership to just Twitter and building a blog. While you grow your leadership efforts, be sure to write and develop whitepapers, ebooks, Webinars, special reports, and maybe even podcasts.

# The Big Deal about Thought Leadership

So, why should you become a thought leader? Does it help with your career? Do you make more money as a thought leader? Take a look at your own industry. Who are the thought leaders? Take a look at Twitter. Who are the thought leaders on Twitter? Who writes the articles in the trade journals or blogs about the issues week after week? Who's the keynote speaker at your trade conference?

If you aren't sure, ask people who have been in the industry for a while. Ask them whom you should be paying attention to, and subscribe to those thought leaders' newsletters, read their blogs, and attend their speaking events. The more important thing you could do is check to see if they are using Twitter. It's a great way to keep track of the content that the individual thought leaders are sharing. And then do what those thought leaders do.

If one of the thought leaders writes an article about a new marble manufacturing technique, write an article about it, too. Be sure to give proper credit and even link to the blog that gave you the idea to write your article, but make sure you offer your opinion about the technique and maybe even the author (politely and diplomatically, of course).

Or say you sell high-end audio-video components, and Bravia comes out with a brand-new 70-inch 1080p flat-panel LCD HDTV. You want to review it on your blog, and then push the post out to your Twitter followers.

When people do online searches for the latest marble manufacturing technique or flat-panel TV, your blog may come up as one of the top search results. If not, you can use Twitter to promote your content and bring people in. When more people come in, more people will recognize you as an expert in that field. When more people accept your expertise, even more people will come to your blog and add you on Twitter because of your expertise, and so on.

When more and more people accept your expertise in an area, you become a thought leader for that industry. In turn, you will see a massive increase in Twitter followers and their usage of your content.

## Being a thought leader can help your career

Ask yourself this question: Assuming you can afford anyone, if you have to make a hiring decision between someone who's relatively unknown in an industry versus someone who's widely regarded as a leader in the industry, whom are you going to pick?

A smart employer will always pick the person who's obviously well-versed in the issues the company is facing. Such people know more about the industry, continually educate and improve themselves, and in general, make themselves more valuable to the organization. (Of course, not every employer is that smart, so if you miss out on a job opportunity despite what I tell you, you didn't want to work for that company anyway. Trust me.)

Depending on what your goal is, here are some ways you can make yourself a thought leader:

- ✔ **You're looking for a job with a certain company:** Do your research to find out what issues the company is facing, as well as whether those issues are company-specific or industry-related. Blog and tweet about them from a "how would I solve this" or "things to avoid" point of view. Then, while you go through the hiring process, point the hiring managers to your blog as an example of the kind of work you do; your blog can show the managers that you know your stuff. Then when you go to work for the company, continue to write about these problems online, and grow your blog and Twitter following. Not only will you help your employer by giving the company more exposure and enhancing its reputation, but your competitors will soon start paying attention to you, too. And competitors tend to pay their rivals' desirable employees a lot in order to get those employees to jump over to their company. (I'm just sayin'. . . .)

Before you start blogging in your new job, make sure to familiarize yourself with any policies your new employer may have about staff blogging. You don't want to join the ranks of employees who have become job casualties because they broke the rules.

- ✔ **You're working as an entrepreneur:** Follow the same model discussed in the preceding bullet, but use it to show clients that you know what you're doing. Review journal articles and news articles about your industry (and your client's industry). Write case studies about clients you've already helped. If you find you're answering the same questions via e-mail over and over, turn the answers into blog posts.

- ✔ **You're trying to build a public-speaking career:** Don't limit your blog to just the written word. Also post videos on your blog (also called *vlogs*), excerpts of speeches you've given, or a video presentation of your regular blog post. (But if you are recording a video of you speaking, just make sure you're putting out your best work. If you *uh* and *um* your way through your vlog, potential clients may think that's what they'll get when you're onstage, so they'll pass on you for this year's keynote speech.)

LinkedIn (www.linkedin.com) is an important tool that you can use to help develop your thought leadership. On LinkedIn, you can connect with people in your company, your industry (through their Groups feature), or from your professional past.

Answer questions in the LinkedIn Answers section and participate in discussions in the Groups you belong to: In both places, feel free to refer people to your blog and articles (just don't be spammy). LinkedIn provides a great way to reach people in your industry and help you continue to build your credibility.

## *Being a thought leader can help increase your sales*

The best salespeople don't sell products; they solve problems. A client has a problem (the need to develop a marketing strategy for Twitter, for example), and he or she is going to buy from whoever solves that problem (that would be you, once you are done reading this book).

But you obviously can't call your customers on a daily basis to find out their latest pains. In some cases, they may not even know. But when they figure it out, they probably won't call you to see whether you have a solution. Instead, customers will head over to Google and start looking for a way to solve their problems. So, what will they find? Some trade journal or newspaper articles? An out-of-date Web site? Your competitor's blog?

If you're doing your job well, your blog will appear near the top of their search results. This obviously means you are applying a fair share of Search Engine Optimization. Given how broad this topic is, I recommend you learn about it by reading *Search Engine Optimization For Dummies* by Peter Kent (Wiley).

Having your blog appear at the top of the results in a search engine also depends on your writing. When you're writing about a specialized topic, you have a good chance of landing a top spot in what's called a long-tail search. In terms of searches and search results, a long-tail search is the kind of search that not too many people make: Those people are determined to find an answer to a very specific question, and those are the folks you want finding you. If you rank at the top of enough long-tail searches, you start to see some real traffic to your blog.

Now, here's the kicker: Your solutions and your posts shouldn't mention your brand or company at all.

"But," you may wonder, "how are the customers supposed to know that my product can help them?" Customers will figure out that they should use your product because you're going to come across as someone who knows what you're talking about (which is the case, of course!). You write about a problem that they have and show that you know how to solve it. You create the solution and explain how it works. In turn, you will share the finding on Twitter, which will drive more traffic to your Web site and build your Twitter brand.

For example, say you sell high-volume digital printing. Your biggest competitor isn't another digital printer — it's the traditional ink-and-paper printers. Your post on printing postcards doesn't have to offer every solution. You can write about how digital printing can solve the need for high-volume printing in a convenient and affordable way. You just don't want to include statements such as "our digital printer" or "we sell digital printing." Your customers are smart enough to figure out for themselves that you sell digital printing, especially after they read your Twitter bio (which I discuss in the following section).

# The Importance of Your Twitter Bio

Thought leadership starts with one of the first things new followers find out about you: your Twitter bio. (See, I made that sentence all dramatic with the colon, but you probably already knew what the section was about because it has that really big heading right above it.)

You can use your bio to explain yourself in 160 characters, which is 20 more characters than Twitter allows in regular tweets. Your bio gives you the chance to tell the world who you are, what you do, what you like, and how you roll.

## Writing the right bio

The right kind of bio conveys one or two basic ideas so people who see it understand what you do. Don't make the mistake of trying to cram as much stuff into the bio as you can. Just give a basic idea about who you are and what you do. Or, if you're creating an account for your business, talk about what your company is and what it does.

Here are a few examples of good bios. The first group of examples say what the person does, which is useful in the case of consultants and other people who offer their services; it helps Twitter users who read the bio to easily figure out how/if the person can help solve their problems.

> A socially creative Indianapolis resident.
>
> Humor writer, copywriter, professional blogger, and social media guy.
>
> Passionate about small business marketing, networking, and social media.
>
> I run an Indian art advisory based in Delhi. I would qualify as an amateur bike restorer, natural-born traveler, and professional socks collector.

The next group of bios are also good examples, showing what the company does. As in the case with personal Twitter accounts, providing this information helps those who read the bio to better understand how the company can assist them with their needs.

> Remember everything using Windows, Mac, Web, iPhone, BlackBerry, Palm Pre, Windows Mobile, and more . . .
>
> Year-round, professional Equity dinner theater with Broadway musicals, plays, children's shows, and concerts.
>
> Start, Grow, and Track your Campaigns — Web marketing software for everyone, made by ### Co.
>
> ### Tape is the original elastic therapeutic tape used by professional athletes and medical practitioners. Supports and offers instant pain relief.

The last example even lists a benefit to the user in instant pain relief. But they all say what the people or businesses do, what drives them, and on a personal level, what interests them.

If you choose to include benefits to potential customers in your Twitter bio, don't confuse a feature with a benefit. A *feature* is what something does, a *benefit* is what the customer gets from it.

For example, a feature would be: "Our windshield wiper is made from heavy-duty polymers that outlast all other wipers in the industry." This is fairly irrelevant to most customers. How does it help them? That is where the benefit comes in: "Our wiper lasts three times as long as other wipers, which means you save $30 per year in wiper purchases."

Short is better than long. Just because you have 160 characters to write your bio doesn't mean you need to use all of them. If you can do it in 100, leave it at that. You guessed it: The first bio I listed ("a socially creative Indianapolis resident") is mine, as you can see in Figure 14-1.

Twitter bio

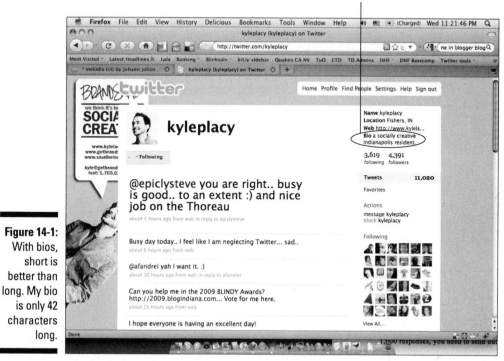

**Figure 14-1:**
With bios,
short is
better than
long. My bio
is only 42
characters
long.

# Avoiding the wrong bio

The wrong Twitter bio is actually a missing one. At the very least, people will
think you don't want anyone to know that much about you. At worst, they'll
think you're a spammer who couldn't be bothered to make a bio for a throwaway account that'll be gone in five days. And somewhere in the middle,
other Twitter users will think you're just someone who tried Twitter for a few
days before giving up.

If you're worried about anonymity, consider the following thoughts before you
worry unnecessarily:

✔ **You're already on the Internet.** You don't have any online anonymity.
   Don't believe me? Google your name, city, and state to see what results
   you get. In some cases, you may even get your phone number and
   address. If you're on Facebook or other social networks, depending on
   your privacy preferences in each of them, your information may or may
   not be visible among the search results.

- ✔ **You don't have to include personal details about yourself.** You're only as visible as you want to be. If you want some privacy, list your state but not your hometown. If you want to localize your presence so that potential customers know you are based close to them (not a bad idea, if you ask me), include your city or town, in addition to the state.

- ✔ **You can always protect your updates.** However, I don't recommend protecting your updates for marketing purposes. You can't build a following if you hide your updates from people. You'll find protecting updates useful only if you keep your small circle of friends closed to the rest of the outside world.

You create a not-very-good bio if you try to cram in as much information as you can so that you can tell everyone who you are. A too-wordy bio might say

```
Father,husband,son,Internet marketer,public speaker,
business writer,soccer fan,lover of goth death poetry,
collector of funny hats,fan of Minor League Baseball
```

This isn't a horrible bio because it does let your new followers know what you do. But the list is cluttered — it crams in as many words as it can by leaving out some spaces, doesn't lend itself to readability, and tries to be all things to all people.

Remember, you're a marketer. If you want people to know about your company or product, talk about it. If you have a personal account, talk about that side of you — specifically, your marketing efforts.

Finally, don't list yourself as something anyone else can lay claim to. For example, a lot of people call themselves Twitter experts or social-media experts after only having a few hundred hours of practice using Twitter or simply having an account on Facebook.

A big mistake in writing a bio involves using it for spam. A spam bio makes all these great and fantastic claims about the product or service, and about how you can *make money fast.* The following are examples of bios that will label you as a spammer, and people won't follow you:

```
Hi cutie I spend my time exercise reading my email but
mostly playing with whipped cream more on my bio link

Make Money Social Media Consultant,Twitter Make Money
Guru, SEO consultant, TwitterFastCash.com President,
Real Estate Specialist, Equity Investor, Entrepreneur

http://www.####.com/hop/#####Code Click Here For The
Best Videos How To Make Money Online!
```

```
GET YOUR FREE BEAR MARKETING SYSTEM THIS HAS 6STREAMS OF
INCOME ALL BEING PROMOTED WITH A SNGLE WEB ADDRESS GO TO
MY WEB URL ABOVE AND GET YOUR FREE SYSTEM 2DAY

Greetings friends. When I have a large enuf following I
will reveal many new ways to make money online for Free!
Visit my Blog for details :)
```

The one thing these bios (except for the first one) have in common is money making. They're blatant sales pitches that read like the worst spam you can find in your e-mail Inbox, such as ways to buy little blue pills, Internet stocks, and cheap counterfeit watches. Twitterers usually block people who have these kinds of bios and report them to @spam.

# Becoming a B2B Thought Leader

In short, being a B2B thought leader is about providing value. Provide valuable content, ideas, and solutions to your Twitter followers, your customers, and your colleagues.

Pretty easy, huh?

Not so fast. Becoming a B2B thought leader requires time and effort. You have to provide valuable content on a regular basis. You have to speak at industry events whenever possible. You have to write blog posts and articles. And then you have to promote it all on Twitter. But you'll probably find the whole process pretty easy, after you get the hang of it.

## Sharing your content

Sharing content is the name of the game in developing thought leadership. Believe it or not, the goal is to give away your information and your ideas. Why? Because people will think that if you're giving away *this* much, you must have so much more brewing beneath the surface (just make sure that you actually do). As a result, people are more likely to hire you or buy from you because they want some of your magic mojo — or, at least, the solution to their problems.

You can share your content in two ways: by hand or automatically.

I discuss how to share your content by hand in more detail in Chapter 11. For now, just follow these basic steps to manually share your content, such as a blog post:

1. **Create and publish your content.**

2. **Copy the content's URL and switch to TweetDeck (described in Chapter 5). Paste your URL in the Shorten URL text box, as shown in Figure 14-2, and click the Shorten button.**

   Alternatively, copy the post's URL and go to your favorite URL-shortener Web site. Shorten your URL, and then switch over to your favorite Twitter app and paste the shortened URL in the message window.

3. **Create a new tweet and type** New post: **followed by the headline of your content.**

   Copy and paste the headline if you have to. Make sure the whole tweet is around 110 characters so that people can retweet it.

Using tweets to share your blog posts or other content isn't actually hard, but it can get tedious, especially if you have ten other things pulling you in different directions when you're supposed to be promoting yourself. In that case, you may want to use the automated method.

Paste your URL here

**Figure 14-2:**
With TweetDeck, you can conveniently share your content.

I recommend using automated tweets only if you're simply automating what you'd do by hand if you had more time or patience. I don't recommend automating tweets for spamming or sending out junk over and over.

To send automated tweets to share your blog posts or other content, follow these steps:

1. **Create an RSS feed.**

   All blogging platforms natively offer RSS feeds as a way for you to syndicate the content you post on your blog. You can also set up an RSS feed with FeedBurner (www.feedburner.com) for free.

2. **Set up an account with Twitterfeed at http://twitterfeed.com.**

   You can either register your e-mail and a password, or use OpenID if you already have an account.

   *OpenID* consists of a login name and password that you've created elsewhere, but that you can use in nearly 50,000 different sites. You may find OpenID especially useful because you don't have to remember a lot of different passwords. You can get an OpenID at http://openid.net.

3. **Authenticate yourself with Twitter.**

   You can authenticate yourself through the use of your Twitter username and password, or you can use the OAuth process, as shown in Figure 14-3.

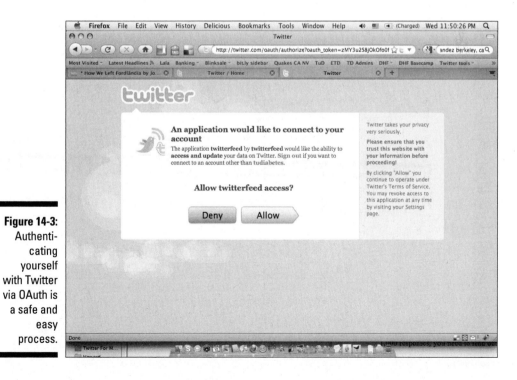

**Figure 14-3:**
Authenticating yourself with Twitter via OAuth is a safe and easy process.

OAuth works by sending you to Twitter from another Web site (Twitterfeed in this case). You authenticate yourself in Twitter if you aren't signed in at the time and allow (or deny) access to the application so it can connect to your Twitter account. Although Twitterfeed is a trustworthy service, the advantage of using OAuth is that you don't have to share your password with Twitterfeed.

Allowing Twitterfeed to connect to your Twitter account will make it possible for it to automatically post on your Twitter account, pulling content from your blog through your blog's RSS feed.

Other Web apps still ask for your Twitter password. Most of them are honest and don't do anything nasty to your Twitter account, but a couple (none that I have recommended) have been known to hack a person's account for nefarious purposes.

4. **Adjust your Twitterfeed settings.**

   Twitterfeed offers a number of options to let you tweak your automated posts, as shown in Figure 14-4:

   - *Update Frequency:* How often you want to have Twitterfeed pull content from your blog's RSS feed and how many new updates you want it to pull each time.

   - *Post Content:* Whether you want to include the title and the first few characters of each post (title and description), the title only, or the description only.

   - *Post Link:* Lets you choose among a large list of URL shorteners.

   - *Post Sorting:* Lets you choose the order in which posts get sorted, with pubdate being the best option (based on publication date).

   - *Post Prefix:* Allows you to add a prefix such as **New post:** in front of all posts added to Twitter. You don't need a post suffix, but you can add one if you want.

   - *Post Suffix:* The same idea as the post prefix, but at the end of all posts added to Twitter.

   - *Post Filter:* Lets you add keywords to be used in order to auto-approve new posts.

5. **Click the Save Feed button.**

Now, you just have to focus on creating your content. Twitterfeed helps with the rest.

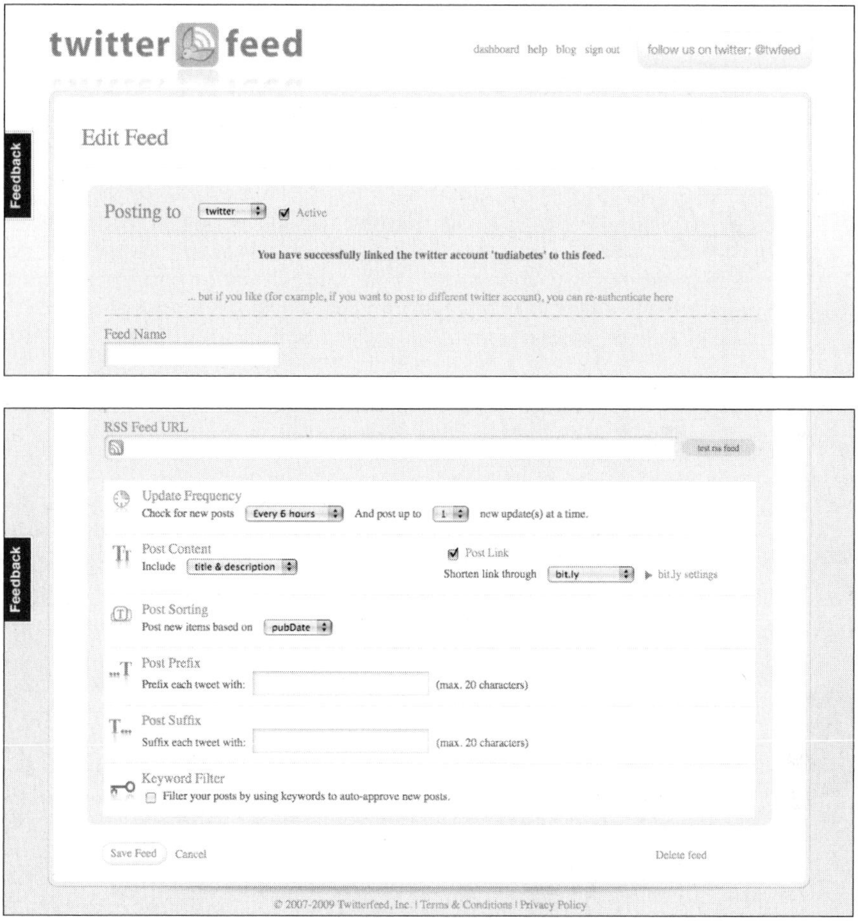

**Figure 14-4:**
Twitterfeed
lets you
adjust the
settings for
each feed.

## Sharing others' valuable content

I talk about retweeting in Chapters 2 through 4 — it's just a way to forward someone else's message to your own followers. You just click the Retweet button on a person's avatar in your favorite Twitter application. (*Note:* Twitter.com doesn't have a retweet button, so you may want to use a different application if you're a heavy-duty user.)

The rules for retweeting are the same as the rules for providing thought leadership: Provide value. Retweet articles and posts that are related to your industry, but don't retweet silly or personal stuff. If someone you follow mentions that he's going to dinner with his mom, you don't need to retweet that message. But if that person writes a blog post about the five ways your industry can improve financially, retweet it.

When you retweet, not only do other thought leaders reach a new audience, but they also see that you think enough of them to retweet their work. Do it often enough, and they may do the same thing for you, too. If another thought leader is popular enough, you can reach a much bigger audience than you've been able to find so far.

## Collaboration is key

You can develop and improve your own thought leadership by working with other thought leaders. Ask them to write guest posts for your blog and ask whether you can do the same for them. Cite and link to each other's posts and articles. Draw inspiration from their work, and write helpful commentary (or polite-but-thorough counterarguments) about their posts.

If these thought leaders are more established than you, and you start appearing in their posts or as a guest writer on their blogs, some of their credibility transfers over to you. Their followers will assume that if the thought leaders like you, they should like you, too. You can gain new readers and followers who are also interested in what you have to say, simply because the original thought leaders believe you're someone they can work with.

# Part V
# The Part of Tens

"I think you're just jealous that I found a community of people on Twitter that worship the yam as I do, and you haven't."

# In this part . . .

Here are ten reasons why you can't skip the Part of Tens chapters:

1. You're already used to 140 characters. Why stop there?

2. The opinions of millions of Twitter users helped develop this part.

3. You can easily tear out these chapters and hang the pages on your wall.

4. You must know what you can't do on Twitter (which Chapter 16 explains).

5. Bill Gates did it. You should, too.

6. Chapter 17 gives you a list of the top ten professionals you should follow on Twitter.

7. Chapter 18 gives you a list of the top applications to use while driving, changing the radio station, and talking on your earpiece.

8. Did I mention the top ten professionals and thought leaders on Twitter?

9. The best things come in groups of ten. Well, except maybe for donuts.

10. Ten is an awesome number. If you put the "one" sideways, it looks like someone is winking at you.

# Chapter 15

# Top Ten Do's on Twitter

*T*his chapter lists the top ten best practices to use when you're marketing yourself and your product(s) on Twitter.

## Do Be Honest

You're honest in your life, in general, right? Honesty is king when it comes to using Twitter for marketing purposes. This concept can relate more to the public-relations side of business, but never lie when it comes to sharing content on Twitter.

People come to respect you for being honest when you use Twitter. When they respect you, they can help drive traffic to your Web site by sharing your content, and that simple step is an important key to success on Twitter.

## Do Have a Sense of Humor

Humor goes a long way when sharing content on Twitter. If your followers find a certain comment funny, they may retweet and share that content with their followers. The entire idea of using Twitter for marketing is to get the people who already follow you to share your content with the people who follow them. That's viral marketing at its finest.

If you're having trouble being funny in 140 characters or less, find a couple of quotes from comedians, such as Jerry Seinfeld or Jim Gaffigan, and tweet them out to the masses. These quote tweets can help you share valued content and promote your funny side. You don't need to be funny to use a funny person's content. Also, make sure you add the name of the comedian or person being quoted.

You may be wondering why (as a serious business owner/marketer) you are sharing comedic content to the masses. Quote tweets that have to do with humor tend to be retweeted more often. It's important to keep trying different strategies to grow your follower base. This is just one way to keep your followers more enthralled with your content.

# Do Interact with Your Followers

Start interacting with your followers before you ever try to ask them to share your content. I talk about the concept of asking how you can help others before they help you in Chapter 8. The same concept applies when you are interacting with your followers, your tribe. Interaction means you have genuine conversations with individuals.

# Do Use TwitPic

TwitPic is a service that allows you to share pictures from your mobile devices directly to Twitter. You can find more information about the service at www. twitpic.com. Using TwitPic while you promote through Twitter can help you live up to the idea of transparency and show some type of personality through your business.

If you want to build brand awareness and create a brand identity through Twitter, you need to connect with people on levels they don't expect. Share a picture of your kids (or maybe your pets if you aren't comfortable showing your children in such a public forum), and you may have a potential client connect with you because he or she wants to ask about your children or has the same breed of dog. You can use these pictures as another touch point in the world of social-media marketing and Twitter.

Keep in mind that too much of something is never a good thing. Make the pictures you post memorable. Don't, for example, take a picture of a random dog in the street and say, "Oh, he's cute!" You're just going to annoy people. For example, you may want to start by posting a few pictures of yourself and your family from your recent vacation and move on from there.

# Do Tweet on a Regular Basis

A long-standing rule says you should try to tweet at least five times a day. You could tweet in the morning, during lunch, and in the evening. This number doesn't include the @replies or direct messages that you should send based on who connects with you throughout the day.

If you don't tweet on a regular basis, you're going to sink into obscurity in the Twitter world, and people will forget you. Stay visible so that people take notice and start communicating with you.

# Do Use a Profile Picture

Use your personal picture in your Twitter profile. This picture shows the face behind the brand. Use your logo as your Twitter icon only if you have a business account as well (for example, @Brandswag).

People want to know faces, not logos, because it makes you seem a little more human on a technology-driven tool. If you don't have a decent picture that you can use as a profile picture, consider having a professional (or, at least, a good amateur) photographer take your photo.

If you want to use a personal profile as a business account, a nice way to show that is to place your business logo beside your face for your profile picture.

# Do Fun Stuff Every Day

Content on the Internet can get boring or repetitive after awhile. The same concept applies to movies and TV — you can watch documentaries for only so long before you want to see a good comedy or action thriller. I give plenty of advice about sharing relevant and great content throughout the book, but remember that it's also important to share fun stuff occasionally.

# Do Stick to a Schedule

In Chapter 5, I talk about the importance of time management when using Twitter. That little piece of advice is monumental when you use Twitter as a marketing strategy. In order to be successful in marketing on Twitter, you need to avoid becoming overwhelmed. The only way to prevent being over-whelmed is to ration and manage the time you spend on Twitter.

Keep to your schedule and don't stray from it. Your Twitter success depends on it!

# Do Say Thank You

Using common courtesy, such as saying please and thank you, is a pretty simple concept, but you might be surprised how often people don't use it in the online world. If someone from your Twitterati decides to share your content, make sure that you thank him or her for sharing. People share content on Twitter for two reasons — they want cewebrities or Twitterati to notice them, or they really liked your content. Whichever reason applies, thank them for sharing your content.

# Do Add Your Twitter Name to Your Business Card

One of the more successful strategies to integrating Twitter into your daily life involves adding your Twitter name to your business card. Not everyone knows what your Twitter name is when it appears on your business card, but many do. And you need to connect with people on multiple levels because the more times you connect with individuals, the better chance of them remembering you and what you do. (Gone are the days where you could meet a person once and he or she would remember you for a lifetime. Well, did those days truly ever exist?)

When people connect with you on Twitter because they saw your username on a business card, that connection is ten times more valuable than just randomly connecting through Twitter itself because you now have more than one way to communicate with those individuals.

# Chapter 16

# Top Ten Don'ts on Twitter

This chapter lists the top ten pitfalls, mistakes, and practices to avoid when you're using Twitter to market yourself and your product(s). Take note! This is some of the most important content in the book!

## Don't Auto-DM

I discuss the pros and cons of auto-DMs in Chapter 7, but it's important enough to mention the concept again. *Never* hard sell an individual on your product or services through automatic direct messaging.

No user in his or her right mind likes to receive an automatic and un-human message selling your product or service. You can send a simple auto-DM of "thank you for following," but I recommend you send all DMs personally, not automatically.

## Don't Say It on Twitter When It's Better Said in Person

It's extremely important to avoid having simple or private conversations through the main Twitter feed. For example, if you want to ask a friend if he would like to attend a party, that question is best asked through DM (direct messaging). A conversation between two people should be made through the Twitter feed only if it adds value to the rest of the group. (If knowing that a person is attending a party with someone else provides value to you, you probably should find a hobby.)

Figure 16-1 shows an example of an exchange of a simple conversation between two people that's not giving any substance to the group.

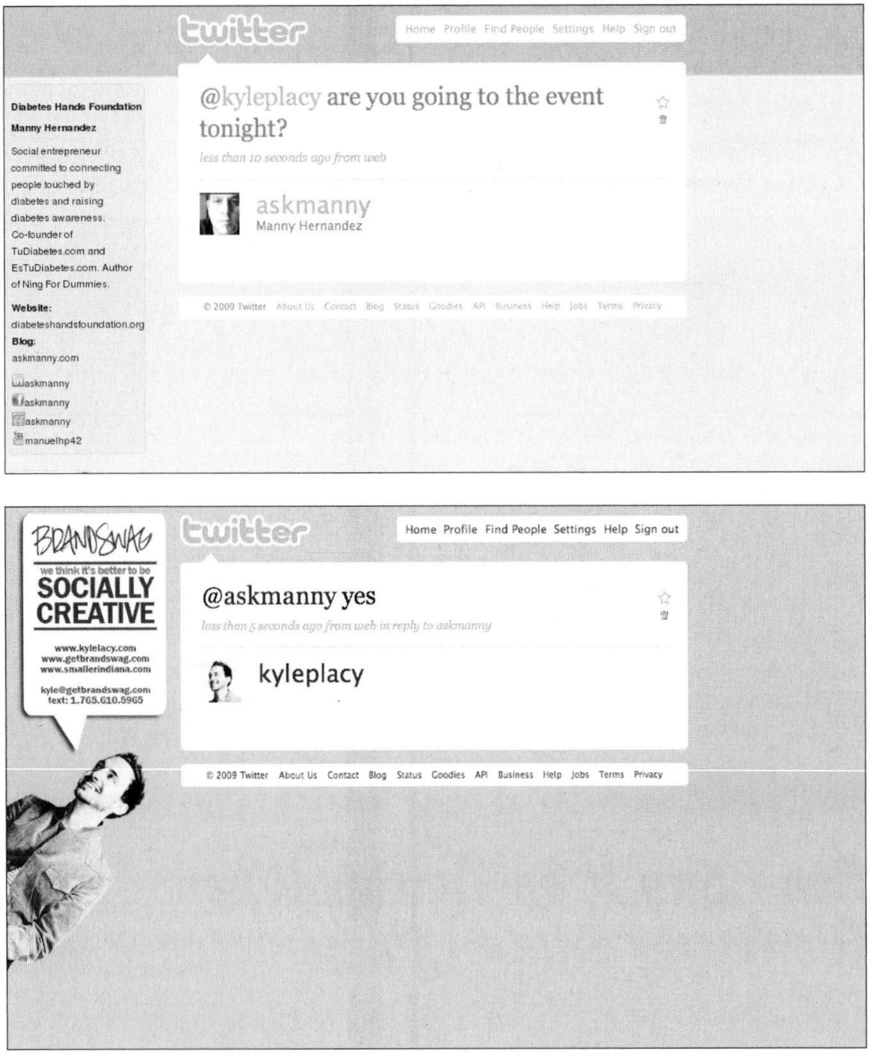

**Figure 16-1:** These twitterers should have exchanged their messages in a DM, in person, over the phone, or by text message.

You can best discuss something as simple as asking whether someone is going to an event through text messaging, e-mail, direct messaging on Twitter, or a phone call. No one wants his or her Twitter feed taken over by your one-on-one conversations.

# Don't Gather Too Many Followers Too Fast

If you browse through the people following you on Twitter (your Twitter tribe), you may find individuals who are following a huge amount of people compared to the number of people following them. These people simply follow as many twitterers as possible without gaining their acceptance and getting them to follow back. Start slowly — create a core group of people you're following who return the favor by following you.

You can broadcast a message to as many people as possible, but shouting your message out to a group of people isn't the point of Twitter. You're trying to create relationships with individuals who have a trusting group of followers and can help spread a message.

# Don't Forget Your Marketing Strategy

Never, ever forget the strategy that you've been developing. Following your strategy can lead to the success of your Twitter marketing campaign.

You can stray from your strategy every now and again, but remember to come back to your original plan. Your strategy is the lifeblood of your Twitter marketing.

# Don't Follow for the Sake of Following

Establish a clear strategy when it comes to following individuals who follow you. Many people add everyone who follows them. You can use this approach if you want to keep up on everyone who's following you on Twitter.

Or you may want to add the people who converse with you on a daily basis to the list of people you follow. If they respond to tweets or retweet some of your content, make sure you're following them before their next tweets. This is important because they may want to thank you through direct message or start an important conversation. If you aren't following the users back, they can't direct message you.

# Don't Use the Web Platform

Don't use the Twitter Web site after you sign up and set up your account. Although casual users don't have a problem using the Web site, you need more robust features to succeed with your marketing strategy on Twitter.

Rather than working through `www.twitter.com`, use a Twitter app, such as TweetDeck, the Seesmic desktop application, or HootSuite, because they all have features that are better suited to using Twitter productively. See Chapter 5 for more about using Twitter apps.

# Don't Create Too Many Accounts

Don't create a Twitter account for absolutely every function, event, or marketing campaign you're doing for your business. Create one personal account and one business account. You may need to create an account for a product (for example, the developer of QuickBooks, Intuit, created `@QuickBooks` for business customer service), but don't try to create an account for every single marketing strategy and campaign.

If you overdose on accounts, you can become overwhelmed and not be able to compete in the marketing and consumer world of Twitter.

# Don't Give a Hard Sell

*Hard selling* is the ability to sell your product or service without asking anything about the individual with whom you're communicating. You should do no hard selling on Twitter. By using Twitter, you can create content-rich relationships with people, and then slowly start sending them content connected to your product or service.

If you tweet or direct message only about your products, you're doomed to fail. Nobody wants to hear a hard sell about your products. People want to know how you can benefit them, not how they can buy, buy, buy from you.

# Don't Ignore Others

Do you enjoy walking up to someone and speaking, only to be ignored by that individual? Of course not. Nobody likes being ignored. Extend that idea to Twitter: When someone responds to you on Twitter, make sure that you return the favor.

When people communicate with you by replying, retweeting, or sending out a message, thank them or reply to them in kind. If you communicate, instead of ignoring people, they're much more likely to reply, retweet, and send out your content.

# Don't Have an Uneven Following/ Follower Ratio

Keep track of how many people you're following and how many people are following you back on Twitter. If you're following a large number of people compared to the number of people following you back, it suggests that you're just trying to gain a huge amount of followers, rather than actually communicating.

For example, if you're following 64,000 people and have only 4,500 following you back, it gives the impression that you aren't genuine in your use of Twitter because you're constantly trying to add followers and not creating great content. Try to keep the following-to-follower ratio nearly even.

# Chapter 17

# Top Ten Thought Leaders on Twitter

In This Chapter

▶ Talking to the Internet-marketing experts

▶ Finding out about the latest social-media research and tools

▶ Getting advice on how to run a business

*T*housands of people can provide value to you as an individual and provide support to your business on Twitter. However, a few individuals tend to stand out among the rest when it comes to interaction, the content that they share, and number of followers. You can help your Twitter marketing plan by following the thought leaders I feature in this chapter and seeing how they successfully use Twitter's viral marketing power.

The individuals listed in this chapter are thought leaders in specific industries on the Web. They can help you take the dive into the online marketing environment! The information that they share is driven toward people who use Twitter and want to be successful. Plenty of people who use Twitter might offer you more value compared to other users, so you simply have to find those individuals. To search for the thought leaders of Twitter, see Chapter 8.

## Jay Baer

Twitter username: @jaybaer

Web site: www.convinceandconvert.com

Jay Baer may not have as many followers as some of the other individuals in this chapter, but he has exceptional content when it comes to Internet marketing and public relations. If you want to find out about brand crisis management and brand identity, you need to follow Jay.

The best thing about Jay is that he's responsive and helps people out when it comes to using the tools of the Internet. Be sure to track him down and start a Twitter conversation with him. You won't regret it.

# Chris Brogan

Twitter username: @chrisbrogan

Web site: www.chrisbrogan.com

You might want to follow Chris Brogan for plenty of reasons other than the sheer number of followers he has, and his following ratio. Chris shares great content and isn't afraid to talk about the personal side of life in his tweets.

He also can discuss concepts and ideas pertaining to marketing on the Internet in a way that makes you feel like you're having a one-on-one conversation with him.

He shares extremely valuable content in relation to marketing through social media and offers his personal thoughts on the online world of business.

# Jason Falls

Twitter username: @jasonfalls

Web site: www.socialmediaexplorer.com

Jason Falls is the founder and CEO of Social Media Explorer, an online communications and social media marketing firm. Jason is an excellent speaker and creates content that individuals who may not be well versed in the Internet marketing world can easily understand.

You can find in-depth content on Jason's Web site — and you can't find better online content about corporate-level social-media use.

# Loïc Le Meur

Twitter username: @loic

Web site: www.loiclemeur.com

Loïc Le Muir has been instrumental in creating desktop applications and other useful tools for Twitter and the Internet. He's the brains behind the Seesmic desktop application, as well as the Seesmic video-sharing and content-development Web site.

Loïc provides value on Twitter because of his ability to stay ahead of the curve when it comes to the development of online technology. As a user, you need to make sure you stay up-to-date with the latest social media tools.

# Jeremiah Owyang

Twitter username: @jowyang

Web site: www.web-strategist.com/blog

Aside from the fact he works for Forrester Research and is one of the main providers of social-media research and information, I recommend following Jeremiah Owyang because he shares great content. You can't find a better dissector of great content (both his own and others) than Jeremiah.

If you want to stay up-to-date on the facts of the Web — and social media, specifically — you won't be let down by Jeremiah's content.

# Katie Paine

Twitter username: @kdpaine

Web site: www.measuresofsuccess.com

Katie Paine is the queen of measurement and valuing return-on-investment in the world of social media when you are using online tools, such as Twitter. She's a kind of revolutionary in the world of public relations and online marketing. So, her content is bleeding edge and business-altering (in a positive way).

She has been called the Queen of Measurement. She lives up to that name every day by creating great content on Twitter and her blog, which has to do with ROI in social media.

# Brian Solis

Twitter username: @briansolis

Web site: www.briansolis.com

The social media world has been whispering that Brian Solis is one of the most enlightened individuals on the scene because of his ability to create tools and sites that change the way people use social media both for time and business management. He's the principal of a company called FutureWorks and has written books about Internet marketing. And Brian is an accomplished tech-leaders photographer. He shares images of parties and events, and you can find the majority of them on Flickr.

# Scott Stratten

Twitter username: @unmarketing

Web site: www.un-marketing.com/blog

I can give you one *huge* reason to follow Scott Stratten on Twitter — engagement. The amount of updates that Scott creates shows his level of engagement with the individuals following him.

If you can find a more beloved Twitter user than Scott, please let everyone know. He helps individuals by sharing content that allows them to make the best use of Twitter and other social-media sites.

# Gary Vaynerchuk

Twitter username: @garyvee

Web site: www.garyvaynerchuk.com

Gary Vaynerchuk is the founder of Wine Library TV, a world-renowned Internet-marketing genius, and a brilliant speaker. If that isn't enough to convince you to follow him, he talks to almost everyone who responds to him. If you had to chat with as many followers as he has, you might feel a little overwhelmed. But Gary Vaynerchuk takes it in stride.

Be sure to check out his Web site, and if you need inspiration (or maybe a kick in the pants), watch one of his videos.

# Carrie Wilkerson

Twitter username: @barefoot_exec

Web site: www.blogbarefoot.com

You can't find an individual better at encouraging and empowering people to succeed than Carrie Wilkerson, the Barefoot Executive. She may be the happiest and most content Twitter user, and she shares great content, as well!

You can gain in-depth knowledge of how to run a business successfully and have a purpose behind running the company. Carrie openly shares a ton of information that is extremely important in the world of marketing and communications.

# Chapter 18

# Top Ten Tools to Use for Twitter Productivity

*W*hile you slowly work through the ins and outs of using Twitter to drive business and increase your brand awareness, how do you manage all the followers, replies, groups, friends, and direct messages? You can find hundreds of productivity tools available to help you out. I mention some of the tools described in this chapter elsewhere in this book, but others are new. Dive into the top ten tools to use for Twitter productivity and do some business!

## bit.ly

```
http://bit.ly
```

In the world of tiny URLs that allow you to track clicks and conversations, bit.ly reigns supreme. The Web site and sidebar application are easy to use, but they both pack quite the punch when managing conversations over a specific platform.

So, why should you use bit.ly? You need to give yourself the capability to shorten long URLs from blog posts or Web sites that have great content you want to tweet to your followers. bit.ly gives you the capability to shorten, share, and track the URL.

You can very easily view your links in realtime and track information sharing while it happens, which I have to admit, is really awesome!

# HootSuite

```
http://hootsuite.com
```

TweetDeck (which I talk about in the section "TweetDeck," later in this chapter) gives you the capability to organize and manage followers, and HootSuite is just as powerful when it comes to the world of Twitter productivity. HootSuite gives you the capability to manage multiple Twitter accounts, add multiple editors of the same account, pre-schedule your tweets, and measure traffic. If you're looking for a tool to help you stay productive throughout your day and not be held hostage by the time-suck police, HootSuite is where you should turn.

HootSuite enables you to view clicks and where each click originated based on region of the world. It also enables you to view your more popular tweets, as well as how many clicks you've received over a given time period.

By far the most valuable option in HootSuite is the capability to *pre-post* tweets (meaning write tweets in advance) to publish throughout the day. You may find the pre-post feature valuable when it comes to managing your time period.

# Nearby Tweets

```
www.nearbytweets.com
```

Nearby Tweets is a tool for those twitterers who want to connect to individuals in their general location. Nearby Tweets is a Web site that allows you to search for people on Twitter based on geography. You can use the search results to build customer relationships and monitor what customers are saying in realtime.

Nearby Tweets is still fairly new at the time of this writing, but it plans to roll out some helpful tools in the future, such as premium business tools, that allow you to find nearby businesses on Twitter, and a page where you can set your default location.

# SocialToo

```
www.socialtoo.com
```

SocialToo is an overall management tool for your relationships on social-networking sites such as Twitter, Facebook, and MySpace. The Web site and profile service give you the tools to auto-follow, auto-unfollow, and auto-direct-message those who follow you, and you can also get daily stats surrounding new follows and unfollows (much like Qwitter, which is described in Chapter 8). Overall, the tool can really be beneficial when it comes to measuring stats and time productivity. It also enables you to share surveys in order to find out more about the people following you.

Oh, and Jesse Stay created SocialToo. (Jesse is, by far, one of the coolest users on Twitter.)

# TweetDeck

```
http://tweetdeck.com
```

You can't find a better tool out there for managing and organizing your Twitterati than TweetDeck. You can use TweetDeck directly from your desktop, and it manages followers, friends, replies, direct messages, groups, and any other Twitter feature you could possibly imagine. TweetDeck gives you the capability to create groups that can cater to any type of subject. For example, if you want to pull a feed from Twitter that has to do with Barney and children's stories, you can do just that by using TweetDeck.

You can also download TweetDeck on your iPhone and use it when you're away from your desktop. You can easily use and manage this program. Built off the Adobe AIR platform, it's your direct link to everything for your Twitter profile.

# twhirl

www.twhirl.org

twhirl is social-networking desktop software designed by the people who brought you Seesmic. The twhirl application is built in the same realm as Twitterific, TweetDeck, and HootSuite (all discussed elsewhere in this chapter). You can run twhirl on both Windows and Mac platforms. If you're familiar with sites such as FriendFeed and Seesmic, you may want to use twhirl because of how each site operates. twhirl gives you the capability to connect to multiple Twitter, laconi.ca, FriendFeed, and Seesmic accounts.

You can let twhirl run in the background while you work, and it gives you random pop-up windows that display new messages. twhirl has a couple of other cool features worth mentioning for this productivity chapter, such as enabling you to post messages to multiple profiles on other social networking sites, such as Facebook and MySpace. You can also record a video by using a Web cam and recording directly on twhirl, and then share the video on the video side of Seesmic, http://video.seesmic.com.

# Twilert

www.twilert.com

Twilert is the tool for the paranoid person in all of us. Twilert gives you the capability to receive regular e-mail updates about tweets that contain the name of your brand, product, or service, or any keyword you could possibly want to find. You can set up the service extremely easily, and you can use it to stay on top of the conversations surrounding your specific keyword.

You can also use the service at http://search.twitter.com to search for keywords being used on Twitter, but Twilert gives you a more consistent feed from the world of Twitter. You can experience keywords being updated on a live basis.

# Twitter Grader

www.twittergrader.com

HubSpot (www.hubspot.com), the people who brought you Website Grader (www.websitegrader.com), realized that Twitter users needed to track and rank users based on certain criteria on Twitter. Twitter Grader was the answer to that need. The site allows you to track and measure your (and others') relative Twitter power. The calculation is based on a combination of different factors, including your number of followers, the power of your followers, and the number of updates, clicks, and retweets.

The Web site offers you a completely egotistical look at the world of Twitter, but it can give you some valuable tips in the areas of top tweets, content you should share, followers you should add, and how you can use Twitter more productively.

# TwitterFriends

```
www.twitter-friends.com
```

TwitterFriends enables you to track and dissect the important network behind your Twitter profile: your followers. The Web site calls this network the *relevant net.* By searching stats on your username through TwitterFriends, you get the top ten people who communicate with you the most. Who's your biggest fan on Twitter? TwitterFriends can tell you.

The tool also gives you average stats, such as replies received per day, replies sent per day, how many tweets you send per day, your Twitter Rank (which is a breakdown of where you "numerically rank" among Twitter users) in the world of TwitterFriends, and the size of your follower network.

TwitterFriends is a valuable tool when you want a bird's-eye view of your Twitter profile and your Twitter usage.

# Twitterrific

```
http://twitterrific.com/
```

Twitterrific is similar to TweetDeck (which you can read about in the section "TweetDeck," earlier in this chapter), but it's designed for use on a Mac. Twitterrific has an excellent user interface, and it is small enough not to hoard your entire computer screen. It gives you the same type of capabilities as TweetDeck, but it offers more keyboard shortcuts for the Mac user. The application is designed to let you view as much or as little information as you want when you use Twitterrific on your desktop.

You can also download Twitterrific on the iPhone as an application.

# Appendix

# Great Twitter Marketing Ideas in 140 Characters or Less

The one thing that keeps my love for Twitter growing in leaps and bounds is the people I interact with. Twitter is a mind-trust of brilliant people from all over the globe dedicated to one thing: sharing great content.

I asked folks from the world of Twitter to share some thoughts on how to use Twitter as a marketing tool; many marketing experts replied by tweet, so all the advice in this appendix comes to you in nuggets of 140 characters or less.

# Marketing

@DavidSpinks If you're not seeing results, it's probably not Twitter's fault, it's how you're using it. That's ok. Reevaluate why you're there and apply.

@BeerFoxTM Have you written a lot? Tweet the titles of all articles you have written, and each URL, so your followers can easily find them.

<Anonymous> Marketing is about promoting what your expertise is & how that is advantageous to someone else. Now get tweeting that!

@watsonk2 Tweet 80% content that readers will find helpful and 20% self promotion. A good mix will get you farther than 100% promotion.

<Anonymous> Find the perfect balance between the quantity of your tweet versus the quality.

<Anonymous> If business has taught you anything it is that you have to pick a niche. Apply that to Twitter.

@Arsene333 Think of Twitter as your own public relations campaign.

@KevinEikenberry The 3 Twitter Marketing P's to use twitter effectively, be provocative, provide value, and most of all, be personable

<Anonymous> Since becoming a Twitter user, a link in each tweet back to my web site has increased traffic

@whalehunters Understand your business purposes for spending time and energy on Twitter

@taskwum Content is king

<Anonymous> Employ a content lure strategy. You point users to help content in exchange for influence

@tushin Don't overplan or overtest. Just do it and see how it works.

@VisitFingerLake Watch, learn, and listen — then jump on in. You can't understand social media until you use it.

@pmhub Do not put all of your eggs in one basket. You will get overwhelmed.

<Anonymous> Twitter marketing is cheap, easy, and effective. If you can't do it alone get some help.

@MrBusinessGolf My thoughts are the best market to be in is the market you create.

@coffee_online If it smells of marketing then you're going to convince noone. That includes spraying fake camouflage scent to cover your tracks

@socialjulie Good marketers can focus on intricacies with a short lens and can then strategize with a long lens and with a strong ROI filter

@makeseriously If all of your links point back to you chances are I am going to ignore you

@JasonFalls Don't think Twitter can't be used for something. You can sell, broadcast, activate, converse, and share.

<Anonymous> Provide value and I will watch for more.

@addresstwo a drawing at a tradeshow. They have to tweet a link from your booth to enter. I got a ton of traffic off a tweet-to-win back in may.

@LeahsGotIt Most imp., be genuine. Ppl will smell it if you're being a ratty salesperson. Yell 'n sell just as annoying in tweets as on TV.

@socialjulie Marketing on Twitter is really a stripped down type of marketing. It's authentic communication; no other approach will work.

@bradpiercephd "If you make people think they're thinking, they'll love you"

@joshmiles Want to recruit your employees or coworkers to Tweet? First take a minute (in person) to explain what to do and why they should.

@MattMacbeth Tip: learn how 2 Twitter by following & learning from a "Twitter mentor"; there R folks who R good at this — pay attention 2 them

# Promoting Your Brand

@UTFCU Use Twitter to promote rates, products, and special events. People will appreciate it!

@DunnMich Twitter about how you're promoting your business, or how you're getting paid, give followers something they can use!

@TimPiazza When you trend, trying to follow your brand is like riding in the front of a roller coaster. Every moment thrills and scares.

<Anonymous> You are the brand!!! Nothing else. You're selling yourself as a person and showing that you are worthy of being followed.

@Alonis DO NOT PUSH YOUR PRODUCT. There, in 26 characters. ;

@azvibe Don't use Twitter if all you're going to do is promote the latest and greatest or ask for help for your business. Be yourself!!

@bnyquist Don't constantly or ever change your avatar as it's one of the main consistencies in your online branding.

@brianspaeth If you murder someone, don't Tweet about it. Bad for the brand

<Anonymous> Putting a real name and face on your identity allows customers to associate with your brand on a personal level

@photogeneve if you are a business, don't always try to promote! Share things you find interesting, and others might too

# Building Relationships

@divinewrite Help people.

<Anonymous> Be the first to share. Get an RSS feed of topical news for your industry and post a link as soon as breaking news hits the search engines.

<Anonymous> Use Twitter as way to grow your networks on other social media channels. It can be the hub of your social media wheel, each channel a spoke

@mooshinindy Be yourself on twitter. People will either love you or hate you for it but at least it's you.

@appellatelaw If someone you know has good news (e.g., been promoted), but is too modest to Tweet about it, you might consider Tweeting about it yourself.

<Anonymous> Like in Shakespeare the more interesting characters are rounded, not flat or static. So be well rounded (or appear to be).

<Anonymous> B human. dont B the person who only talks abt their product/service. Interact w/ ppl (RT, DM, etc) on a personal level.

<Anonymous> Don't be all over the place. Be known as the go to page for a topic, and as a reliable source for information on that topic.

@jennielees Pay it forward — giving is as good as getting, and social capital is invaluable. It's not all about you anymore.

@Chadrichards identify, engage, respond, repeat ;)

@JillHarding Simply be genuine and share useful information as in time it will come back to you.

@chuckgose Broadsting is great for TV. Not for Twitter. Participation is a two-way street. Get to know your groups and they will get to know you.

@fleurdeleigh Be mindful that your horse precedes your cart. Relationships are key.

@gambitfauri BROADCASTING is one thing. LISTENING is a major thing and REACTING is the real thing

<Anonymous> Have fun. Meet people. Share ideas. They will visit your website.

@augie_malson develop/build relationships with your (potential followers) 2. use a background image that connects to your other sites.

@PhillipM If you can't have a vested, genuine interest in your followers then you are in the wrong business

@yougonetwork Build relationships through interaction and remember quality of content over quantity will get you the right followers

@unmarketing Take 5 min daily to reply/retweet others, nothing about you. Engage, interact, build.

@LindsayManfredi Twitter should be about relationship building and trust. Use it wisely and people will get that. Please don't try to sell to me.

<Anonymous> Building communities that will be sticky takes longer than a few tweets — tweet early and tweet often.

<Anonymous> Be shockingly honest. Usually at least one person connects with that.

@sarahrobinson Always remember you were a beginner once too.

@jennypratt Honestly, I really don't care what you have for lunch. But I do care to know about the ideas you have for your biz

@donschindler Be a friend. Be a resource. Be yourself.

@askfrasco Twitter is a give and take relationship, you have to contribute yourself in order to have others contribute to you.

@homestarstaging It's called a "social network" for a reason build your network online as you would in real time.

@socialarts Find something that you care about, make it your goal to share that passion with followers, without expecting ANYTHING in return

# Engaging in Conversation

@calamity7373 Create a dialogue with your followers, don't just push promotions about your brand in their face.

@virtualewit Twitter is a conversation. Take some time to listen to what is going on and respond, don't just talk at people.

&lt;Anonymous&gt; Don't just talk about your product, talk about your area of expertise. And the key talk — have a dialog with your customers or potential customers.

@hatmandu don't just use auto-follow tools to spam legions of people — instead, create individual conversations

@followthecolson Twitter is not a scripted dialog. It is an open conversation between you, your followers and your potential followers.

&lt;Anonymous&gt; Make sure you're able to talk to the people who follow you. Make sure you're on when they're on, and free to chat.

&lt;Anonymous&gt; DON'T BE STUCK UP! Talk to the people who took time to mention you, follow you, and/or DM you.

@roundpeg Focus on building conversations and relationships and the followers will come

@gioias Build relationships. Share ideas and info with people who have similar interests and then meet them offline

&lt;Anonymous&gt; Remember that Twitter is about communicating, not marketing. Focus on adding value to the conversation, not selling something to someone

&lt;Anonymous&gt; Listen. Listen. Listen. And engage in conversations. Do not spam.

&lt;Anonymous&gt; Tweet about other people's stuff.

@krisplantrich Don't be a tweet hog! 15 tweets in a row gets irritating

@AlaneAnderson Don't be the JERK at the party that just wants to sell u. smthing.

@briancarter Tweet funny stuff in funique (fun+unique) ways. Funky ways works too. Funquee.

@authorlisalogan Don't answer "What Are You Doing?" Instead: Reply, Retweet, and Respect (by following back those who follow you)

@jennypratt Be Bold. Have an opinion. Talk to strangers and have fun!

&lt;Anonymous&gt; When tweeting, you don't need to make it all about you

&lt;Anonymous&gt; Staying on message in Twitter is dangerous. Learn to adapt and listen to what they are telling about your service/product

@tonymarshall Remember that it's called "tweeting," not "squawking."

@smquaseb Twitter is an ongoing conversation you participate in. It isn't about how much info you can shove out, it is about communicating.

@blakenquist Don't talk AT people. Talk TO people. (or Don't broadcast. Engage.)

@JustShireen Talk. Interact. Respond. It should be a conversation, not a sales pitch.

# Retweeting

@makingcjc learn how to RT (re-tweet) it not only helps you stay active, but lets people know what you're interested in

@mayhemstudios "Retweet" is a powerful tool on Twitter; helps to build your brand, following, trust & seen as an expert in your field.

@KristieKreation Don't just retweet, post links and post quotes!! Make sure you carry on conversations so others know a little about you.

@SandyDfromNJ Twitter is a great place to clarify your vision, mission & message. Are you being Re-Tweeted?

@douglaskarr Find out who is tweeting your links with Backtweets http://backtweets.com/

@chrisfyvie If you expect people to RT your post leave 20–25 characters for convenient RTs!

@MacksMind Speak simple. Share your passion. RT the best words of others.

@briancarter Expertise, sex, news, controversy, and humor get retweeted. Making fun of yourself is my favorite.

# Following and Followers

@bradjward Don't get caught up in the numbers game. 100 relevant followers on Twitter is worth more than 1000 followers any day of the week.

@sarahebuckner It drives me crazy when people don't post for a few hours, then post 9 times in a row. If they do that a lot, I unfollow.

<Anonymous> First — Get followers. Second — Keep followers. Sounds easy right? It's actually not. It takes patience and hard work.

@Arsene333 Before you click send ask yourself "Would I follow this person solely based on this one tweet?" If yes, clink send.

@jecates Following thousands of people hoping to get their attention is more likely to get you blocked than followed

@greenphare Listen think then react. Don't tweet just because. Many following doesn't mean you are a "superstar"

@ericblonde Be a person to follow — not just a Twitter account.

@Aislinnye Make friends with your followers and tweet then as you'd like them to tweet you

<Anonymous> Follow people outside your niche. I've read books I would have never known existed all from random tweets.

@claymabbitt With every tweet you're either giving people a reason to retweet or you're giving them a reason to unfollow

@lookwebdesign Twitter is as good as the people you follow

@LeahsGotIt Encourage followers, all R potential customers. If 1 posts abt being down, send a cheer-up tweet, they'll remember U well 4 it.

# Using Twitter Wisely

@ForwardSteps Want your blog posts fed to Twitter? In friendfeed setting, you'll see Twitter publishing

@krisplantrich All tweets are read — not just your branding or marketing ones. Be careful what you tweet!

<Anonymous> Keep your business and personal life separate. Would you like to see someone you were considering to do work for you drinking on a boat?

<Anonymous> Twitter works best when integrated. Use it to supplement blogging and other social media efforts

@unmarketing Twitter is a conversation about your business/industry whether you're there or not. Your choice.

@BeTheLink I might be crazy enough to believe Twitter can lead Social Awareness movements. Lead people to involvement

@wowbroadcasting Add the Twitter icon to your website.

@karamartens Twitter is a great equalizer. CEOs, gurus, and regular joes all have to make the best of 140 charac.

@jennypratt Twitter bios rule. If say something interesting about yourself in 140 characters imagine what you can do with stuff you really care about?

# Index

## Business/Accounting & Bookkeeping

Bookkeeping For Dummies
978-0-7645-9848-7

eBay Business
All-in-One For Dummies,
2nd Edition
978-0-470-38536-4

Job Interviews
For Dummies,
3rd Edition
978-0-470-17748-8

Resumes For Dummies,
5th Edition
978-0-470-08037-5

Stock Investing
For Dummies,
3rd Edition
978-0-470-40114-9

Successful Time
Management
For Dummies
978-0-470-29034-7

## Computer Hardware

BlackBerry For Dummies,
3rd Edition
978-0-470-45762-7

Computers For Seniors
For Dummies
978-0-470-24055-7

iPhone For Dummies,
2nd Edition
978-0-470-42342-4

Laptops For Dummies,
3rd Edition
978-0-470-27759-1

Macs For Dummies,
10th Edition
978-0-470-27817-8

## Cooking & Entertaining

Cooking Basics
For Dummies,
3rd Edition
978-0-7645-7206-7

Wine For Dummies,
4th Edition
978-0-470-04579-4

## Diet & Nutrition

Dieting For Dummies,
2nd Edition
978-0-7645-4149-0

Nutrition For Dummies,
4th Edition
978-0-471-79868-2

Weight Training
For Dummies,
3rd Edition
978-0-471-76845-6

## Digital Photography

Digital Photography
For Dummies,
6th Edition
978-0-470-25074-7

Photoshop Elements 7
For Dummies
978-0-470-39700-8

## Gardening

Gardening Basics
For Dummies
978-0-470-03749-2

Organic Gardening
For Dummies,
2nd Edition
978-0-470-43067-5

## Green/Sustainable

Green Building
& Remodeling
For Dummies
978-0-470-17559-0

Green Cleaning
For Dummies
978-0-470-39106-8

Green IT For Dummies
978-0-470-38688-0

## Health

Diabetes For Dummies,
3rd Edition
978-0-470-27086-8

Food Allergies
For Dummies
978-0-470-09584-3

Living Gluten-Free
For Dummies
978-0-471-77383-2

## Hobbies/General

Chess For Dummies,
2nd Edition
978-0-7645-8404-6

Drawing For Dummies
978-0-7645-5476-6

Knitting For Dummies,
2nd Edition
978-0-470-28747-7

Organizing For Dummies
978-0-7645-5300-4

SuDoku For Dummies
978-0-470-01892-7

## Home Improvement

Energy Efficient Homes
For Dummies
978-0-470-37602-7

Home Theater
For Dummies,
3rd Edition
978-0-470-41189-6

Living the Country Lifestyle
All-in-One For Dummies
978-0-470-43061-3

Solar Power Your Home
For Dummies
978-0-470-17569-9